Theo**Media**

Theo**Media**

The Media of God and the Digital Age

BY ANDREW BYERS

CASCADE *Books* · Eugene, Oregon

THEOMEDIA
The Media of God and the Digital Age

Cascade Books
An Imprint of Wipf and Stock Publishers
199 W. 8th Ave., Suite 3
Eugene, OR 97401

www.wipfandstock.com

ISBN 13: 978-1-61097-988-7

Cataloguing-in-Publication Data:

Byers, Andrew.

   TheoMedia : the media of God and the digital age / Andrew Byers.

   xii + 240 p. ; 23 cm. Includes bibliographical references.

   ISBN 13: 978-1-61097-988-7

   1. Mass media—Religious aspects—Christianity. 2. Mass Media—Influence. 3.
Christianity and culture. I. Title.

BR115 .T42 B66 2013

Manufactured in the U.S.A.

To my conversation partners at CODEC and "37A"

Contents

Acknowledgments

This "acknowledgments" section is not a perfunctory ornamentation thrown in for the sake of writing protocol. Books are communal endeavors, and my amateurism in media studies and theology has required the assistance of many guides for whom I am genuinely grateful. First, I want to thank the friends to whom I gave not only a manuscript but also a short deadline for reading it: Matt Orth, Dr. Tim Hutchings, Chris Juby, Caz Weir, Matt Godfrey, Paul Jones, and Joel Busby. Their feedback was honest, constructive, and much of it made its way into the final draft.

Professor Walter Moberly also deserves my thanks. He lent his ear over coffee to let me sound out some of my thoughts about media in the Old Testament and allowed me to read portions of his manuscript for *Old Testament Theology* before its publication. The thoughtful nudging and prodding with well-crafted questions brought a welcome degree of clarity (though he is certainly not responsible for any shortcomings in my theological reading of the Old Testament!).

I also want to thank two groups of colleagues with whom I was in constant interaction while writing the book. CODEC (Christian Communication in the Digital Age) is a research institute at St John's College at Durham University. It is more than an "institute": CODEC is a *community*, one that pairs theological thinking with an enthusiasm for new media. Dr. Pete Phillips and Dr. Bex Lewis kindly (and daringly!) took me on board as the "theological consultant" for CODEC's blog, www.BigBible.org.uk. Many of the ideas presented in this book were first tested in blog entries for that website.

The other group of colleagues I want to thank consists of my daily companions in biblical and theological study. Just off an old medieval street behind the Department of Theology at Durham University is a lackluster hole-in-the-wall study room. I am honored to have a desk there amidst fellow PhD students who have become a tremendous source of friendship, wisdom, and laughter. Always eager for heated theological discussions, I kept bringing up media issues during our lunch break to see what would happen. Those countless interactions sometimes affirmed and sometimes corrected my thinking, forcing me to write more carefully.

There are also two groups of university students I would like to thank, both of whom endured my preaching on media and the Bible in the early stages of this book. The sermon series out of which the concept of "TheoMedia" grew was delivered to the students of University Christian Fellowship in Birmingham, Alabama back in 2010. The students attending the 2012 "House Party" event sponsored by Kings Church Durham sat through my second sermon series on TheoMedia. Both groups of students offered lively interaction and posed helpful questions.

The two people who most deserve my thanks are Rob O'Callaghan and my wife, Miranda. Rob has been one of my best friends for years. He also just happens to be the best copyeditor I know. It has been a humbling and joyful experience to have a wiser theologian and a better writer graciously devote himself to sharpening my own theology and writing. And I could not imagine writing without the help of Miranda. I often realize that she understands what I want to say better than I do. Along with making countless sacrifices in giving me time to write, she has lovingly guided my thoughts, tweaked my questionable grammar, and encouraged me to move abstract concepts into the earthy realm of everyday life.

Finally, I want to thank Rodney Clapp for taking me on as a low-profile author. Wipf and Stock has honorably put the technology of printing and bookmaking in the service of theology, not the other way around. Their in-house publishing apparatus allows Cascade Books and their other publishing lines to take on authors regardless of whether or not they have a large public platform guaranteeing book sales. The primary criterion is that the author holds some promise of delivering a worthy project. It is an honor to have my own project marked with Cascade's logo; and I hope I have honored their investment.

PART 1

Media Old and New

Chapter 1

Introduction
In Search of a Script:
Is the Bible Media Savvy?

Discerning what characterizes the socially constructed worlds people around us inhabit places us in a better position to address the generation God calls us to serve. Doing so, however, necessitates that we conceptualize and articulate Christian beliefs—the gospel—in a manner that contemporary people can understand. That is, we must express the gospel through the "language" of the culture—through the cognitive tools, concepts, images, symbols, and thought forms—by means of which people today discover meaning, construct the world they inhabit, and form personal identity.

—STANLEY GRENZ AND JOHN FRANKE[1]

"Daddy, my homework is to do a project about somebody important in history."

"Yeah? Who do you think you will study?"

"Um, I think . . . Jesus." I am proud, of course. The little guy is seven years old and already at risk of being stereotyped as a preacher's kid, supplying the right answers in Sunday school and doing homework projects

1. Grenz and Franke, *Beyond Foundationalism*, 159.

3

on Jesus in primary school. But his curiosity about Jesus is sincere so I am keen to encourage him.

Along with being a dad and a minister, it just so happens that I am also a doctoral student focusing on the Gospels and thereby uniquely qualified for the parental task of guiding this homework project. With dense books on New Testament studies weighing down the shelves behind me, I pose my first questions as my son's self-appointed research supervisor: "So where do you think you would go to find out about Jesus? What are the best sources?" (Bibliographies are a big deal, you know.) Before he is able to respond, his big sister passes by in the hallway and knowingly provides an answer.

"Google! That is the best place to go to find out anything about anything!"

I am aghast. After a decade of life in the twenty-first century, my eldest child somehow knows intuitively that Google is the end-all and be-all for knowledge. The response I am anticipating is "the Bible" or "the four canonical Gospels." I am hoping that maybe early Christological hymns or ancient creeds of the church will be identified as potential bibliographic material. Instead, I am given the name of an Internet search engine.

To my relief, it occurs to me that my daughter has no idea that Jesus is the subject matter of this homework assignment. Still, I am unsettled that her reflex as a digital native is to say "Google" at the instant a question arises about sources.

As much as I want to protest, though, she is on to something.

Though Christian scripture is surely a better source than the Internet for understanding Jesus, Google could very easily direct my son to an online version of the Bible. If he types "Jesus Cappadocian Fathers" into the search field, within seconds of hitting "Enter" he could begin learning patristic Christology without having to rush off to the university with my library card (assuming his father's personal collection on those shelves is found wanting for the advanced research needs). After a few clicks on my laptop he could instantly begin reading the Nicene Creed. He could be staring at maps of ancient Palestine within seconds. Google could offer him timelines, charts, images of archaeological artifacts, and artistic depictions of first-century life.

So could my wife's thick study Bible, but it is all the way up the stairs.

If you are thinking, "C'mon, don't be ridiculous—just send the kids upstairs to fetch that study Bible," then what informs your suggestion?

Is the media format of a screen inferior to the media format of a book? Why so? And if you are wearied by all this internal wrangling and trying to figure out why I am hesitant in letting my son do an innocent Google search, then what suppositions underlie your bewilderment? Ease with the media format of the screen? Is it pragmatism? Displaying one of the Gospels or Philippians 2:5–11 on the computer screen is more convenient than having my children hunt down and thumb through that unwieldy, page-bound study Bible. If pragmatism is a motivation, though, is it okay to make all our media decisions on the basis of whatever seems most practical at the time?

READING AN OLD SCRIPT IN A NEW AGE

That little episode with my two oldest children took place within sixty seconds. It is one scene out of countless others in which I am regularly forced to make decisions about media technology. The questions continually raised by these little interactions have ricocheted in a vast blank cavern in my head, exposing the absence of a biblical frame of reference for understanding and appropriating the new media that have suddenly dawned on the scene.

Does the Bible actually offer such a frame of reference for new media? Can sacred ink voice wisdom for understanding Facebook, Google, Angry Birds, avatars, and online Jesus research?

I just finished reading an impressive book by an astute writer offering a sophisticated critique of our media culture. Though the author wrote as a Christian, there was very little engagement with the Bible. Another book I just finished reading draws from scripture haphazardly to show that a golden age of techno-utopia awaits if the church would just jump aboard the new media train. The dual messages are 1) the Bible has little to say about media culture, or 2) you can make the Bible say what you want about media culture when it seems to be reticent. Both cases contribute to the nagging sense that the sacred texts of our faith have little to do with life in the digital realm.

The conviction underlying this book is that Christian scripture is not only the best source for understanding Jesus but also the best source for understanding Google. The church has been adequately provisioned with a robust script for guiding our task of thinking about media. As a "script," the Bible offers an authoritative vision that gives shape to how

5

the people of God conduct themselves in the unfolding drama of life.[2] The rich theological traditions of the church help interpret this script for its continual reenactment on the contemporary stage.

This book is a product of my ongoing process of stumbling onto the stage of the digital world. Like a theater company staging a Shakespearean play with twenty-first-century language within a current-day setting, I am trying to read that old script well enough to make some faithful performance or improvisation in a brand new media culture.

FROM PAPYRI TO PIXELS: DOES THE BIBLE NEED AN UPGRADE?

It is hard to see how an ancient collection of documents can serve as such a script in a cutting edge digital era.[3] The authors of our sacred texts and the bygone leaders of the church's theological thinking did not foresee the luminous powers and capabilities of twenty-first-century media technology. Can our doctrinal heritage and those age-old creeds really guide how we read the script in our current mediascape?

Everything at our fingertips today seems to require updates or upgrades. Our gadgets and their programs are so acutely self-aware of the perpetual threat of antiquation that they tell us periodically when we need to check for the latest downloads to stave off their irrelevance. Like us, our devices are averse to becoming outdated, and we have taught them how to speak up and let us know when they sense they are getting old. Heeding their alerts is to our advantage, of course. No one wants the burden and incompatibility of outdated stuff.

So is the Bible in need of an update?

We have to acknowledge that the Bible's content is old. *Very* old. New translations occasionally appear and electronic versions are now available, but in spite of these updates in language usage and media form, the raw textual material of the Bible has been canonically stabilized and

2. By "script" I am relying on Kevin Vanhoozer's media-related imagery of Christian theology as a dramatic performance. See Vanhoozer, *The Drama of Doctrine*, 115–185; see also his essay "The Voice and the Actor." Also helpful, with different nuances, are Brueggeman, *The Bible and Postmodern Imagination*, 64–69; and Wells, *Improvisation*, 59–70.

3. John Dyer points out that the biblical Abraham and Abraham Lincoln would probably have more in common with each other than with those of us living in the technological landscape of the twenty-first century (*From the Garden to the City*, 21).

left unchanged for centuries. The canonization process firewalled the Bible so that it resists additions, downloads, and new uploads.

We all know what happens to media products that resist adapting their content to shifting cultural trends and technological advances. They risk that most dreaded twenty-first-century malady of slipping into *irrelevance*. So does "antique" mean "antiquated" when it comes to the sacred text of the Christian church?

The high-speed velocity of technological innovation reinforces the suspicion that we are a civilization developed so far beyond the ancient contexts out of which scripture grew that words once etched into stone or penned to papyrus are surely outdated and out of touch. Western society is ever poised on the cusp of the celebrated *next* and the anticipated *new*. While Christian scripture has remained a fixed, stable corpus of really old poems, songs, tales, laws, and letters, the civilized world has impressively gone on to invent gunpowder, discover a heliocentric solar system, harness electricity, and create that ephemeral matrix of the Internet.

Of all the advanced sophistication we regularly observe and experience, few areas of technological prowess are more all-encompassing in the daily lives of Westerners than that of media technology. So we are asking in this book, *is the Bible media savvy*? *Is Christian theology media competent*? Can the ancient medium of scripture offer fresh words for new media? Is there a compelling theological vision in those inked pages for twenty-first-century mass media and communications technology?

Yes.

The idea of "media" is bigger than formats like an email, a tweet, or a blog post. A medium is not just a gadget like a TV or an iPad. More fundamentally, I am understanding "media" as means of communication or revelation.[4] Though scripture says nothing about digital media, it is enormously invested in communicative and revelatory *means*. God speaks. He reveals. Humans respond and interact in diverse ways with him and with one another. Media formats and media gadgets will feature throughout this book, but our primary task is to understand how scripture portrays media as a concept. So to retrain what we think about "media," we are going to make a pilgrimage of sorts throughout the entire biblical saga, tracing the narrative plotlines of the epic story of Creation,

---

4. Philosophical theologian Nicholas Wolterstorff is careful to make the distinction between revelation and discourse/speaking, hence my definition of media as means of *communication* and *revelation*. See his chapter, "Speaking is not Revealing," in *Divine Discourse*, 19–36.

Fall, Redemption, and Re-Creation to show that the idea of media is a central theme of the church's most sacred text.[5]

So how can the narrative of scripture speak to us about the concept of media? Here is a quick overview . . .

MEDIA AND THE BIBLICAL STORY

We should acknowledge first that although there is such a thing as "new media," the actual concept of media is as old as the hills. This is true literally, because the hills themselves are a form of media.

God's media. Or, we could say, "TheoMedia." Media production began with God.

As self-revelatory artistry, creation can be understood as divine media. Silicon Valley has nothing over the one who made valleys and silicon. Big shot marketing firms perched within the glass and steel of metropolitan skyscrapers may actually have the sky itself as a competing media product.

The aesthetic media of God's creation was produced by another form of divine media. The slope of the valleys and the rise of hills beneath glorious sky blue all came about through the medium of holy speech. Divine words addressed the primordial cosmic blankness, and ever since "let there be . . ." sounded in the dark, creation has served as a means of divine revelation and divine self-communication. The idea of media goes back to the decision of the Creator to create, to produce by his word self-expressive artistry in the glimmer of star and the flutter of wing.

The divine medium of holy speech soon became interactive with other speakers. Amidst the sounds of the buzzing and whirring in this fresh new world, divine monologue became *dialogue*. Words produced Eden, and then words echoed in Eden. Pristine words, words directly from the mouth of God, words dense with splendor and power, laden with the strength to birth solar systems—such words were addressed to and comingled with the voice of human beings. These lovely new

---

5. John Dyer's *From the Garden to the City* takes a similar approach in understanding technology in general, working through the biblical story and addressing media issues as they arise. I read Dyer's book twice during my research, both times after having crafted the approach and plan of my own book. I was pleased to find a solid resource making a similar trek through the biblical story. It is the best work I know of on technology that is accessible for non-specialist readers yet rigorously biblical and theological.

creatures with whom the Creator shared such open, unhindered communication were themselves designated as holy media.

That's you. And me.

Unlike the other creatures, human beings were fashioned in God's image. The most fundamental vocation of humanity is a *media vocation*, that of divine image bearing. Though the rest of creation reflects divine glory and beauty, Adam and Eve were endowed with an even more intrinsic capacity for conveying God's character and intentions in the world.

So the opening page of scripture is soaked in media-related themes. Here is what we have thus far in this brief overview of the biblical story: the medium of God's word produced the media of creation, including Adam and Eve, chief media agents who uniquely shared divine likeness and enjoyed open, unhindered communication with their Maker.

Then there was this serpent.

A new voice from somewhere offstage interrupts Eden's ongoing dialogue. Satan volunteers his hermeneutical services as an interpreter of holy speech. *Did God really say that? Let me clarify. Let me explain.* The unambiguous words of God about that intriguing tree are garbled up a bit and then re-presented, re-transmitted. The serpent offers himself as deceptive *medium*, as an intermediary, as a communicative agent between two parties—two parties never intended for intermediation. His uninvited voice is inserted between human ears and God's direct address.

The serpent interposes himself as an unsolicited *mediator*.

It does not follow, however, that "media" as a concept is bad or satanic just because Satan appears as a mediator in the opening of the biblical story. Remember, God came up with the idea of media, making the repeated observation "it is good" of creation and of the media agents of his image. And another Mediator will make an appearance in the biblical story about whom nothing bad can be said.

It is important to recognize, however, that the "Fall" of humankind comes about through the uncritical embrace of a plausible yet unsanctioned media source.

The results of heeding this interrupting mediator can be described in terms of a cataclysmic media obstruction. Sin effects communication loss. The first result of harkening to this unreliable media source over the TheoMedia of God's unambiguous words is the horizontal damaging of interpersonal relations between Adam and Eve. "Naked" and "unashamed" they were. No secrets. There is a total openness to the other.

But that uninterrupted, unmediated state proves short lived. At the taste of illicit fruit the cover-ups begin. Dark secrets enter the scene of human-to-human communication. Then they hear a sound once received so warmly and now understood as ominous—the sound of their Maker's approach.

"Where are you?" God asks.

This is the sound of a great gash ripped between two intimately bound parties. "Where are you?" is the sound of an epic communications disaster. "Where are you?" is the sound of a transmission loss of biblical proportions. *Did you heed some other voice?* The second result of sin is a loss of human-to-God communication. Yielding to the influence of an unauthorized mediator left humanity and God in need of continual mediation . . .

We have only made it past the first three chapters of the Bible. This account of Genesis 1–3 is seminal for all that lies ahead in this book.

As we proceed in our brief overview of the saga of scripture, we find that one of the greatest external threats to the redemptive program of God continues to be that of alluring and unauthorized media sources. The image bearers were naturally image producers. The Creator's chief media agents began creating their own media products. Much of the production was marked by beauty. But much of it was smeared by something twisted, by some corrosive influence now embedded deep within humanity's veins. Some of the media produced by these fallen creatures were explicitly produced for fallen purposes.

The visual and aural space of our own physical and social context today is voluminously occupied by ads, images, and sound bytes. Our term for this is "media saturation." As in the ancient world, a lot of the imagery today is wholesome, while much of it is not. In spite of the long chronological toll from the earliest days of the Bible to this day, not that much has really changed. Visual media dark and perverse haunted the ancient landscapes of Egypt, Canaan, Babylon, Greece, and Rome—the imagery of pagan religion and pagan empire. Often promiscuous in nature, often covered with silver or gold and commonly minted on coins—we should note that worldly media's partnership with sex and money is almost as old as those hills. And sadly, the lovely hills of divine media became the domain of this dark media as pagan altars and idols were positioned "on every high hill and under every green tree"—that phrase is common in the Old Testament.[6] It is the biblical language for "media saturation."

So how was Israel to maintain its distinct identity in a media saturated world?

*Theo*Media saturation.

In the Book of Deuteronomy, Israel is poised on the plains of Moab and eyeing the Promised Land across the River Jordan. They could almost taste those streams of milk and honey. But Canaan's geography was besmirched and littered with media. There were no billboards or digitized screens, but the poles, idols, and hand-wrought altars of idolatry were aplenty. Hence God's call to TheoMedia saturation, a call issued in one of the most heavily weighted passages of Scripture: the *Shema*.

Readers familiar with the New Testament will recognize the commandment Jesus deemed "the greatest": "Hear, O Israel: the Lord our God, the Lord is one; you shall love the Lord your God with all your heart, and with all your soul, and with all your mind, and with all your strength" (Mark 12:29–30; cf. Matt 22:37). Though familiar with the commandment, we may be less so with its context. It comes from Deuteronomy 6:4 opening the passage known as the *Shema* (from the Hebrew "to hear"). The context of the *Shema*—the words Jesus designated the most binding command on our lives—*is a call to media saturation*. It is a call to be saturated with the TheoMedia of God's words. Love the Lord your God with all your being, Israel, and

> These *words*, which I am commanding you today, shall be on your hearts. And you shall teach them diligently to your children and shall talk of them when you sit in your house and when you walk by the way and when you lie down and when you rise. And you shall bind them as a sign on your hand and they shall be as frontlets between your eyes. You shall write them on the doorposts of your house and on your gates. (Deut 6:6–9; emphasis added)

The words of God were to saturate the daily grind of the Israelite family. They were to feature orally in conversations in the fields and in the home. Bound to the hand, stuck between the eyes, and emblazoned on the entranceways of the home, the TheoMedia of God's words were also to occupy the visual space of God's people. In a world rife with unauthorized

6. Deut 12:2; 1 Kgs 14:23; 2 Kgs 16:4; 17:10; 2 Chr 28:4; Jer 2:20; 3:6; 17:2; Ezek 6:13.

media sources, the Israelites were commanded to esteem their God as their primary media source, holding fast to the TheoMedia of divine words, embracing a life saturated by holy speech.

They fail. Misguiding visual media proved more alluring than the verbal media of scripture. This is not to say that visual media is "bad" and verbal media "good." As we have just seen, the words of the *Shema* were to be visually rendered as well as orally shared. God is dazzlingly visual at times in his media making (just think of creation!), and the sacrificial system was a multimedia worship exercise that engaged the full range of the senses. But God's form could not be visually rendered, and the other deities seemed irresistibly tangible in their graven representation. For many, looking at idols replaced listening to Torah. Israel's plunge into spiritual collapse corresponded with its media preferences: dark, twisted, and idolatrous media over TheoMedia.

You might recall that there was a famous spiritual revival under King Josiah. The renewed devotions of God's people in his day corresponded with a return to TheoMedia when a dusty old scroll of scripture (likely Deuteronomy) was discovered during a Temple repair job. That revival was short lived. And Israel went adrift in a sea of propaganda, imagery, and rhetoric from pagan gods and pagan empires.

Originally destined as the bearers of God's image in the world, humanity—both Gentile and Jewish—had become shaped by the world's unwholesome images and untruthful words. The once uninterrupted interaction with God was now clouded; the transmission was lost in the distracting white noise of worldly media. Such a disastrous media situation required a media "eucatastrophe," to borrow a term coined by J. R. R. Tolkien.[7] That media "eucatastrophe" (an event of catastrophically *good* proportions) finally took place.

It was the Incarnation. The TheoMedium of God's Word became flesh.

The public announcement of what Jesus has done on our behalf as the God who took on flesh is called "gospel." It is a media term. In the genre of a eucatastrophic newsflash, the TheoMedium of the gospel is the breaking news that our King has arrived and conquered, that the mediated distance between humanity and God is to be bridged through the work of the Incarnate Christ, a new Mediator who has come from

---

7. Tolkien, "On Fairy-Stories," 153.

offstage as abruptly as that serpent of old. And this Mediator is hailed as the untainted "image of the invisible God" (Col 1:15).

In the wake of bloodied cross and vacated tomb, a new TheoMedium was formed. Indwelled by the Spirit, that society we call "church" was created as a new TheoMedium in the world in the sense that we as the church are now being restored as bearers of God's image. And we are entrusted with divine media forms like the sacraments and biblical preaching by which we are shaped and transformed. The covenant we call "new" has set us on a trajectory that ends with the end of intermediation: "they will see his face" (Rev 22:4).

The cosmic communications disaster that resulted in God's "Where are you?" (Gen 3:9) will end with "Behold, the dwelling place of God is with man" (Rev 21:3). To the first mediator's "Did God actually say?" (Gen 3:1) Christ the final Mediator will respond with, "Behold, I am making all things new" (Rev 21:5). Sin has effected a cataclysmic communications disruption answered by God's decision to close that distance through means of revelation and communication—TheoMedia—by which he not only presents himself to us but actually restores us into his precious company.

So let's revisit our earlier questions: Is the Bible media savvy? Is Christian theology media competent?

Absolutely. The explosive tide of new media technology has hurled the people of God into waters uncharted, *but not unchartable*. As a medium featuring media-related themes, the Bible as script is competent to address a media saturated society. It has been doing just that from the days when it was first chiseled into stone, inscribed onto scrolls, and bound in parchment or vellum codices. No reconfiguring upgrade is required for the content of Christian scripture.

NOT NECESSARILY AN UPDATE, BUT HERMENEUTICS

There is, however, the urgent need for careful and rigorous *hermeneutics*, that is, biblical interpretation. We do not need to trade in our Bibles for a more relevant, newfangled source for understanding media. But we do need lively and faithful interpretation of our ancient texts under the guidance of God's Spirit.

To embrace the task of hermeneutics is to acknowledge that the Bible was produced from contexts dramatically different from our own (see the next chapter). It is also to acknowledge that the Bible is not in the form of a well-ordered catalogue of dos and don'ts applicable for all times and seasons. If I want to know whether I should let my kids watch a particular movie, I cannot turn to the Bible's index listing of "Secular entertainment; Children." As a minister in university contexts, I've yet to find a section in the Bible on "Physical Intimacy in Dating" to which I can direct students when they have those sorts of questions. If only we had clear rules and regulations set in black and white, right?

But if that were all Scripture offered, the continual emergence of scenarios unforeseeable to the biblical authors would make download-able updates an unending necessity! The rules and regulations Scripture *does* provide are often modified or even upended as the larger biblical drama unfolds (good news for bacon lovers, right?). So fresh (yet truthful and orthodox!) interpretations rather than new content uploads are ever needed within the church.[8]

ABOUT THE BOOK

This book is a hermeneutical project in the church's wider efforts of try-ing to understand the technological mediascape of the twenty-first cen-tury. The purpose is not to offer a how-to guidebook to help churches incorporate communications technology into their worship and witness. I am hoping to provide something more foundational. The point is to make some headway in constructing a theological frame of reference for understanding and appropriating media in the digital age and in the ages to come.

The Book's Strategy and Layout: Reading for Reorientation

On offer here is a *reading*. After a few more chapters of introducing and situating our topic of media (Part 1), this book will take a brisk plunge into the biblical story, tracing the idea of TheoMedia throughout the Bible's "salvation-history." That phrase simply denotes the biblical vision of God's unfolding saga of redeeming humanity and all of creation. At-tention will be given to the sights, sounds, words, and texts constitut-ing the media of our own day, but as indicated above, our interest lies

---

8. For more on this, see my blog post "Technological Upgrades and Christological Hermeneutics."

primarily with the sights and sounds of Israel's God in the Old Testament (Part 2), with his use of spoken and written words (Part 3), and with the "media legacies" and "focal media practices" established for the church by Christ's Incarnation, life, death, Resurrection, Ascension, and Return (Part 4). The final chapter will offer a summary of our discoveries, sketching the "rough overarching theological framework" for understanding media. The last few pages cast a vision for the church's use of its own media forms (preaching, spiritual gifts, the sacraments) in a media saturated society.

This extensive "reading" of Scripture is designed to baptize our senses so thoroughly into biblical ink that our faculties of understanding media in our day can be reoriented according to biblical logic. The church is embracing (and sometimes rejecting!) media technology faster than it can be theologically assessed.[9] What I hope this book will provide is a theological lens through which we can make sound evaluations when it comes to the media appearing so rapidly in the digital age. We need an interpretive grid that will shape and inform our media instincts.

The Book's Perspective: Between Technophobia and Technophilia

I will go into more details later, but when I originally approached this writing project I was somewhat of a technophobe with a chip on my shoulder. While interfacing new media with the Bible in my research, however, I began experiencing a shift in perspective. Though some of my preconceived suspicions have been confirmed and even intensified, many have been relieved. To a certain degree, the redemptive potential of media technology now strikes me as quite astonishing. So this book is no outraged condemnation of the digital age.

Neither is it an unqualified endorsement of the limitless communicative powers of the Internet, with the implication that Christians who refuse to get on board with all things digital and pixelated are cultural curmudgeons who, as Twitter might put it, are likely to "miss out."[10]

9. From the *Dictionary of Scripture and Ethics*: "[t]he moral challenges surrounding technology are exacerbated by the fact that new technologies are appearing at an exponential rate, threatening to outstrip the pace at which Christians can evaluate them." Hatch and Kallenberg, "Technology," 764.

10. "Don't miss out" is a message that sometimes appears in emails sent to me by Twitter to keep me in the social media game. See the TheoMedia Note following this

There are a number of Christian books, blogs, and articles out there representing these contrasting poles in the church's thinking about media technology (we will get to those in chapter 3). My own treatment walks between the aisles of the technophobes and technophiles.

The "TheoMedia Notes": Blogging Through the Book

Interspersed between many of the book's chapters are "TheoMedia Notes." These brief sections are like blog posts that will complement the discussions in the larger chapters, usually addressing the practical side of the concepts we will be addressing. Some Notes are longer than others, and some are more conceptual than practical. They are not superfluous add-ons. The reflections found in these Notes are integral to the book's underlying conviction that the ancient text of scripture is to inform the daily reality of our lives.

A Word about Vocab (and Media Wars)

Writing as an amateur in media and theology, there are some words I have had to learn or gain a better grasp of while working on this book. We have already defined "media" as means of communication or revelation. When I refer to "new media," I have in mind online social media. The "mass media" of Western societies in the form of commercialized ads will be getting some press as well. I will spend some time on "news media" in chapter 13 (focusing on cable news networks), but aside from TheoMedia Note 2, "entertainment media" does not get much attention in what follows.[11]

We have also already used the terms "TheoMedia" (plural) and "TheoMedium" (singular) to refer to the media employed specifically by God for communicating or revealing himself. TheoMedia can be formal in that they have been specifically commissioned as divine media, e.g., prophetic speech, the Tabernacle complex, etc. They can also be informal or ad hoc, like when God utilizes something according to the need of the moment, e.g., Balaam's donkey or the writing on the wall in Babylon.

---

chapter.

11. For entertainment media, see the recent study by Laytham, *iPod, YouTube, Wii Play*.

I should mention here that a host of media-related controversies will soon begin to surface. Sometimes I address these tensions directly, at other times rather subtly. Though I hail from a Protestant tradition emphasizing "word-media," we will soon observe that TheoMedia are so vast and varied in form that they appeal to the entire range of our senses. Media scholars sometimes use the impressive-looking word "sensorium" to refer to our various means of sense perception in communicating or receiving communication (seeing, tasting, touching, smelling, hearing).[12] Today and throughout history, friction has persisted among various Christian groups as to which sensory organs are to be prioritized when it comes to "doing church." Visuality and sight-related media are sometimes set at war against orality (referring to spoken word-media) and textuality (referring to written word-media). Put more concisely, images and words are often pitted against one another. We will see as the book progresses that some of these tensions are valid.

Many are not.

WHAT THE BOOK WILL NOT OFFER

There is one final point to make in this introduction. Remember that I have called "rough" the "overarching theological framework" I am developing here. That interpretive grid will not serve as a hermeneutical key for unlocking all the mysteries faced daily by those of us who are struggling to understand our faith and our media use. And others would perhaps offer readings of media in the Bible's salvation-history that differ from my own. When I write "rough," I mean it.

Jason Byassee has written an essay on social media subtitled "An Underdetermined Response"[13]—"underdetermined" because hermeneutics does not always offer a tidy, concise, and definitive quotient, sum, or product. Alan Jacobs points out that a society's decision to embrace certain technologies with sweeping consequences takes a long time to assess. In writing about the specific technology of the "codex" (that handy media format of pages bound together along the same margin, essentially what today we call a "book"), Jacobs writes,

---

12. For a brief overview of the idea of "sensorium," see Ong, *The Presence of the Word*, 1–16.

13. Byassee, "Practicing Virtue with Social Media." Byassee writes in n. 17 that he is borrowing the term "underdetermined" from Fowl, "Stories of Interpretation," 32–61.

> . . . only in the last half-century has a sound understanding be-
> gun to emerge of the relations between emergent Protestantism
> and print culture, and many of the details are still highly con-
> tested. So it may be far too early to grasp how a shift away from
> the codex might affect culture as a whole, or even the part of it
> that Christianity represents.[14]

Neil Postman, in spite of his adamant defense of print culture's superiority to screened culture, also expressed reserve about sweeping statements:
"we must be careful in praising or condemning because the future may
hold surprises for us."[15] Along similar lines, when it comes to the effects of
an electronic age on biblical interpretation, A. K. M. Adam has suggested
that we can at best "make provisional observations" and "hesitantly anticipate" what awaits "beyond a fog bank, over an unfamiliar horizon."[16]

Though it is satisfying as a writer to make bold, confident assertions, it seems best to offer a reading along with a theological frame of
reference that are both tentative and open to modifications by readers
and interlocutors as we grow and learn together. "Rough" is intended to
provide this qualification.

On the other hand, we cannot just plod haphazardly into the digital
age with the hope that the historians will one day figure out what the
church did well and not so well when new media dawned on the scene. A
retrospective assessment of the past does not help us in the present. For
today, we must put forward some form of theological guidance, carefully
reading an ancient script to negotiate an urgent present in anticipation of
a rapidly unfolding future.

To that end, I want to venture two claims here at the outset that will
be prominent throughout all that follows, both of which have already
been suggested above. First: *if God himself creates and employs media,
then there must be a theological logic that can guide how we produce and
use media and communications technology today.* Here is the second
claim: *Christians are called to media saturation, but the primary media
that are to shape, form, and saturate our lives are the media of God—Theo-
Media,* the communicative and revelatory means God employs to share
himself and to influence humankind as his image bearers.

---

14. Jacobs, "Christianity and the Future of the Book," 28.

15. Postman, *Amusing Ourselves to Death*, 29.

16. Adam, "Interpreting the Bible at the Horizon of Virtual New Worlds," 159.

TheoMedia Note 1

When Our Social Media Talk Back

We should neither try to demolish technology nor run away from it. We can restrain it and must redeem it.

—ALBERT BORGMANN[1]

As we turn to the Bible as a source for understanding our twenty-first-century digital culture, we should note that there are a lot of sources out there offering wisdom on how we should understand and use new media. Among them are the new media themselves.

Twitter has a voice.

The powers that be in their San Francisco office have taken to emailing me every now and then. There is apparently some concern around their conference table that I am drifting out of touch with the world's goings-on since my tweet sending and tweet reading are registering low of late (maybe that is why they sent an email, not a direct tweet). They gently nudge me in these emails to get back into the game: "*Don't miss out*. Stay up to date on what's happening" (emphases original).

Graciously, they send a list of tweets from other people more faithful in their tweeting that inform me of online articles I will surely find of interest. One link directed me to a story at *Christianity Today*'s website about Twitter and a major Christian conference.[2] In a gesture of impressive magnanimity, Twitter execs are giving attention to church leaders.

1. Borgmann, *Power Failure*, 8.

2. Bailey, "Twitter Reaches Out to Christian Leaders at Catalyst's 'Be Present' Conference."

As it turns out, theology and parish ministry are among their concerns. If you don't believe me, you can send a direct message to @Pontifex and ask the Pope himself.

On another encouraging note, WordPress is really helping me along in this blogging thing. I noticed not too long ago that the WP team began providing accolades upon my reaching a certain number of entries: "Congratulations! This is your 160th post!" Then they started setting attainable objectives: "Next goal: 165 Posts." I also noticed that formatted into the bottom of the "new post" screen is the inspiring exhortation, "Just Write."

It is nice for us Christians to get all this attention from social media firms, with Twitter helping clergy extend their reach and with WordPress coaching writers along in their blog ministries.

But in all honesty, WordPress might say "Congratulations! This is your 160th post!" even if my previous 159 were all about how to cheat on one's spouse or how to hurt lots of people really badly. And when Twitter rejoices with my ego when I get some online attention via their channels ("Andrew Byers, you were mentioned in a tweet!"—note the exclamation mark), it is unlikely that they have noticed whether I was being praised or slandered in those 140 characters. Now, I really like WordPress, and I am sure they would condemn any blog sponsoring dangerous activities. I am also growing in my appreciation of Twitter. Surely no one in their San Francisco office would delight in online mud slung in my direction. And for the record, I think it's great that the Pope has a Twitter handle.

The point here is that social media does not just amplify our voice—they have voices themselves. "Don't miss out. Stay up to date on what's happening." "Next goal: 165 Posts." "Just write." "What's going on, Andy?"—that's from Facebook. And let's not forget YouTube's imperative, lacking no subtlety, of "broadcast yourself." We do not just talk *through* social media. Our social media is talking to *us*.

Twitter's apparent anxiety over my tweetlessness and WordPress's enthusiasm over my pressing of words are about *activity*, not *content*. Neither of these fine and upstanding companies are weighing the validity of my blog posts or my occasional tweets based on their theological integrity or stylistic sophistication. "Just write." But just write *what*? Anything? *Just write* . . . because writing creates posts, and posts create traffic. Traffic is activity. And somewhere down the road for a dot-com, activity is income.

Social media companies are providing us with a platform. It is not their job to police poor grammar or correct bad theology promulgated through their channels. As media platforms, Twitter, Tumblr, Blogger, and Wordpress offer remarkable opportunities for conducting God's mediated voice into the cybersphere. I just think it is important for us to recognize that behind the graphics on the screen are corporations with budget goals, profit plans, marketing strategies, and other business-oriented agendas. These are not necessarily corrupting influences. But they are there, barely perceptible in those imperatives ("just write") and questions ("what's happening, Andy?").

Responsible use of media technology means we that rely on more authoritative voices to govern our online activity than those coming from executives poised in their corporate suites. As Christians, we take our theological and technological cues from elsewhere.

Chapter 2

Contextual Gaps
Media Commercialized and Secularized

Now while Paul was waiting for them at Athens, his spirit was provoked within him as he saw that the city was full of idols.

—ACTS 17:16

Social space—the areas in which life was lived—for pagans was thus in a sense alive with images, mythologized. The statues in the temples and around the cities, the reliefs on the altars, the busts and statuettes of the home, etc. all, with varying degrees of intensity to be sure, figured the divine or, better for ancient polytheism, the divinities. The notion of a secular, separate realm devoid of religious penetration is of course a modern invention (if not itself a fiction). For ancient pagans, space was religious.[1]

—KAVIN ROWE

[T]raditions of "public service" and other obligations of broadcasting gave way . . . to an orientation toward "markets" and "marketplace forces." Product

1. Rowe, "New Testament Iconography?," 307–8.

cross-promotion in children's television programming, the increasing practice of "product placement" in film and television, and the cross-promotion of films, television, and popular music are all examples of this blurring of traditional boundaries. The media have become integrated into—and are in many ways the basis of—the larger economic project of the creation, marketing, and consumption of cultural commodities.[2]

—STEWART M. HOOVER

My life as a father, husband, chaplain, and a doctoral student in biblical studies comprises a bizarre and richly layered media medley. Within my weekly visual grasp is a hodgepodge of sights that includes films by Pixar and DreamWorks, pages in Karl Barth's *Church Dogmatics*, clips from "Thomas the Tank Engine," webpages on theology blogs, and homespun, impromptu skits in the living room starring each of my four kids. My ears are filled with the sounds of solid, theological preaching at my church, loud cries of discontent from the backseat of my car, cheery tunes from the Wiggles, haunting ballads from Bill Mallonee, and raw hymns from Chuck Hooten. My reading consists of dense monographs on New Testament theology, young adult fiction like *The Hunger Games*, news articles in *The Economist*, arduous essays in academic journals, the Gospels in Greek, and Bultmann in German (well, I am trying). Yet I also read Facebook status updates from friends, tweets from people who tweet, ads on café bulletin boards, tales about Robin Hood or King Arthur, and catchy rhymes by Dr. Seuss. I can spend painstaking hours laboring over the wording of a sermon on a difficult text and the next thing I know I am flipping the pages of a children's picture book and interjecting unrelated questions like "Do you need to poo poo?" and "Can you say 'I love Dada?'" in goofy, high-pitched inflections. After a day of crafting a single paragraph for an academic essay I can walk in the door of my home and hear my little boys humming the John Williams score from *Star Wars*, and just before reading bedtime Bible stories I might find my little girls dancing to Beyoncé's "Single Ladies" (thanks to the influence of my dearly loved and fun-loving sister-in-law).

It may seem a bit odd to suggest that the Bible stories my family and I come across at bedtime may have something to say about this complex

2. Hoover, *Religion in the Media Age*, 29.

collage of media in our daily lives. Moses did not envision my sons' fascination with a galaxy far, far away and a long time ago. When Paul wrote the so-called "love chapter" (1 Cor 13) he was not anticipating my daughters' delight in dancing to some hip hop ditty about a young man's failure to propose (nor was he writing about romance at all, for that matter). There are massive cultural, geographical, religious, and socio-economic gaps between my day and the days when Moses received the tablets and when ages later the Apostle was dictating epistles. As we begin reading the script for a rough theological framework for understanding media, we should acknowledge the two major differences between media in the ancient realms of the Bible (the ancient Near East and the Hellenized Mediterranean realm) and our own realm of twenty-first-century Western civilization.

SECULARIZATION, COMMERCIALISM, AND THE BYGONE DUALISM OF ANCIENT MASS MEDIA

When God cried out through his prophet Amos, "Take away from me the noise of your songs" (Amos 5:23), he was not referring to all that secular music blaring from Assyrian radio stations. There was no "secular" music (or radio stations, of course). Amos was actually talking about Israel's songs of *worship* (a frightening reminder that so-called holy activity does not necessarily evidence holiness itself!).

In our contemporary context, Western Christians have inherited a pluralistic world that has infamously forged a chasm between the sacred and the secular (the latter generally referring to religious neutrality). No such chasm existed for most of human history. Old world sights and sounds were infused with religion— "space was religious," as Kavin Rowe puts it in the epigraph above. This is not to claim that Hittites, Persians, Israelites, or Greeks never sang a folk song about love and loss (see Song of Songs) or never penned poems about a hard day's work (see Ecclesiastes). But the worldviews of the ancient Near East and the Greco-Roman realm were decidedly religious, so any song or folk story was subsumed beneath an overarching metanarrative in which gods and goddesses played primary roles. For Israel in the Old Testament, any song that honored another deity other than or alongside their "one" God, or any tale sponsoring an alternative account of the world's governance or formation, was deemed *idolatrous*.

There persisted in antiquity a noticeable dualism (that is, a direct and opposing tension) between the media of God and the media of the world. The latter consisted of public imagery and events (what we often call "mass media") sponsored by the cultures and nations surrounding and often infiltrating the subcultural domain of God's people. The former were sourced in God or directed toward him through particular spiritual disciplines or by approved means of ritual worship. Since religion was inseparably woven into the fabric of the ancient contexts, "worldly media" was easily recognizable as worldly, and also idolatrous.

Though we tend to think of "media" as contemporary phenomena, the roots stretch throughout the timelines of human civilization; and historically, "media" has been an *explicitly religious concept.*

The sharp dualism between media's religious connotations are less obvious in our own time. The relatively recent process of secularization in Western societies, resulting from a scientific worldview, has dampened the overt religious rhetoric and drained almost dry (but not entirely) from our societies what was once a widespread sense of the mystical and numinous. Public media's religious overtones are quite minimal (though religious *under*tones do persist at times).

Along with secularization, the other predominant force that influences public media today in ways unknown to the world of the Old and New Testaments is commercialism. The public sights and sounds glaring and blaring along our streets and building complexes are not religious media but *commercialized* media. Rather than alluring idols of gods and goddesses, we have alluring ads for goods and services.

Urban centers in the ancient Near East and later city-states like Rome, Alexandria, and Antioch could certainly boast at times of thriving commerce, but the agrarian nature of those societies and the absence of a widespread consumer base with coinage to spend meant that little signage and few consumer marketing strategies were required. The range of purchasable items was drastically less than it is for us today, so media campaigns bombarding the masses with the latest gadget or adventure tour were quite unnecessary.

YET SIMILARITIES . . .

Commercialization and secularization have brought about the most obvious differences between the media of ancient and contemporary societies, but we should note that gold has never lost its glitter nor silver its luster. What I mean is that cold hard cash (which would have been literally cold and hard in Egypt, Canaan, or Corinth) was still the apple of many an ancient's eye. As noted in the previous chapter, ancient world media at times paired the visual gleaming of costly metals with the visual portrayal of sexuality (phallic symbols and heaving breasts were not uncommon characteristics of idolatry).

Also, no form of entertainment or communication today is entirely eviscerated of religious meaning. Westerners may assume their consumerism is innocent of religion, yet shopping is one of the most consistent activities to which we are sometimes religiously devoted.

Secularization has eliminated from media the names of gods and goddesses and the terminology of worship, but that does not mean that today's media are never idolatrous. In Colossians, "greed" is equated with "idolatry" (Col 3:5; cf. Eph 5:5). Sure, we don't worship graven images, but Paul's pairing of greed with idolatry should give us contemporary shoppers pause. Perhaps even more disturbing, Jesus seemed to personify material wealth as an alternative god named "Mammon" (Matt 6:24; Luke 16:13).[3] Our lust for stuff (and perhaps our unintended religious allegiance to the Mammon-god?) can now be awakened and deepened by twelve-second television clips or by banner ads on a webpage. Most of us are exposed to hundreds of these every week.

Commercialism and secularism have depersonalized the gods, but we consumerist moderns have not abandoned sect-like loyalties to forces emblematized in gleaming and sexualized imagery.

"CULTURAL EXEGESIS"

But I *do* need a car to get my family from point A to B, right? What about a laptop for writing a theology book? Don't churches need expensive sound systems so that the preached word may resound in every ear in the sanctuary? Should Western consumerism really be understood as synonymous with the cultic devotion of past civilizations? Surely the manufacturers of automobiles, computers, and microphones are not in league with some undercover pagan conspiracy. Spending hours hunched over

---

3. Miller, *The Ten Commandments*, 46. See also Betz, *The Sermon on the Mount Including the Sermon on the Plain*, 454; and Moberly, "Toward an Interpretation of the Shema," 144.

a keypad and screen does not make me an idolater, right? We middle and upper class folks in westernized societies may love to shop, but we do not bow prostrate before our new SUVs, smartphones, and flat screen TVs while singing songs of gadget adoration (well, except on the release days for new Apple products). And many of those standing in the factory lines managing the machinery coating new car bodies with glossy enamel and many of those writing programs for the latest electronic devices may well be Christians.

Are they blaspheming by virtue of their daily grind?

A secular, commercial, and pluralistic civilization blurs the distinctions between that which is sourced from God or the gods. If I saw minivans gilt with gold on the dealership's lot and marked by a "BAAL" inscription on the hood, I would certainly shop elsewhere. I would never buy a smartphone that displayed "Ra, the Sun God, loves you" on its screen every time I turned it on.

The point here is that the dualism between media's spiritual or religious sources and functions is less clear these days than it was for the Hebrews, Israelites, and even the first Christians we read about in our Bibles. Most of us will readily acknowledge that beautiful stories of redemption and grace can emerge amidst the smut of a seedy, back-studio film produced by non-Christians. Powerful ministry can result from the use of a cunningly marketed laptop. Gold romanticized as the source of ultimate joy in steamy, sexualized commercials can instill healthy gravitas in the bride and groom who stand before God exchanging solemn vows. Rap lyrics of jolting violence and raucous sexuality can sometimes offer brilliantly insightful commentary on the dark side of an urban culture many of us wish to ignore. The Bible itself does quite a job of displaying divine beauty in the midst of unnerving depravity, and Paul's instructions on whether or not Christians should eat meat offered to idols show that some lines have always been fuzzy. Today's commercialism and secularization have blurred the lines that once demarcated media as holy or profane. Connections to idolatry are less explicit in our modern-day context, and even explicitly unhealthy ideas embedded in public imagery or events can coincide with healthy, even biblical, ideas.

What are we to do?

Something Kevin Vanhoozer calls "cultural exegesis"[4] is required of us. We have to be good readers not only of our Bibles, but also of our

---

4. See Vanhoozer, *Everyday Theology*.

culture. The discernment needed for assessing our media-saturated lives is to be premised on the former. Though the contextual gaps are vast, studying scripture can offer us wisdom from ages past when the source and focus of media were very clear indeed. The challenge is learning how to rely on this biblical wisdom today in discerning what is holy, unholy, both, or neither amidst the noisy and complex host of media influences around us.

Those practicing this cultural exegesis, however, are not coming up with the same assessments. Their *biblical* exegesis is quite mixed as well. We should take a look at the vast range of opinions and assessments on offer when it comes to media technology and the church. And you should probably know more about where I am coming from as I offer my own.

Chapter 3

Harbingers of Gloom and Glory

Christian Responses to Media Technology

[I]n every tool we create, an idea is embedded that goes beyond the function of the thing itself.[1]

Each technology has an agenda of its own.[2]

—Neil Postman

The vehicle of Twitter is, in many ways, the ultimate medium for disciple-ship. . . . The real question is not "Would Jesus tweet?" but "What would Jesus tweet?"[3]

—Leonard Sweet

A melodramatic modernism or postmodernism, one that underscores the

1. Postman, *Amusing Ourselves to Death*, 14.
2. Ibid., 84.
3. Sweet, "In the Beginning Was the Tweet," lines 16–17; 131–32.

revolutions and ruptures that come with electronic communication, is not particularly helpful and is pretty much based on an illusion . . . . I attempt to deconstruct the satanic and angelic images that have surrounded, justified, and denigrated the media of communications. We are dealing with an old story rather than a new one. Although the computer and the satellite have reduced time to a picosecond, an instantaneous present, and the globe to a point where everyone is in the same place, this is simply the latest chapter in an old tale. The habits of mind and structures of thought that seem characteristic of our age, particularly the talk of a communications revolution and exalted hopes and equally exaggerated fears of the media, are repetitions so predictable as to suggest undeviating corridors of thought.[4]

—JAMES W. CAREY

We are sitting on the sofas for Family Movie Night. Everyone is eating pizza and having a fine time. It occurs to me that the sun is setting. Part of the living room becomes ablaze with the fiery gold of another dusk, a time of day when the ceaseless flight of celestial objects becomes visually obvious. In this wondrous movement, the sun's fading rays cast a glare on the screen. My kids groan in dismay. I blockade the digitally mastered soundscape from my ears and consider the conversations we are not having over a table and suffer a twinge of guilt. When I pause to notice how glued my kids' eyes are to this screen distorted by the garish intrusion of fiery gold, I feel bad that a sunset—one they are missing—has become the occasion for annoyance . . .

I am having coffee with a friend. The sense of Christ's presence in our midst grows stronger with each exchange. My cell phone is buzzing. The conversation intensifies and takes a more serious turn. My cell phone keeps buzzing. My friend's tone adjusts as he begins to confide. We have leaned in more closely over the table, closing distance. My cell phone—it is still buzzing. *What if that is my wife calling? What if one of the kids is sick at school?* I am hoping my friend does not notice that I am in two conversations, one with him, and one with myself over whether or not to start a third conversation. To suspend the powerful interaction

4. Carey, *Communication as Culture*, 2.

taking place over this table would be rude. To ignore the buzzing feels irresponsible . . .

A writing project is due. I want to type "conversation" but I have already overused the word in my text. So I open the Internet browser to find an online thesaurus. The bold print signifying an unopened email appears on the iGoogle page as I click the bookmarked link to the thesaurus. But that bold print is screaming. The unopened email is back there, a mere two clicks away on a previous webpage, waiting for me like a corked bottle suddenly washed ashore bearing concealed contents. "Colloquy," "discourse," "parley"—these are too formal for my replacement of "conversation." "Powwow" and "chin-wag" will certainly not do. A half-naked woman is staring at me on the left side of the screen, an ad for a cell phone, maybe, or for a new car or maybe for luggage (probably not for a sweater or a jacket). My hand is oddly positioned over the left side of my screen, shielding the ad as I read through a list of hyperlinked words. "Chat" is simple enough—*of course, why didn't I come up with that on my own?* But I do not make it back to my writing project for another ten minutes. I have to open the contents of that mysterious bottle that washed ashore into my inbox. The thesaurus was helpful, but I now feel as though I wasted time. There is the outline of a barely-clad female selling luggage or what-not lingering in my peripheral vision, and the faint thought arises that maybe I am outsourcing my brain's reserve of vocab words to the data banks of the Internet . . .

CONFLICTED

Many of my friends are untroubled by their experience of the sort of scenarios offered above. *C'mon, we're in the digital age. Get used to it.*

My own experience of the digital age, however, comes with regular conflicts of conscience. Watching movies with my family affords us a time of rest and relaxation over a good story. It can also become an unhealthy escape from reality and limit our time for those unplanned but often meaningful chats that arise over a dinner table. Checking to see if my wife is calling on my cell phone signifies that my relationship with her is prioritized over all others. It is also a interruption at the coffee shop table. I legitimately needed to look up a word while writing a book that I hope brings some edification to the church. The online thesaurus is presumably the quickest way to do a vocab search, except that

I often allow myself to be allured by the distractions of new emails or status alerts that sabotage the supposed speed (and printed versions of the *Merriam-Webster Dictionary* do not allow ads with half-naked people in the page margins).

I tend to be an all-or-nothing sort of guy, so for the sake of relieving a conflicted conscience I want to either embrace the digital age wholeheartedly or chuck it altogether and flee for one of those diminishing un-digitized outposts of rustic simplicity that must be out there somewhere.

Neither option is feasible, and neither will do. I have too good a script to be this conflicted.

STUMBLING INTO THIS WRITING PROJECT

Clearly, I have not written this book on media and theology because I am a techno-guru. I like Mac products, but you are not going to find me waiting outside the Apple Store on product release dates. In spite of the bouts of internal wrestling, neither am I a technophobe hoping to toss a vindictive wrench into the virtual machinery. But when my interest was ignited a few years ago by these conflicts of conscience and by media-related concerns in pastoral ministry, a wrench was certainly clutched within my fist.

I first encountered "electronic mail" during my final year as an undergraduate student. According to the tech department at my university, this new mode of communication obligated me to memorize a lengthy "email address" (whatever that was) shot through with random periods and interjected with a strange symbol I had never even noticed on typewriters or computer keyboards ("@"). As it turned out, there was also a "password" to commit to memory. It was all so tedious that I casually ignored this initial introduction to the World Wide Web in the halcyon days of the mid-1990s when life was still uncomplicated, pristine, and absent of distractions.

Seven of my past ten years in ministry have been spent among university students. When I assumed a pastoral post on a small North Carolina campus at the turn of the century, I quickly found that within just six years of my departure from undergraduate life the struggles of my slightly younger friends regularly included media issues my peers and I never had to deal with when we were students. (These media issues in-cluded relational spats incited through "Instant Messenger" or addictions to Internet pornography.) After four years of working with these dear young people, I then spent two years pastoring a small, mostly elderly congregation that cared little for the burgeoning gadget market (aside from flat screen televisions, which began appearing in the homes of these retired farmers and factory workers). Neither were they interested in the exciting new world of social media that was suddenly flourishing online.

When I re-entered college ministry in 2008 I found that I could hardly get a response from a late teen or twenty-something through any other means except by sending a text message from my outdated cell phone (oddly enough, my unsalaried undergraduate friends always seemed to have the better phone, like the pensioners in my previous flock always had the more advanced TV).

Even after a couple of years out of the campus scene, the pastoral problems related to media technology appeared to grow more intense. Misrepresentations on Facebook, online theological debates that got out of hand, promiscuous interactions with strangers through a variety of other social media outlets—these issues and many others were the topics of countless conversations over coffee and in my office. The porn addictions had become all but universal among the guys. While working as a server at a nearby restaurant that was great for dates, my wife kept finding young couples with their eyes glued not to each other but to the screens of the cutting-edge phones they both held in their laps while texting or Googling or whatever-ing.

Burdened by the effects of these media-related entanglements and by the new habits with technology that I observed in my young friends, I began worryingly considering the future of my four little kids. The probability is quite high that my two daughters will date teenage males whose pubescent introduction to sexual interrelation will have been shaped by "gonzo porn," the sexually brutalizing imagery that is pushing pornography to its extremes and currently flourishing on the Internet. I was overwhelmed envisioning my sons' future online addictions and frightened at the prospects that all four of my children might be unwittingly exposed to "sexting" once I succumb to the cultural winds and the logistical realities of our society and supply them with their first mobile phones.

Woe betide us.

It was in the midst of these pastoral and parental anxieties that I began preparing a sermon series on media, gearing up for a homiletical takedown of the twisted covens spawning all this malevolent techno-wizardry. It makes sense, I suppose, that when I first began reading media studies I was a naysayer and somewhat of a Luddite (one of our day's most despised labels). In the name of pastoral and parental urgency I arraigned media technology, summoning it to a theological court for judgment. Surely we were better off without all this newfangled stuff so laden with temptation and so capable of distortion. And surely the Bible would provide ammunition for my sermonic raillery . . .

SKETCHING THE SPECTRUM

I have since calmed down a bit.

Those anxieties were possibly exaggerated at the time, but the concerns that ignited them are nonetheless very serious, painfully real, and in need of urgent pastoral and parental attention. But ranting out of the limited perspective of my personal preferences and inclinations would be no good to anyone. I needed a *theological frame of reference* (even if it is "rough").

So how are Christians crafting a theology of media? And how are we practicing the "cultural exegesis" mentioned in the previous chapter?

One of the challenges in the academic study of media and religion is identifying how people of faith respond to media technology. As noted in the concluding line of the previous chapter, these responses vary drastically along a wide range of dispositions.

On one end of the spectrum is an optimism quite alien to my own disposition when I started work on that sermon series a few years back. For many Christians, all the new media technology is jolly good fun and an unprecedented ally in the work of the gospel. Some proponents go so far as to assign Pollyannish powers to media technology, as if it places utopia within our grasp. Other enthusiasts tend to view media as neutral conduits by which content is transmitted—"neutral" referring to either the morality of the medium or its power to govern how it is used, or both.[5] In this "instrumentalist" view, media are neither good nor bad in and of themselves.[6] The ethical merit of a media form is determined by how it is used. For example, the Internet can be used for viewing porn (which Christians would affirm as ethically wrong), yet it can also be

5. I am relying on media scholar John Ferré, who labels this approach to media technology by religious groups as the "Media as Conduits" perspective. See Ferré, "The Media of Popular Piety," 84–86.

6. Borgmann, *Power Failure*, 122–23.

used for evangelizing. These uses, however, say nothing about the Internet's moral status as media.

Pragmatism strongly governs how Christians with this perspective engage media technology. If television gets the word out, televangelism is legitimate; if Twitter expands the influence of a pastor, then tweeting is good. On this end of the spectrum are media advocates for whom the ministerial possibilities via screens are "virtually" limitless (pun intended). Their rhetoric often casts an idealistic vision of technology's benefits and at times criticizes (subtly or blatantly) those backward media skeptics stuck in their old-fashioned ways and failing to see the emerging horizon of a bright new era for both church and society. Plenty of books have emerged espousing varying degrees of this optimism (though televangelism is not championed quite as often as it used to be).[7]

On the naysaying end of the spectrum, where I found myself a few years ago, are those heeding the prophetic frowns of intellectuals like Jacques Ellul, Neil Postman, and Malcolm Muggeridge.[8] These leading twentieth-century observers of society's embrace of technology warned that to regard a medium as an innocent conduit is to be deceived. Embedded within each technological product or mechanism is a veiled value system inimical to society. Ellul warned that all life was being philosophically reconceived in technical and therefore utilitarian terms. "Technology is ideology," wrote Postman in his classic critique of the Age of Television.[9] In spite of his decades as a broadcast journalist who helped pioneer televised news, Malcolm Muggeridge publicly recanted of his participation in the field and proudly admitted to having tossed out his telly.[10] A collective concern of these astute thinkers is that a medium actually shapes (and thereby often corrupts) the content conveyed.[11]

In media studies, this is called "technological determinism."[12]

7. A brief sampling includes Rice, *The Church of Facebook*; Drescher, *Tweet If You Heart Jesus*; and Sweet, *Viral*.

8. Ellul, *The Technological Society* and *Propaganda*; Postman, *Amusing Ourselves to Death* and *Technopoly*; Muggeridge, *Christ and the Media*.

9. Postman, *Amusing Ourselves to Death*, 157.

10. Or removed his "aerials." For background insights into Muggeridge's rather shocking claims (though at times very inspiring, in my view) in his 1977 lectures at All Souls, Langham Place (chaired by John Stott), see Grant, "Christ and the Media."

11. Ferré calls this approach "Media as Modes of Knowing"—see Ferré, "The Media of Popular Piety," 86–88.

12. Marshall McLuhan was also a technological determinist; however, he was enthusiastic about the exciting possibilities of media technology (I am grateful to Tim

For example, television may broaden the church's message, but the message itself will have to conform to the limits and the warping influences intrinsic to that technological product (the media is deterministic). As portrayed in the fictional settings of dystopia in E. M. Forster's "The Machine Stops," Aldous Huxley's *Brave New World*, George Orwell's *1984*, Ray Bradbury's *Fahrenheit 451*, Don DeLillo's *White Noise*, or even in Suzanne Collins's depiction of the Capitol in *The Hunger Games* trilogy, these warping influences of media technology are so efficiently masked that they are ignored by the benighted masses until some jolting crisis occurs . . . assuming the characters awaken to the crises' call.

Failing to recognize the inherent influences of the medium itself (technological determinism) results in the technology we use actually using us, as the logic goes.[13]

The bright and dark sides of media are thus depicted in the spectrum sketched above. Ratcheted to extreme degrees, we have what communications scholar James Carey has called "happy pastorals of progress" on one end and "grim narratives of power and domination" on the other.[14] But there are multiple authorities along both sides. Who is right? Which perspective toward media technology is more theologically legitimate to guide the church's experience with media in the digital era?[15]

Though many of my suspicions toward media and technology remain, I have recently begun listening more charitably to the media enthusiasts. As it turns out, I have much to learn from their pragmatism, and maybe even from their optimism. Though I felt somewhat backslidden when I cried "uncle" and opened a Facebook account a few years back, I have to say that scanning those status updates helps me keep up with friends now that I live overseas. As squeamish as I was about blogging, I have to admit that it seems to sharpen my theological thinking. It also allows for interactive feedback. Though a bibliophile struggling with Nicholas Carr to maintain the neural pathways conducive for long-form

Hutchings for clarifying this for me). See McLuhan, *Understanding Media*; for a brief but representative collection of McLuhan's writing on his ideas of a medium's impact on its message, see McLuhan, "The Medium is the Message," in *Media Studies*, 38–43.

13. A sampling of respectable books along this more cautionary side of the spectrum directed to Christian readers include Schultze, *Habits of the High-Tech Heart*; Hipps, *Flickering Pixels*; Challies, *The Next Story*; Boers, *Living Into Focus*; and Dawn, *Unfettered Hope*.

14. Carey, *Communication as Culture*, 9.

15. Walking a fine path between these opposite poles is Dyer's *From the Garden to the City*.

reading, I nonetheless find so much material online that spurs me on in the faith, even if the media formats are too limiting to give a full account of the issues at hand and even if the text is embedded with those distracting, sky-blue hyperlinks.[16]

But allow me to flip-flop a bit. Blogging can become vainly tied to hiking up the stats. Facebook can be exhibitionist and voyeuristic. Those hyperlinks really do distract. So how is a Christian to negotiate not only the range of voices, but also the irreconcilable notion lingering in the back of our minds that all this media saturation is paradoxically both good and bad? More to the point: how do we practice faithful spirituality in the digital age? Is media technology a necessary evil we just have to learn to live with in the twenty-first century? If so, then constructing a godly life in a digital age of media saturation can feel quite impossible.

THE MESSINESS OF MEDIA: DREAD AND EXCITEMENT IN THE DIGITAL AGE

If we accept the view that technology and media are inherently dangerous, we begin thinking that life is deterministically enslaved in our inescapable media culture. We have to identify the Internet and smartphones as necessary evils. The vigilance some of us feel compelled to maintain can become paralyzing. But after a long day of worrying over technology's influences, we have photos from the family vacation to edit and then upload so that grandparents can see how cute the kids were on the beach, we have toys to order online for a nephew's birthday, and suddenly we detect a beeping sound indicating an incoming text from mom checking to see if we got home safely. Communications technology seems unavoidable, and often quite helpful. As nobly as we might wish to resist the digital revolution, most of us will conclude that we should still reply to those emails at work. As irresponsible as it may have been to linger haplessly on Facebook, we might be remiss to log off without offering some consoling comment to the friend with the disheartening status update. Are we destined for a life plagued by necessary evils?

Sort of, yes. Ex-Eden life is just that way. The church has never known any other context.

---

16. I am referring to the dilemma of online reading and neuroplasticity addressed in Carr's book *The Shallows*.

Life in this world is messy. *Media* are messy. The Corinthian Christians were hard-pressed in the first century to find any meat that had not been sacrificed to some idol before it got to the city market; likewise, our lives today are entangled with our culture's trends, interests, and operations. The church has been born for such messy entanglements. God never assigned the church to a pristine world. The halcyon days before the Internet were really not that halcyon. As the church, we have always worshiped, shared meals, and served our neighbors in the thick of cosmic, social, and cultural messiness. Negotiating new media in a media-saturated culture is just one of our most recent messy tasks in a long line of others.

The authors I cited above as representatives of media suspicion are, to varying degrees, sensitive to the practical difficulties of living as Christians amidst such entanglements. Most Christian writers on media do not decry communications technology with such broad strokes as to incite ethical and moral dilemmas every time we hear the chime of our laptops as they boot up. But as media and religion specialist Heidi Campbell points out, there is the assumption in the extreme, distilled version of this more cautious perspective that

> media technology use will always shroud and distort human culture, so that we are left only with the ability to respond to its power or educate ourselves against its control. This approach often allows only for acceptance or rejection of technology in light of religious values. It does not leave room for considering how religious values may lead to more nuanced responses to technology or the creative innovation of aspects of technology so they are more congruent with core beliefs.[17]

The harsh skeptics who point to technological determinism could well jeopardize the church's witness in society and miss opportunities in this media culture conducive to growing and strengthening the church.

Even so, I cannot cast my lot entirely with the media enthusiasts, some of whom would seem to think that Jesus's birth before the digital age was surely a miscalculation of providence. As a Millennial or even a Gen-Xer, he could be tweeting and blogging his way into so many more hearts. The motivations for getting on board with new media may in some cases stem from the cultural inferiority complex that bedevils us as Christians—in order that the world (especially those hip Millennials)

17. Campbell, *When Religion Meets New Media*, 48.

cannot accuse us of irrelevance, we may rush too hastily to assimilate media technology into our lives. Also, media enthusiasm sometimes derives from our media addictions—playing with the games and gadgetry is so fun that we must quickly forge a theological frame of reference in which Angry Birds, iPhones, and multiple tweets per hour make perfect sense.

At times, media enthusiasm may well be no more than uncritical cultural assimilation.

The gist of what I am getting at here is that a wholesale rejection of communications technology is absurd; and championing media technology without a rigorous process of discernment is equally absurd. From Albert Borgmann: "Contrary to what the technological determinists would have us believe, we are not simply and entirely under the sway of technology. And *pace* the instrumentalists, we are not normally elevated above technology as wakeful and rational choosers."[18] Skepticism or enthusiasm alike should be premised on something deeper than an aversion to or an excitement over all things new. What we need is a (rough!) theological framework premised on something more enduring and authoritative than our media preferences, or our penchant for electronic devices, or our fears of technology, or our media anxieties. We need a theological frame of reference that refuses to coddle our media addictions and refuses to justify our harangues against the techies. Only a theological framework informed by the script of the church's sacred texts can be expansive enough and objective enough to account for the nuances and apparent paradoxes of living faithfully in a media-saturated culture. Though the Bible may not have much to say specifically about tools, machines, and computer software, it has quite a bit to say about humanity, God, and how we communicate. Only a theological framework founded on these biblical realities is big enough for such a sticky media mess.

Articulating such a theological framework is the lofty goal of this book. But remember, it is going to be "rough." Maybe even a little messy.

"THE RELIGIOUS-SOCIAL SHAPING OF TECHNOLOGY"

I have been flip-flopping across the spectrum sketched above to sound out my own internal conflicts that, I am guessing, may well be echoed in

18. Borgmann, *Power Failure*, 123.

the hearts and minds of many of my readers. We have seen that neither extreme on that spectrum will do (and few writers are positioned at the farthest edges). If we find in the script of our sacred texts that God is a communicative God of means, of agency—of *media*, and if human beings are beneficiaries of divine media and are sometimes divine media themselves, then surely there is a form of enthusiasm that is theologically valid. It also stands to reason that media suspicion is also biblically legitimate because human beings, as means and beneficiaries of God's communicative activity, are fallen creatures.

Our concern in this book is primarily with the makers and users of media: broadly speaking, God (so "theology") and human beings (so "anthropology"). To overlook the divine and human characters behind media and attend primarily to communications technology and media forms is misguided. A "technology-centered" approach directs attention primarily to the medium itself, wrangling over whether it is to be viewed as an innocent conduit or as a means endowed with potentially distorting properties.[19] Arguing over this idea of technological determinism might obscure the *theology* of media that insists there is a divine figure ("*Theos*") involved somewhere in the way communication works in this world. The technology-focused approach may also lead us unwittingly to overlook media's *anthropology*, by which I mean the complex human dynamics informing media's production and reception.

Heidi Campbell has proposed a more nuanced approach for understanding religion and media: "the religious-social shaping of technology."[20] She has found in her extensive observations that although communication technologies have the capacity to influence their users, religious groups often resist those influences and bring their theological traditions to bear on how they use them. In other words, although religious folks may indeed be shaped by the technologies they employ, at the same time they exert their own influences on media, incorporating communications technology within their existing conceptual grids and

19. See Campbell, *When Religion Meets New Media,* 49, where she contrasts "technology-centered" with "human-centered" approaches to religious perspectives on media technology.

20. Ibid., 57–63. Campbell is expanding Ferré's third approach, which he calls "Media as Social Institutions" (see Ferré, "The Media of Popular Piety," 88–90). Campbell's religious-social shaping of technology model has informed my approach here as I have tried to understand media by studying Christianity's sacred texts, the history of media reception and use, the authority structures that make media-related decisions, and the ways Christians interact during processes of media discernment.

forcing some degree of theological compliance. Studying the appropriation of media by religious traditions in this way moves beyond the dichotomized spectrum in which technology is seen in varying degrees as
either good or dangerous. As John Dyer succinctly puts it, "Technology
should not dictate our values or our methods. Rather, we must use technology *out of* our convictions and values."[21] Heidi Campbell's ongoing
work demonstrates that Dyer's challenge is not an idealistic rant but an
exciting possibility.

Our focus on TheoMedia (the media of God) in the Bible will soon
begin, but before devoting space to media theology, we need to take a
close look at media's anthropology. When we look at human nature, it
makes sense why there is such a wide spectrum on media philosophies.
It makes sense why media can be so irreconcilably good and bad at the
same time. It makes sense why the media can be so messy. It is because
we ourselves are so messy. So we will close this introductory section looking at two anthropological convictions about humanity found in Genesis
1–11 that are central to the Christian theological tradition and that help
explain why our consciences get so conflicted in this media age. The first
conviction is that human beings are made in God's image. The second
conviction is the doctrine of original sin. Understanding these two realities helps us understand why media can be so dark . . . and yet so bright.

21. Dyer, *From the Garden to the City*, 25.

TheoMedia Note 2

The Mediation of Sex and Violence

Our primary source for sex ed is not our mom, dad, the local health provider, or our middle school science teacher. It is not the church, the Bible, a priest, or a pastor. Our primary source for understanding sex and sexuality is the entertainment industry. The expectations of what sex is supposed to look like and sound like are established in our society by way of screens.[1]

This is an odd way to learn about sex. When two people are so inter-relationally bound together that they can be called "one flesh" (Gen 2:24), there is a stark absence of media. Sex may well be the most unmediated communicative act. When sexuality is displayed by way of a screen, it is a bizarre instance of mediating the unmediated.[2] If media form and content are at all connected, the imagery and acoustics of screen-based technology are rather unfavorable means for communicating the wonder, power, and mystery of sex.[3]

Most of what we know about violence probably comes from screens as well. This means that our understanding of the most gruesome re-alities of human existence is supplied by high-paid fight choreographers and carefully orchestrated stunt techniques. Makeup artists have taught

1. Naomi Wolf: "Young men and women are indeed being taught what sex is, how it looks, what its etiquette and expectations are, by pornographic training—and this is having a huge effect on how they interact." See her article "The Porn Myth."

2. I have used this phrase regularly in teaching on sexuality to university students, but I recently discovered that John Dyer uses the same phrase. See his *The Garden and the City*, 129–30; 163.

3. Though I should note here that my friend Dr. Tim Hutchings wisely reminded me that sex has always been portrayed through a variety of media forms throughout history.

us what wounds look like and how people bleed to death. For most of us, what we know about choking, stabbing, and firing an automatic weapon has been learned not in an emergency room, in a dark alley, or on a battlefield, but in a cinema. When I see violence in films, I am excited and entertained. On the few occasions I have seen violence in real life, my stomach got knotted up and there was this awful metallic taste in my mouth.

Something we are quite accustomed to on those big screens are shooting sprees. They happen all the time in some of the biggest block-busters. The guy with the gun is often identified as the hero, and we cheer him as he vanquishes the foes.

When shooting sprees happens in real life, the shooter is identified as a maniac.

Arnold Schwarzenegger would have me know that the images and acoustics relayed through screens and surround sound are easily dis-tinguishable from reality—the lines are only blurred for crazy people.[4] And secular media sources are continually reminding me that no certi-fied think tank has published scientific research proving definitively that violent behavior is directly linked to media sources. We are too advanced these days to rely on common sense without a scientific study. Of course, when scientific studies do come out, they are sometimes disproved by the study that follows a week later. It is a hard lot relying on scientific studies if you are, say, a coffee drinker. I keep finding out that coffee is destroying me only to learn a week later that it is extending my lifespan. So though I respect the scientific studies, I am not holding out for the definitive report that will settle this whole violence and media debate.

If I might be unscientific for a moment and make a broad sweeping claim, I would like to suggest that reality perception has always been a problem for humans in every age. And today, when it comes to realities we rarely experience, it is easy for us to allow unconsciously the mediated presentations of those realities to dictate how we understand them. Vio-lence is a case in point. Those of us living in areas of town that the zoning laws keep relatively safe and uneventful rarely see real brutality (except for those who witness or experience firsthand the horrific instances of domestic battery taking place behind closed suburban doors).

We also tend to allow entertainment media to dictate how we per-ceive realities we *do* regularly experience, but perhaps not in the way we

4. Alexander, "Schwarzenegger Discusses Violence and Newtown Shootings." See the comments by Clapp in his blog post "Newtown and Movie Violence."

want to experience them. Sex is the most poignant example. Our fantasies create a demand that cinematographers and pornographers rush to supply.

Schwarzenegger is probably right about most of us being able to recognize fact from fiction. But that does not mean that we will rationally choose the former over the latter. Our fantasies are so overwhelming that when we find them readily available on our screens we sometimes let them override reality, consciously or unconsciously. And if screen-mediated sex becomes the standard for what we expect in sexual experience, then we have allowed folks like porn producers, sound technicians, cameramen, and surgically altered actors to dictate our take on real intimacy.[5]

We have also allowed them to define our expectations for what the bodies of our sexual partners should look like, particularly female bodies. In her oft-quoted article for *New York* magazine, Naomi Wolf wrote, "For most of human history, erotic images have been reflections of, or celebrations of, or substitutes for, real naked women. For the first time in human history, the images' power and allure have supplanted that of real naked women. Today, real naked women are just bad porn."[6]

Expectations are also shaped by entertainment media's depiction of sex within ridiculously unrealistic settings. For most folks, sex happens within a complicated matrix rife with all sorts of joys, burdens, and unresolved relational tensions. But *sex with context* does not sell or amass online "hits." Our fantasies are of *decontextualized sex*. This is sex that does not come with questions like, "Is the baby monitor on?" or "Do you think the kids are asleep?" Decontextualized sex does not have to deal with whether or not the dishes have been left dirty in the sink or whether or not there are clothes spinning in the dryer. It does not take into account the previous discussion in the living room over financial difficulties. No

---

5. There are a number of secular writers who have depicted the emptiness, injustice, and sheer ludicrousness of the porn industry. The best exposés I have found are Wallace's essay "Big Red Son"; Hedges's chapter "The Illusion of Love" in *Empire of Illusions* (55–87); and Dines's powerful study *Pornland*. Due to the subject matter, these works are profoundly disturbing. Prospective readers: take caution.

6. Wolf, "The Porn Myth." Prior to the quote above, she described this tragic state of affairs: "Here is what young women tell me on college campuses when the subject comes up: They can't compete, and they know it. For how can a real woman—with pores and her own breasts and even sexual needs of her own (let alone with speech that goes beyond 'More, more, you big stud!')—possibly compete with a cybervision of perfection, downloadable and extinguishable at will, who comes, so to speak, utterly submissive and tailored to the consumer's least specification?"

one has a headache or a cold. There is no alarm clock to set for the morning and it never happens to be "that time of the month." Rarely do the on-screen sexual partners share an elaborate history of hurts and joys.

Then again, Hollywood has its exceptions. I do not recall being entertained by the first twenty minutes of *Saving Private Ryan*. That cinematic depiction of D-Day's violence rightfully horrified and repulsed me. And at times sexual relationships are indeed portrayed with a vivid dose of reality. Sex can be much less glamorous in real life, and sometimes better than a camera can capture. There are some filmmakers who do a fine job portraying the former and leaving the latter alone. Mediating the unmediated has its limits. We have noted already that God can convey truth through unlikely means. Though I think the medium of film often misrepresents violence and sex, there are occasional moments when divine beauty and wisdom are presented on screen.

Even so, I recommend the Bible as a more faithful resource. It may seem a bit archaic and backwards to suggest that Christian scripture is a more reliable source for understanding sex than our current-day entertainment industry. Understandably, women especially might cringe at the suggestion that ancient texts from a patriarchal society have something helpful to say about their sex lives. Accounts of the escapades of powerful men with harems is surely a distasteful source for sex ed (even though some of them may not have been quite as bad as Christian Grey).[7]

What I appreciate about the Bible is that sex and violence are treated with such stark honesty. The violence is ugly and the sex is contextualized within reality. In many respects, the Bible is much more politically correct than many of our media sources today. The sexual oppression of females is becoming a mainstream component of entertainment media—porn's brutal dehumanizing of women keeps surfacing in pop cultural outlets,[8] and E. L. James is signing movie contracts. In spite of the male-dominated milieus of antiquity, those old texts of scripture are honest about sexual oppression and express a divine compassion for women like Rahab (a prostitute), Haggai (a surrogate sex partner), Tamar (who had to pose as a prostitute), and Bathsheba (a victim of coerced sex). All four of these women appear in Christ's genealogy, embedding sexual redemption as a theme within messianic hope. The Bible also expresses divine displeasure

7. The reference, of course, is to the male protagonist in E. L. James's *Fifty Shades of Grey*.

8. See Dines's chapter, "Pop Goes the Porn Culture: Mainstreaming Porn," *Pornland*, 25–46.

at the sexual injustices of men like Judah, David, and Solomon. These men are also in Christ's genealogy—redemption is available even for the perpetrators. And the Bible's own erotic literature celebrating the glory and fun of sex emphasizes mutuality among the partners and places their romance within a realistic context—the lovers in Song of Songs are continually beset by a host of difficulties and tensions as well as delights.

One of the most urgent refrains throughout this book is that Christians are called to media saturation, but the media that are to saturate our lives and dictate our perception of reality are TheoMedia, the media of God. My point in this TheoMedia Note is that many of us are allowing secular media to influence our perception of two of the most critical issues the church must address in society: sex and violence. The Bible is more honest about both than our entertainers.

Chapter 4

Media Dark and Bright
Image Making by Fractured Image Bearers

...Although now long estranged,
Man is not wholly lost or wholly changed.
Dis-graced he may be, yet is not de-throned,
And keeps the rags of lordship once he owned:
Man, Sub-creator, the refracted Light
Through whom is splintered from a single White
To many hues, and endlessly combined
In living shapes that move from mind to mind.
Though all the crannies of the world we filled
With Elves and Goblins, though we dared to build
Gods and their houses out of dark and light,
And sowed the seed of dragons—'twas our right
(used or misused). That right has not decayed:
we make still by the law in which we're made.

—J.R.R. TOLKIEN, "ON FAIRY-STORIES"[1]

I looked at my hand right, the hand with which I painted. There was power
in that hand. Power to create and destroy. Power to bring pleasure and pain.

1. Tolkien, "On Fairy-Stories," 144.

Power to amuse and horrify. There was in that hand the divine and the demonic at one and the same time.

—FROM CHAIM POTOK'S *MY NAME IS ASHER LEV*[2]

The previous chapter closed suggesting that the reason media has a side so dark and one so bright, both of which are inextricably entangled, can be explained by looking beyond technology to the human dynamics behind its production and use. So this chapter is about media's anthropology. The reason for the brightness is that we are media makers made in the image of God (the *imago Dei*, as it is rendered in Latin). The reason for the darkness is because sin has somehow corroded our faculties for displaying divine beauty and character.

These dual realities—that we are made in God's image and yet debilitated by sin—are affirmed for me every day. Being a dad affords quite a vantage point for observing human nature. The doctrines of the *imago Dei* and original sin make the best sense of what I experience personally every day as a human being, and they explain perfectly what I see at work in my kids . . .

EXTENSIONS AND DISTORTIONS OF GOD: THE *IMAGO DEI* AND THE *INCURVATUS IN SE*

When Communion was served recently at our church, I rose with the toddler in my arms as soon as the invitation was extended and went to receive the bread and wine. My desperation for Jesus was too intense to wait and piously reflect in the seat. I just needed him. Not in two minutes, not in one. I needed him then and there. I needed bread and wine to remind me of his presence.

Returning to my seat, I found my seven-year-old son distraught and on the verge of tears. My wife had just joined the Communion line with our older daughter. I had baptized her the previous year, and my wife and I have decided that our kids will wait on taking the elements of the Lord's Supper until baptism (not a conviction enforced by our church or one we would hold others to).

---

2. Potok, *My Name Is Asher Lev*, 319.

This little boy who chose Jesus as his focus on that homework project has not yet been baptized.

He wanted the bread (not the wine, so much). Oh, for that bread. He was hungry. I sort of wanted to correct his attitude: *we do not take Communion because we want a snack*. I thought better of it. Hunger is real. The bread is real. The tangibility of it all is intentional. I explained to him again the meaning of the elements. In childlike, innocent fashion the little guy's desire for a snack, his palate's delight in our church's style of Communion bread, and his yearning for Jesus were all bound together quite beautifully. Beautifully, but also tragically since his daddy has this policy of no pre-baptism Eucharist.

By denying him the bread (he still had no interest in the wine), my little boy seemed to think I was denying him of something more. And I was. I shared the gospel with him again, affirmed to him Christ's love. *That bread is for you, little guy. It is yours. Jesus wants you to feast on it, to never get tired of it, to munch it and taste it over and over again. It is for you . . . forever.* But I also want to honor baptism as an initiating sacrament that binds one into the family of faith nurtured on the sacramental bread and cup. He was nearly in tears. The boy wanted the body of our Lord, broken for him. He was desperate. He did not want to wait two minutes. Not one minute. He needed something at that very moment.

His mother and sister returned. My daughter, then nine years old, discreetly stuck out her hand as she walked past her grieving brother to get to her seat. In one motion, her little fingers swiftly opened his and secretively placed something inside.

A tiny piece of bread.

That scene was one of the most powerful moments of mediating the Eucharist I have ever witnessed. A big sister had snatched an extra morsel and surreptitiously fed a little boy hungry for the bread of his Lord. Nothing short of divine beauty—the beauty of the *imago Dei*—was on display in that moment.

Of course, moments later they could be yelling and scratching and kicking each other.

That is exactly how I witness divine beauty in my home. One minute there is holy splendor radiating from a smiling little face, and within seconds that face is contorted with fierce rage because there will be no more sweets until after dinner. We human beings can demonstrate the divine image quite remarkably in our lives. Then someone tells us we cannot have or do something we want, like more chocolate before supper.

Or like forbidden fruit off a lovely tree.

It was claimed in chapter 1 that humans are divine media agents. Along with the rest of creation, human beings were designed to radiate the beauty of the Creator. Our responsibility and capacity for serving as divine media is heightened uniquely among the other creatures because we alone were entrusted with the divine image. A central dimension to this image bearing is to exercise the benevolence of God's divine rule as royal representatives: "Let them have dominion . . ." (Gen 1:16). The meaning of divine image bearing is the subject of an ongoing dialogue throughout the centuries. There is no space to plumb its theological depths here, but along with the regal vocation just mentioned, we can say that bearing the image of a *creating* God certainly implies that human beings were intended to produce artistry depicting and conveying the splendor and character of the great Artisan King.[3]

Some media scholars consider Marshall McLuhan's work misguided or outdated today, criticizing the technological determinism with which he is associated or perhaps decrying his so-called originality.[4] But his definition that a medium is an "extension of man"[5] takes seriously the inseparable human components integral to technology and media. Marked by the *imago Dei*, the holy likeness of the supreme Artist, human beings are extensions of *God*. We serve as living referents of both his reign and his creative artistry, extending the wonder of God into the divine handiwork of the fields, forests, vales, and hills beneath our footfalls. As claimed in chapter 1, image bearing is a media vocation, a calling to serve as divine media in the world. If media technology extends from us, and we extend from God, then there are divine components at work in our media making and media use.

But we are not only extensions of God. We are also *distortions* of God.

Since the Fall of humanity, we are fractured image bearers marked by divine beauty yet marred by sin. Brightness and darkness are now intertwined and entangled in one big mortal mess.

---

3. On the history of interpreting the *imago Dei* and the assorted suggestions, see ch. 2 in Middleton, *The Liberating Image.*

4. For a recent look at McLuhan's legacy as a thinker and writer (and an assessment of his works' applicability for today), see Jacobs, "Why Bother with Marshall McLuhan?"

5. See McLuhan, *Understanding Media.*

These dual doctrines of original sin and the *imago Dei* are at work not only in how my kids interact, but also in the way they make stuff. Creating is intrinsic to us as created beings. We beget, produce, fashion, and forge. Crafting a piece of wood, trimming the lawn, making up a song, and dabbing a thin brush on canvas are elemental human activities.[6] From the makeshift studios of our dining room table and living room floor, my wife and I are daily collecting what will become boxes of carefully preserved artwork. Though none of it would sell in a reputable gallery, no illustration of a tree or cloud is better than those produced at the tiny fingertips of our kids.

Yet sometimes their creations bespeak a disturbing darkness. Gruesome scenes of blades ripping and lasers slashing. A sign displaying "Keep Out of My Room" crafted in heated anger.

That primeval act of cosmic mutiny in Genesis 3 did something that has affected our creative as well as our relational capacities. As rebel image bearers, our image making can often be characterized by a Latin phrase from Augustine, later used by Luther and Barth: *homo incurvatus in se*.[7] Referring to humanity's centripetal curving in on itself, the phrase captures the inward (and therefore futile) orientation of sinful creatures. It is not that human beings are incapable of producing beauty. But we are regularly rushing off to hide among the trees, masking our secrets with homespun clothing and hanging on the bark behind us handmade signs reading, "Keep Out of My Room."

In following the serpent's mistranslation of God's word in Genesis 3, we have opted for an orientation that is self-ward rather than God-ward. Relationally distanced from the ultimate source of beauty and truth, the mediation of divine reality in the world via fallen image bearers is clouded and debilitated. The Pauline claim that Jesus is the "image of the invisible God, the firstborn of all creation" (Col 1:15) suggests that Jesus bears something that the rest of humanity has in a limited or damaged status. Our media vocation of image bearing has been compromised.

6. For more on this idea of human beings serving God by imaging his creative capacities and thereby creating *culture*, see Crouch, *Culture Making*; see also Kuyper's lecture "Calvinism and Art," in his *Lectures on Calvinism*, 156.

7. For an elaborate and recent treatment of this phrase, see Jensen, *The Gravity of Sin*. I am not the first person to apply the Latin phrase *homo incurvatus in se* to media. My co-blogger Joel Busby does so in his post "Social Media & Theological Discourse [6]: Social Media and *Incurvatus in Se*"; and after making notes about the phrase in my preparatory notes for this book, I noticed that Dyer also uses it in *From the Garden to the City*, 77, 96.

MEDIA TECHNOLOGY AND THE FALL NARRATIVE: SIN, CULTURE, AND COSMOS

The results of sin in Genesis 3 can be categorized as relational, cultural, and even cosmic. These relational, cultural, and cosmic ramifications are central to understanding media and technology. We highlighted the relational effects of sin in chapter 1, how the unhindered interpersonal communication between Adam and Eve was instantly clouded. Once the sugary pulp of that fruit began dissolving in their mouths, they recognized that they were naked and then concealed themselves from one another with clothing. Immediately afterward, they both made a mad dash into the trees as "Where are you?" echoed darkly in Eden. Heeding the voice of the serpent as an unauthorized mediator resulted in the primordial communications disaster that haunts all human relationships and gashed a breach in our interaction with God.

We find in Genesis 1 what is sometimes referred to as the "cultural mandate." Human beings were called to "be fruitful and multiply," to "fill the earth and subdue it," and to exercise "dominion" over the other creatures (1:28ff). This charge to yield families, to proliferate out to the horizons, to govern the earth and its flora and fauna, is a call to create a vast human society that flourishes as the fellowship of glorious creatures fashioned in the image of God. It is a call to form God-breathed culture that teems with life and beauty.

The judgments God utters over the serpent, Eve, and Adam in Genesis 2 all refer back to the cultural mandate. Humanity had been assigned a benevolent dominion over the animal world: "over the fish of the sea and over the birds of the air and over every living thing that moves upon the earth" (Gen 1:26). That vocation is now radically undermined as the serpent and the children of Eve (the human species here, though understood by early Christian interpreters as a prefiguration of Christ) are consigned to perpetual conflict, to the continual plight of back and forth head bruising and heel bruising (3:14–15). Haunting the world is now an ongoing collision of humanity and "an evil being that has assumed form, that is inexplicably present within our created world, and that has singled out man, lies in wait for him, and everywhere fights a battle with him for life and death."[8] Our exercise of dominion is now challenged by another *dominus*, another "lord": the serpent from of old.

8. Von Rad, *Genesis*, 92.

The call to "be fruitful and multiply"—to establish families and societies—is also affected as childbirth is infused with pain (3:16–17) and as marriage is poisoned with interpersonal tension ("He shall rule over you"). The call to govern the plants and the ground is compromised as the latter bristles with painful versions of the former: "thorns and thistles" (3:18). Adam had been placed in Eden to "till" and "keep" the ground (2:15), labors requiring some degree of technology at its most basic level. Yet sin not only hobbles our capacity to relate to God and to one another; it also mars all our cultural enterprises, many of which, as any worker of the "ground" could tell us, include technological processes.

As fractured image bearers in a world labeled as "fallen," we still possess the yearning and inclination to beget, produce, fashion, and forge. We are media producers and technology users. But now that sinful humanity has been relationally disengaged from God as the life-giving Creator, now that a cosmic tension with evil is underway, now that a dystopic friction marks all we do, our self-produced media and our use of technology will often bear the marks of the incurvature of our souls. When we set our hands to creative and technological ventures, we are operating within an entropic realm. Since the entire cosmos has been affected by sin, technology is never developed or applied in pure neutrality.

Writing on the genre of fairy stories, J. R. R. Tolkien remarks that "Man becomes a sub-creator"; and as such, "not all [visions of fantasy] are beautiful and wholesome, not at any rate the fantasies of fallen Man. And he has stained the elves who have this power (in verity or fable) with his own stain."[9] Tolkien goes on to point out that "we make in our measure and in our derivative mode, because we are made: and not only made, but made in the image and likeness of a Maker."[10]

When we make and use media, we are drawing from the artistic reserves of creatures both divine and fallen.

Thus the bright and dark sides of media's anthropology, and thus the messiness of media. The reason it is so difficult to practice cultural exegesis and discern the moral and practical pros and cons of media is because the dual realities of the *imago Dei* and original sin blur together into a foggy haze. The human dimension behind media and technology can be jointly beautiful and corrupt.

9. Tolkien, "On Fairy Stories," 122.
10. Ibid., 145.

THE MEDIA PROJECT OF BABEL: WHEN "CONNECTEDNESS" IS DANGEROUS

Those anthropological lines are not *always* blurred, however.

There are two major structural projects described in the biblical prehistory of Genesis 1–11. The first is a boat, the second a skyscraper. Noah's ark was not his idea. God not only commissioned him to build it. He also provided specific measurements and even identified which construction material to use (gopher wood, of course; see Gen 6:14–16). The first structural feat in scripture is a boat designed by God for the salvation of a small handful of fractured image bearers.

The second structural feat was not God's idea. It was the idea of collective humanity. In Genesis 1:26, God said, "*Let us make* man in our image," and then in Genesis 11:4 humankind said, "*Let us build* . . . and *let us make* a name for ourselves . . ." (emphases added). The city of Babel and its tower depict the *incurvatus in se* of a race of creatures disinterested in their Creator, concerned chiefly with their own self-preservation ("lest we be dispersed over the face of the whole earth"—11:4). This human insistence on becoming a stationary, homogenous enclave is also a rejection of God's command "to fill the earth" (Gen 1:28).[11] Architecture can serve as a powerful media form, and the text is clear that the staggering height of that skyscraper was intended to communicate humanity's impressive prowess and to signify its self-sufficiency, a sufficiency at the tune of staying safely put rather than heeding God's original command to proliferate throughout the nooks, crannies, and broad plains of the earth.

Even God himself is impressed. So impressed, in fact, that he recognizes the need for divine intervention: "This is only the beginning of what they will do. And nothing that they propose to do now will be impossible for them" (11:6). What his media agents have produced is radically divorced from the original intention. The God-likeness and God-relatedness of the *imago Dei* entrusted to women and men is unique and glorious, though now so adulterated and curved inward that it is dangerous. To staunch the damaging potentialities flowing out of human ingenuity, God cast his fractured image bearers out of Eden with its immortality tree, and he cast the Babelites "over the face of all the earth" (11:9).

Before God dispersed Babel's citizens, however, he plagued the primeval human race with a media scourge. He imposed language barriers.

11. Middleton, *The Liberating Image*, 224–25.

Though human beings were created to interact in unmediated community, sin had rendered them dangerous to themselves, to each other, and to the rest of creation. Sin separates, a reality observed in the weaving of garments in Genesis 3 after Adam and Eve's ashamed recognition of their nakedness.

Babel shows us that sin can also *unify*: "Behold," God says, "they are one people, and they have all one language" (11:6).

The uninhibited interaction shared so briefly by Adam and Eve had become a liability—the ex-Eden unity was sin induced and now fraught with frightful prospects. Sadly, the less these curved-in-on-themselves human beings could collectively communicate with one another, the safer all of creation. Thus the linguistic confusion imposed from heaven.

"Connectedness" is the unofficial mantra of social media today. Once online, look out, because "here comes everybody," as Clay Shirky has put it.[12] Connectedness is also a biblical theme, to be sure, but we have to admit it: *human connectedness is often quite dangerous.*[13] Media enthusiasts point out that the connectedness of social media has helped topple oppressive dictatorships of late. However, it should also be noted that the wreckage and mayhem of the 2011 London riots were also assisted by the connectedness of social media.[14]

Though we will focus later on God's work of restoring human connectedness through Christ, we note here that the divine dispersal of humankind from the garden of Eden and from the city of Babel were purposeful disruptions of human connectedness. The imposed exiles from the garden and from that tower were God's preemptive limiting of distorted media projects.

IDOLATRY: ANCIENT MEDIA AT ITS DARKEST

Ex-Eden and ex-Babel, banned from the tree of life and divided up into disparate language groups, fallen humanity still engaged in futile media

---

12. Shirky, *Here Comes Everybody*.

13. My friend Rob O'Callaghan, who copy edited this book before I submitted it to the publisher, made this astute observation concerning the dangers of connectedness: "Especially glaring are unities of race or nation or peoplehood that lead one people to enforce their superiority over others, e.g., the remarkable cohesiveness of Nazi Germany, or of most perpetrators of genocide."

14. Douglas, "Social Media's Role in the Riots."

projects. The most offensive in the minds of the Old Testament writers/ editors is the production of idols.

The comment is regularly made that we contemporary folks are more visual as learners and communicators than our forebears. This may be true if we are talking about literate members of the print culture that has emerged since Gutenberg cranked up his printing press in the fifteenth century. The axiom probably does not apply so easily to the bulk of the populace in most ancient (and even medieval) cultures. Many early writing forms were pictographic, and visual imagery held powerful sway. And the sight of a beautifully crafted idol seemed to wield such infectious, alluring force as to arrest the attention and evoke the fascination of ancient eyes.

We should not underestimate the powerful inclination toward idols in the ancient world. As we have acknowledged, the ancient Near East was saturated with the imagery of locally worshiped deities.[15] It was visually hard to avoid. Even within the geographical and cultural confines of early Israel, a Hebrew family looking for a decent serving bowl could run the risk of having their eyes exposed to pagan celestial imagery on the fine Phoenician earthenware at some of the markets.[16]

Why produce an idol? It seems that the theological rationale behind fashioning idols was to have on hand tangible representations of a deity's presence.[17] We should be cautious not to arrogantly dismiss this rationale as an archaic silliness confined to quirky tribal groups who lived in the dark ages of the distant past. Educated Christians living in the technological age also want a palpable sense of the divine (and idolcraft was no less a technology form than graphic design, even if it is quite "old"). We long to feel, touch, hear, and see our God. Producing an idol is a convenient way to satisfy this characteristic desire of humankind ancient and modern.

Given God's self-pronounced jealousy for Israel's exclusive loyalty, the prohibition of imagery portraying other deities makes sense (Exod 20:4–6; Deut 5:8–10). The Second Commandment also prohibits any visual media portraying God himself—since Israel "saw no form" of him during his definitive appearance on Sinai, no material form was to be

---

15. When Israel left Egypt out of Rameses for the wilderness, they left a land of idolatrous media (see Deut 29:15–16) and Jeremiah lamented that Babylon was "a land of images" where the inhabitants were "mad over idols" (Jer 50:58).

16. Uehlinger and Keel, *Gods, Goddessess, and Images of God in Ancient Israel*, 280.

17. MacDonald, "Recasting the Golden Calf," 25.

made (Deut 4:12; cf. 4:15–16).[18] Humans bearing the divine image are not permitted *to reduce God to* an image. In spite of the creativity intrinsic to God's creatures, they were banned from the ambition of re-creating their Creator.[19]

The reason? It seems as though it is impossible for human beings to produce visual media that accurately depicts worship-able divinity. The inevitable tendency is to fashion a god *selectively*, to carve and shape a deity suitable to our expectations, to give birth to a self-reflecting figurine that ever falls short of divine reality. And once we do pull the form out of the kiln and place our completed work on display, what we have is a pathetic rendering of what is supposed to represent a living, immortal being. The effort to render God in visible form always ends up as "an act of false imagination."[20]

So when it comes to reifying the holy, dysfunctional image bearers will always produce dysfunctional images.

We find in the Old Testament that the penchant for making and honoring idols was overpowering and contagious. The people of God were drawn to idolatrous media like starved addicts to a visual drug. The draw was so strong that the removal of Canaanite religious iconography was an integral dimension to the conquest under Joshua. The visual vestiges of Canaan's pagan media were not just to be removed, but violently obliterated: "You shall break down their altars and dash in pieces their pillars and chop down their Asherim and burn their carved images with fire" (Deut 7:5).[21]

"Break," "dash," "chop," "burn"—these verbal commands were the fate to which all Canaanite media were consigned to suffer at Israel's hands (see chapter 8). Arresting and captivating, the idolatrous media of the Promised Land were to be annihilated lest they become a "snare" (Deut 7:16; cf. 7:25). The punishment for taking up the media production of making idols like the Canaanites? Babel-style exile: "If you act corruptly by making a carved image . . . the LORD will scatter you among the peoples" (Deut 4:25b, 27a). The production of worldly media like idols

18. Mettinger, "Israelite Aniconism," 177.

19. It is possible that the golden calf in Exod 32, and the idols made by Micah in Judges 17–18 and Jereboam in 1 Kings 2:25–33 may have been intended to depict YHWH, even though against his will. See Weeks, "Man-Made Gods?," 7–8; and MacDonald, "Recasting the Golden Calf," 35.

20. MacDonald, "Recasting the Golden Calf," 35.

21. Cf. Deut 12:2–3; Exod 23:24; 34:13.

portraying false gods and of city towers portraying human supremacy resulted in the divine interruption of dispersal and exile.

God is so acutely aware of the *incurvatus in se* of mortal media production that he often gave detailed and specific instructions for anything Israel built for formal or informal means of worshiping him. It was God himself who cast artistic vision for the visual forms put into official use for Israelite religion.[22] We will discuss the elaborate designs for the Tabernacle and its many accoutrements in chapter 6, but it is important to note here that the craftsmen charged with the task of this massive media project, Bezalel and Oholiab, are directly filled with the Holy Spirit (Exod 31:1–11; 35:30—39:43). Since media production by fallen media agents is inherently skewed, external inspiration is supplied from above for the artistic project of God's dwelling place among his people.

This sensitivity to humankind's incapacity to reify the divine in visual form is also seen in the limitations God places on impromptu altars. Elaborate visual projects like the Tabernacle come with elaborate blueprints from God's own lips; but ever since the patriarchs in Genesis, it was customary to build altars in certain places where God did something worth memorializing. Such constructions would add to the media dotting the landscape of the ancient world. Unlike the carefully instructed and Spirit-anointed work of Bezalel, however, God would not tolerate any fancy craftsmanship out on any old hill or alongside any old byway. His preference when it came to impromptu man-made altars was a pile of dirt (Exod 20:24). And if someone was compelled to use stones, then they were to be uncut stones on which no creative energy had been exerted, "for if you wield your tool on it you profane it" (Exod 20:25; cf. Josh 8:30–35).

The vigilant resistance to man-made media depicting God betokens divine mistrust in humankind's creative powers. In bearing God's image, we share his propensity to beget, produce, fashion, and forge. Tremendous beauty can result, but also horrendous rot. Fractured image bearers will naturally yield fractured imagery, at least to some degree; and this debilitation inherent to human creativity is most obvious when it comes to crafting media intended to visually portray God. Whatever comes out of the kiln will fall short of divine reality.[23]

22. The original Temple is clearly Solomon's doing (1 Kgs 5–7), but he took his cues from God's prior instructions on the Tabernacle (see chapter 6).

23. According to the exhaustive archaeological study of Uehlinger and Keel (*Gods, Goddesses, and Images of God in Ancient Israel*), there was no "Yahweh iconography

THE INVISIBILITY OF GOD AND THE MEDIA AND MESSAGES OF IDOLATRY

I mentioned above that it is vogue to criticize McLuhan. Admittedly, his perhaps overworn adage, "the medium is the message,"[24] is often cited in gross oversimplification. The relationship between content and media form is more complex than the amateurs to media studies who so freely cite McLuhan usually note.

My own amateurism notwithstanding, it seems worth pointing out that a sensitivity to the relationship between a medium and its message is often found in the Bible. The first embodiment of scripture was etched into stone (the Ten Commandments), which might well be intended to say something about the density and durability of the content.[25] Additionally, the prophets did more than speak—they sometimes embodied their oracles in the form of vivid displays or actions (e.g., Isaiah's nudity, Hosea's marriage to Gomer, Ezekiel's dung-baked meals). Throughout scripture, we find that form and content are often intentionally yoked, as Jeremiah knew somewhat literally! And the supreme example in all history of the medium fused to the message is the Incarnation, when the Word became flesh.

So what message is conveyed by the visual and tangible medium of an idol?

The theological message of a statue with unseeing eyes, unhearing ears, immobile legs, and silent lips is that the god represented is a useless non-god. The prophets are repeatedly making this critique: "Their idols are like scarecrows in a cucumber field, and they cannot speak; they

in Israel and Judah" (407). They go on to say, however, that "[t]his does not mean that Israelite and Judean women and men would not have recognized an appropriate portrayal of their god in one or another of the pictures presented here" (407). The pictures they are referring to are what they believe to have been artistic renderings of images *symbolizing* YHWH—solar and celestial symbolism, imagery of a tree flanked by animals, etc. (277–81). Their evidence accords with God's command in scripture that no image be constructed of himself, but also evidences an artistic devotion to creating rich visual symbols of God.

24. Again, for a brief but representative collection of McLuhan's writing on this theme, see McLuhan, "The Medium Is the Message," in *Media Studies*, 38–43.

25. Postman (who, incidentally, also defended his references to McLuhan) observed that the emphasis of text over images implied in the Second Commandment is explained by the author assuming "a connection between forms of human communication and the quality of a culture" (*Amusing Ourselves to Death*, 9).

have to be carried, for they cannot walk" (Jer 10:5a).[26] Though the idea of idolatry is to provide a fixed point of connection between the heavens and the earth, the deity idolized is inevitably locked into a blank and uncommunicative stare. The Old Testament's consistent critique of the idol-medium is that it conveys a vain divinity unable to save and unworthy of attention.

God, the *Living* God, will not be so identified.

Another message conveyed by a concretized rendering of a god is that the divinity is tangible, portable, convenient, and handy. The miniature figurines known as "household gods" are in effect domesticated deities.[27] But YHWH is no household god. No house will hold him. And you can't take him wherever you want to go. God leads and is not led. In the wilderness, the people of Israel did not pack up God in their Tabernacle ensemble and march in the direction of their fancy. They moved only when the uncontainable spectacle of the holy cloud and pillar of fire indicated that it was indeed time to move (Num 9:15–23).

The non-medium of God's invisibility also bears a message: no one can put their creative little hands on him. He will not be subject to the whims of his worshipers. He will not submit to a selective chisel. He will not be embossed with precious metals he himself created with a word. The theological message of a God who refuses to be captured in the medium of a visual form is that he is an untamable, unbound, uncontrollable Divinity for whom no limits apply.

Now, the time will come when God does indeed appear in visual form. The message of that medium is that God is willing to be bound, controlled, and even executed on behalf of his fallen image bearers. But that moment in salvation history is the subject of Part 4.

In our current position at the opening of the biblical story, let's consider the invisibility of God, and how that non-medium was celebrated as a signature means of his self-revelation, not as evidence of his absence. Moses instructed Bezalel's artistic team to construct an ark over which God associated his presence. It is not that God was distant or removed from his people by prohibiting his representation in tangible idols. He was present, just unseen, and the invisibility conveyed the message that this is a Deity not to be constrained by space or a physical form (except later on his own terms).

26. Cf. Jer 10:1–11; Isa 40:18–20; 44:9–20; 46:1–2, 5–7; Hab 2:18–20.
27. See Gen 31:33–35; 35:2, et al.

Just ask the cult of Dagon about the invisibility of God. Having captured the ark once in a battle with Israel, the Philistines placed it before the statue of their god Dagon, thereby positioning the enthroned presence of Israel's God before their champion deity. You probably remember what happened.

Dagon was found mysteriously amputated and beheaded in the night (1 Sam 4:1—7:2).

ANCIENT IDOL-MEDIA AND THE DIGITAL AGE? SOME PRACTICAL LESSONS

Understandably, Dagon doesn't get much press today. In any case, media production in the twenty-first century is not invested in promoting personified deities. So what does the discussion above on ancient idolcraft have to do with the media concerns of today?

For one, we should acknowledge that the mass media of any culture, ancient or contemporary, can be powerfully enticing, especially when sex (phallic symbols, fertility goddesses with enormous breasts, or Internet ads with half-naked bodies) and materialism (silver, gold, or flashing dollar signs) are combined. Images sexualized and monetized can have the allure of visual drugs for starved media addicts, even if we have depersonalized the gods and commercialized media's purposes today.

And consider what we have learned in this chapter about humanity's failure to produce media that sufficiently represent God. What can a secular society in which idolcraft is virtually extinct learn from the Old Testament's warnings against idolatry?

These questions brings up even messier questions. For instance, is it okay that icons are used in certain church traditions today? And what are we to make of those glorious paintings of God in the Sistine Chapel? The crayon portraits of Jesus produced in Sunday school—what about those? I mean, my kids are drawing pictures of Jesus every now and then. Should I throw the Second Commandment at them and then break, dash, chop, and burn their artwork?

Iconoclasm—the vigorous protest against any use of images depicting God—seems responsibly sensitive to the *incurvatus in se* of human media production. Israelite religion was certainly supposed to be "aniconic" (opposed to images of their Deity). But many Christians have pointed to the Incarnation as grounds for portraying God in artistic

61

form.[28] By becoming flesh, Jesus made divinity depictable, at least to some degree.

The church has seen violent internal clashes over the validity of artistically rendered images of God, and the ripples have continued into our own day. Disagreements abound (I am making no attempt to resolve them here!), but we should be able to agree that while we can worshipfully produce art, we cannot produce art to worship. Art celebrating divine beauty is a discipline to nurture. Art produced as a substitute for God's presence will fall short of its intentions, and may well constitute an idol.

Another urgent question prompted by the material above is this: what does it mean for a media-saturated culture that the primary media makers are curved in on themselves, infiltrated by the corrupting influence of sin?

One practical lesson to take from the idea that humanity is curved in on itself is that the mass media of our own day must always be understood as the extensions not just of human beings, but of human beings who are sinful and therefore distorted in our wondrous capacities for creativity. A healthy degree of mistrust is biblically necessary in our appropriation of mass media's forms and content. We are theologically compelled to embrace media critically and reflectively.

Here is something else to sink our teeth into: *if Christians are to learn accurately about their God, they must heed media sourced outside of the human realm. We must heed TheoMedia, the media of God.*

A thriving multi-billion dollar industry of marketing and advertising is out there as proof that media can and does influence individuals and entire societies. But the media ultimately appropriate for shaping Christians are divinely issued "TheoMedia" that erupt into our sphere from somewhere offstage and break through the incurvature of our disoriented souls to give life. We are going to turn in the next few pages to our extensive look at TheoMedia in the Bible. But first, let's end this chapter about media's anthropology on a more hopeful note.

---

28. This is the primary reasoning used by John of Damascus in the eighth century controversy over iconoclasm. See Louth's introduction and translation of St. John's *Three Treatises on the Divine Images.*

VALID PHYSICAL AND VISUAL DEPICTIONS OF GOD: YOU AND ME AS THE "IDOLS" OF GOD?

In spite of the *incurvatus in se*, the TheoMedia we are about to study actually include *us*. As divine image bearers, human beings are legitimate material and tangible depictions of God's identity in this world.

In trying to sort out media enthusiasm and media skepticism, we have seen that one of the primary reasons media-related issues are so difficult to discern is because human beings are marked by both the *imago Dei* and by the sin that incapacitates our vocation of imaging our Creator. We are extensions of God and also distortions of God.

But I want us to conclude the chapter acknowledging the potential beauty in our creative capacities and remembering that the biblical story is about the redemption of human image bearers. This means that our capacity for bearing God's image is being restored. Christ has come as a fresh representative of the image of God (2 Cor 4:4; cf. Col 1:15), and by his Spirit we "are being transformed into the same image from one degree of glory to another" (2 Cor 3:18). As the church, we have "put on the new self, which is being renewed in knowledge after the image of its creator" (Col 3:9; cf. Eph 4:20). The image in which God initially fashioned us, which we somehow defamed and failed to honor, is being reforged.

The Hebrew word used for "image" (*selem*) in Genesis 1:26–27 is translated elsewhere in the Old Testament as "idol."[29] It is a word with strong connotations of physicality.[30] To be made in God's image is not just intellectual or spiritual:

> The marvel of man's bodily appearance is not at all to be excepted
> from the realm of God's image. This was the original notion. . . .
> Therefore, one will do well to split the physical from the spiritual
> as little as possible: the whole man is created in God's image.[31]

J. Richard Middleton would qualify the comment above by Gerhard von Rad in this way: it is not "that the image consists in a bodily resemblance between God and humanity, but that the invisible God is imaged by

---

29. *Selem* as an idol: 1 Sam 6:5; Num 33:52; 2 Kgs 11:18 / 2 Chr 23:17; Dan 3:2, 15 [the Aramaic equivalent]; Amos 5:26. For more on the use of image as an "idol," see Middleton, *The Liberating Image*, 25, and Robert Hayward, "Observations on Idols in Septuagint Pentateuch," 52–54.

30. Cf. Ezek 1:26; 28:12; Ps 8; Isa 6:1; Amos 9:1, etc.

31. Von Rad, *Genesis*, 56.

bodily humanity."[32] As creatures endowed with the faculties of speech and movement, of kneading and painting, of carving and writing, redeemed human beings are personalized multimedia embodying the shining goodness and beauty of God.

There is more at work than technological determinism when it comes to technology projects and products; and there is more at work than the inherent fallenness of humankind when it comes to media making and media use. The redeeming power of the triune God is pushing against the constraints of our damaged souls and against the limitations of our technological capacities by forging a new humanity from the empty tomb of the risen Christ. Babel showed us that "connectedness" can be destructive. Pentecost shows us that a different sort of "connectedness" is being established by God's Spirit: "How is it that we hear, each of us in his own native language?" (Acts 2:8).

The restoration of the divine image through Christ does not justify our use of every technology form, and it does not remove human sinfulness from the picture. Our redemption, however—underway and soon to be completed—does give us grounds for expanding our imaginations for how media technology might redemptively function within and for the church. Humans have the capacity to mediate destruction and pain through the technologies of nuclear and chemical warfare.

But we are also the sort of creatures who mediate the beauty of salvation by placing tiny morsels of bread into tiny hands.

32. Middleton, *The Liberating Image,* 25, n. 32.

TheoMedia Note 3

When Screens Are Oracles, Portals, Stages . . . and well, "Screens"

You talk as if a god had made the Machine," cried the other. "I believe that you pray to it when you are unhappy. Men made it. Do not forget that. Great men, but men. The Machine is much, but it is not everything. I see something like you in this plate, but I do not see you. I hear something like you through this telephone, but I do not hear you. That is why I want you to come. Pay me a visit, so we can meet face to face, and talk about the hopes that are in my mind.

—FROM E. M. FORSTER'S "THE MACHINE STOPS"[1]

The "plate" referenced above is what we would recognize today as a screen. E. M. Forster was not much of a sci-fi writer, but the post-apocalyptic short story he wrote in 1909 turns out to have been loaded with eerie foresight. We do not live today in the sort of dystopic realm he creates in "The Machine Stops," but we have to admit that we are indeed a screened people. In our palms, on our laps, and fitted onto the walls of our homes, our local pubs, our classrooms, and our churches—screens are now ubiquitous fixtures in our visual space.

The previous two chapters have made reference to technological determinism, the idea that the content and purpose of media are altered or confined by the technology that makes them possible. Though I do

1. Forster, *The Machine Stops*, 3–4.

not subscribe to a hard determinist view, I do think it is important for us to recognize how various technological media formats are suggestive of certain values and practices. In that recognition we can make strides to avoid the determinative impact of technology on our lives.

So what might be the inherent dangers of using the communications device of a screen? We tend to invest them with curious powers. But then again, we also need to ask if the restoration of humanity into the divine image pushes against the technological constraints, biases, and dangers of screen-use.[2]

SCREENS AS ORACLES

I recently endured a season in my life when I was desperate for God to bring clarity to a number of vocational issues that were up in the air. I was in regular email contact with potential employers and repeatedly checking my inbox for news about applications to doctoral programs. It occurred to me in the midst of this vocational wrangling that there was a time when, in desperate moments of needing guidance for my future, my first impulse in the morning was not to consult the Internet via a screen.

It was to pray. It was to read scripture.

Unknowingly, I was developing a new morning habit: rather than hitting my knees in prayer to listen for God's voice, I was clicking a mouse to get online to see if my future had been revealed by way of a new email.

In the ancient world, there was a name for a mystical medium through which news known only to the gods came to mortals. They called such a thing an "oracle." If you were anxious about your love life, desperate for information about the future, or just plain frustrated and stuck, then you could go to the oracle and beseech some revelatory knowledge from the ethereal realm.

I think many of us treat screens as modern-day oracles, and the Internet is our ethereal realm.

Of course, oracles are not just a pagan idea. An oracle is a divine medium, a means by which a deity communicates. My term "TheoMedia" refers to the oracles of the God of the Bible. And God can certainly use screens to reveal himself to us or to supply some information we are desperately seeking (by way of information received or wisdom gained

2. Some of this material first appeared in an earlier article, "From 'Among the Trees' to 'Face to Face.'"

through various online sources). The problem, I think, is when we depend on the technological capacities more readily than we turn to the spiritual disciplines of prayer or Bible reading (more on this in chapter 11).

Google will almost always deliver information when we use it for a search. But those of us who have searched for God hour by hour, year by year, know that he often does not dispense mere data. He seems quite uninterested in providing immediate info about our futures or about our existential questions.

But he does supply wisdom. He does offer fellowship. These we often need more than the data results of an online search. And every morning, before our feet hit the floor—and our fingers the keypad—he is keen to keep our company.

SCREENS AS PORTALS

A portal is a gateway to a different world, like a magical wardrobe that leads to Narnia. We tend to think of the Internet as an alternative realm, often using *spatial* terms to describe it. We "surf" the web. We visit "sites." The "@" sign implies location. We click to "follow" someone as if they are going somewhere. Staring into our screens can give us the sense of being transported into some other place. Oddly, the Internet is a visible, invisible world—visible on our screens, yet we can't really *see* it.

Dangers arise when we treat screens as portals into some other place. Think about the risky combination of using a phone and driving. By texting with one hand while the other is on the wheel of the car, your mind can get stuck between two worlds—the world in front of you (which includes fast-moving vehicles) and the world of the person you are texting or video-conferencing.

It is also dangerous when we feel that what happens through a screen in a cyber-world can stay in that cyber-world. Someone was telling me recently how a friend was bashing them through Facebook messages and emails, but in their face-to-face encounters there was nothing but sweet sugary smiles. It was as if the communication online did not apply outside cyberspace in the real world.

Also, when we allow screens to be portals into online worlds, we feel as though we can get away with stuff that we can't in real life. In the cyber-realm, you can be a super hero or a buff space marine shooting aliens. You can be someone you are not. You can take on screen names that provide anonymity. You can create an online avatar, an improved version of yourself in a stylized world. You can have naughty little chats you would never have if sitting with that person at a café. If we are not careful, we can treat screens as entry points into a dream world where anything goes.

The thing about portals, though, is that they are bidirectional. Like when the White Witch followed Digory and Polly back to London through that mysterious pool in *The Magician's Nephew*.[3] As many have painfully experienced, online material and interactions have a way of leaching back through the screen and materializing in the flesh and blood reality of our offline lives.

SCREENS AS STAGES

A stage is a public platform. I have used the metaphor of a stage to refer to how we live in the great drama of life. But when it comes to the actual world of theater, it is a general rule that not many people make it "on-stage." A theatrical stage appearance is often preceded by years of hard work, rigorous training, and intimidating auditions. But a screen can afford us a public platform almost instantly, our "audience" being Twitter followers, blog readers, and Facebook friends.

Stages are the domain of *actors*. In a screened culture, it is very easy to put on an act from behind our screens, tweaking the presentation of our persona in our bios and profile descriptions (there will be more on this in TheoMedia Note 8).

Another temptation is to live for applause online. Now, the audience might throw rotten fruit (negative comments, online bullying, etc.). But they just might offer the glorious cacophony of clapping, appearing in the form of increased blog stats, flattering comments, or in large numbers of "likes" or "retweets." Having such access to a stage can subtly encourage us to be more performance-minded in our lives.

The word "share" is extremely significant in social media. It is a good word with connotations of generosity, openness, and transparency. There are fine lines, though, between sharing and performing. Our screens and social media subtly (or sometimes not so subtly!) encourage us to live lives awesome enough to "share." When we treat a screen as a stage, we might feel the need to live tweetable lives eventful enough to warrant

3. Lewis, *The Magician's Nephew*, 78.

regular status updates. If we are not careful, generously sharing ourselves with open transparency could be replaced with a life that is little more than a series of affected performances.

SCREENS AS "SCREENS"

Another definition for a screen is a thin veil that hides or obscures.[4] We can screen ourselves with our screens. I have mentioned the temptation of deceptively tweaking our Facebook and Twitter profiles. When we craft a bio in the third person, it can be tempting to pose as someone else who is admiringly describing us. And a high degree of selectivity is often behind whatever we enter into the "compose" box or the "status update" field.

We have already encountered the first use of screens in human history. It happened in Eden, when Adam and Eve concealed themselves with those impromptu clothes. The very first effect of sin for Adam and Eve was a dark self-recognition that immediately led to the manufacturing of screens. I am not saying that our actual computer screens can be traced back to the very first sin in the Fall narrative. But the idea of screening ourselves from others most certainly does go back to that fateful scene.

THE REDEMPTIVE USE OF SCREENS

In spite of the dangers listed above, screens can be redemptive tools. Remember, media are messy, racked with all sorts of potential for both distortion and beauty. We have acknowledged that God can indeed use a screen in an oracular fashion. He can reveal himself through online interactions with other Christians, through YouTube videos, and through powerful movie scenes. The spiritual discipline of *lectio divina* (divine reading) can actually be practiced online via our screens. Bible apps are now available with all sorts of helpful options for improving our understanding of scripture (though personally, I am much more inclined

---

4. After writing this TheoMedia Note, I came across Boer's related comment that the original meaning of a "screen" is something designed "to separate us" (*Living Into Focus*, 82).

to study scripture through the medium of a book/codex than that of a screen).[5]

It can also be helpful when screens are portals, stages, and "screens." Now that I live overseas I am able to connect with friends and family via screens. The web cam does not physically transport me to my parents' living room, but I can at least interact with them while seeing that familiar setting in the background of their smiling faces. As a stage, a screen allows us to practice the ancient task of bearing witness to Christ in the public arena. And it is even helpful at times when our screens serve as thin veils that obscure or hide. There are folks out there we would never share our lives with unless we had time to build trust face-to-face. Screens permit interactions with strangers while also providing a safe degree of distance (since the Fall, safety is no longer guaranteed in human interactions—"screens" are sometimes *necessary*[6]).

I want to close this Note asking a tricky question: is a *screen* inferior to a *book* as a media format? Though the page-bound codex is greatly revered in the Christian tradition, we should point out that books can also be treated as oracles, portals, and screens (though not so much as stages, unless you happen to be the author!). Flipping a paper page can be just as much an exercise of consulting an oracle as clicking a mouse. Though kids often seem locked in an alternative world they behold through the portal of a screen, I often find my daughter gripping a book and more present in Hogwarts than in our home (and it is always hard for me to leave Middle Earth). You may have heard the phrase, "he is hiding behind that book"—we can be "screened" from others by open paper pages as much as by open browsers on laptops and iPads.

For us bibliophiles who might look down on the screen users with a tinge of media self-righteousness, we should ask if familiarity with our preferred media format is such that we are blind to its particular set of influences. Some of us are screened. Some of us are booked. Most of us are both. All of us need to recognize the technological influences of our beloved media formats as well as their redemptive potential.

---

5. Again, see Jacobs's essay "Christianity and the Future of the Book."

6. My thanks to Rob O'Callaghan for pointing this out.

PART 2

The Sights and Sounds of Israel's God
Multisensory TheoMedia in the Old Testament

Chapter 5

Creation and God-sponsored "Media Events"

[T]he *media* we use for saying things extend far beyond words. . . . Actually all of us use conventional gestures of various sorts to say things: winks, nudges, shrugs, nods, and so forth. The media of divine discourse are even more diverse, or so at least the biblical writers claim. Words, yes; but beyond that, happenings of all sorts: dreams, visions, apparitions, burning bushes, illnesses, national calamities, national deliverances, droughts—on and on.

—NICHOLAS WOLTERSTORFF[1]

The fact that the *Word* creates means that creation is an act of revelation.

—RAYMOND BROWN[2]

It has often been stated that because of Israel's radically anti-iconic stance, it came to prefer forms of revelation that were mediated by word rather than by sight. This assertion, like all such truisms, is to some extent accurate.

1. Wolterstorff, *Divine Discourse*, 38.
2. Brown, *The Gospel According to John*, 25.

> Nevertheless . . . it should not be assumed that because Israel rejected the representation of God in statuary form in the Temple, it thereby rejected all linkages of God to a specific physical domain.
>
> —GARY A. ANDERSON[3]

My recognition that God employs media came at that time when I was securing homiletical artillery for assaulting the evils of the communications technology that were badgering college students under my pastoral care and threatening to undo the innocence of my four small children. I was reading Shane Hipps's *Flickering Pixels* at the time, and his chapter "Media God" help spark my thinking about "TheoMedia."[4] That God himself uses particular media was an idea that failed to add much to my arsenal, though.

I knew from my upbringing in the church that the God of the Bible was relational and communicative. In reading the scriptures it was quite clear that there was such a thing as "divine agency," a phrase simply meaning that God is a God of *means*. The concept of TheoMedia derives from pairing these two concepts together: God is relationally invested in communicating with us, and he uses a variety of means (media!) to do so. So during my sermon research, I began to realize that the foundational elements of the concept of media are actually quite biblical.

If God is determined to reveal himself and interact with us, and if he is indeed a God of means, then our contemporary media culture is not outside the purview of the Bible and the church's theological disciplines. The story that unfolds throughout our corpus of sacred texts is told along the lines of God communicating with us through a rich variety of means. And if our relational God communicates through a wide array of media forms, then surely there is a theological logic from which we can derive insights for faithful media practices in an age of media saturation.

Now begins our study on TheoMedia, beginning with the sights and sounds of God in the Old Testament.

3. Anderson, "To See Where God Dwells," 41–42.

4. In that same chapter "Media God," Hipps briefly lists many of the divine media forms that we are about to study (*Flickering Pixels*, 161–70). Adam has also referenced the media of God in his essay "Interpreting the Bible at the Horizon of Virtual New Worlds," 164–65.

MULTIMEDIA GOD

For some readers, my following claim might come across as controversial. But there seems no way around it: in the Old Testament, the prioritized media of God are more *verbal* than *visual* (with the term "verbal" I am referring to all forms of word-media, e.g., texts and speech). The textual medium of scripture and the oral medium of God's direct or mediated address—much of which eventually ended up in those scripture texts—are given primary weight as the most reliable means by which Israel was to receive God's self-presentation. Accordingly, textual and oral TheoMedia require certain skills, those of *reading* and *hearing*. And the way God has chosen to use self-expressive media determines what media forms his people need to develop proficiency at interpreting and receiving.

Does this mean that the more "visual," then the less "spiritual"?[5] Are those of us who seem more inclined to learn or communicate through visual imagery at a loss or incapacitated in relating to God on his own communicative terms? Is there some sort of divine persecution of the non-readers underway in the cosmos?

If you are among those terrorized by the verbal and reading comprehension sections of standardized tests, the verbal and textual reality of TheoMedia might come across as intimidating, or even disparaging. Despair not: there is no need to equate high verbal schools on the GRE or SAT with higher aptitude for knowing Jesus. For one, our culture of reading today is vastly different from the oral dynamics that held sway during the centuries of the Bible's composition. What it means to be competent with words in recent history may not have translated very well back to the third century BC or the first century AD.

We will revisit verbal TheoMedia in the next major section of the book. In this section on the sights and sounds of Israel's God, we will find that although God resists the idolater's chisel and certainly seems to make serious reading assignments, he displays his character and beauty through means appealing to the entire range of our senses—he is a multimedia God in his revelatory enterprises.

As his image bearers, we are *embodied* and thereby endowed with eyes, ears, hands, noses, tongues, and fingertips. If God himself made us this way, supplying us with a vast "sensorium" (range of senses), and if he wishes to communicate with us, then we should expect TheoMedia to

---

5. I am drawing on a phrase I used in my previous book to describe hyper-spirituality ("more normal" is "less spiritual"). See Byers, *Faith Without Illusions*, 72–74.

be varied, complex, and even *sensory*. The verbal medium of God's word begets the aural, visual, and tactile media of God's world. And human beings were entrusted with artistic skills, not intended for idol crafting, of course, but certainly for creating imagery and artifacts that inspire a sense of the holy. Divine words written and spoken produce and govern all material forms of TheoMedia, as we will emphasize in the following section; for now, our interest is in how God revealed himself to Israel through a range of media that required human senses to do more than hearing or seeing divine *words*, be they spoken or written.

So what did the non-verbal manifestations of God look like and sound like in the Old Testament? They were loud and quiet, resplendent and coaxing, beautiful and terrifying . . .

UNKNOWINGLY SATURATED BY CREATION: OF SKIES AND SCREENS, BIRDSONG AND BEEPS

Creation is the most comprehensive mélange of visual and aural artistry. The glowing and gleaming, roaring and humming, twirling and spinning, cawing and snorting—John Calvin called creation God's "dazzling theater."[6] We often lament the ubiquity of worldly media. We are troubled by the degree to which the sights and sounds of ad campaigns and pop-cultural propaganda are unavoidable and inescapable. But no media form is more saturating than that of creation.

We can delight in the fact that the sky and the ground, the sun and the soil, are more unavoidable and inescapable than the sights and sounds of looming billboards and catchy sound bites.

Yet the billboards and bytes seem to have more of our optical and acoustic loyalty. The TheoMedia of creation is implicitly understood as a gratuitous backdrop for the more important things taking place on our screens or within our structures of fabricated steel, composite plastic, and concrete. For ancient societies less shielded from the dangers and marvels of the natural realm, their metaphors and similes had a starting point in creation:

> Like the cold of snow in the time of harvest is a faithful messenger to those who send him (Prov 25:13a).

---

6. Calvin, *Institutes of the Christian Religion*, 61. See n. 27 on the same page for more references. The "excellence of divine art" is on display in the stars of the sky (53).

All flesh is grass, and all its beauty is like the flower of the field (Isa 40:6b).

The kingdom of God is as if someone would scatter seed on the ground . . . (Mark 4:26a).

So I cringe if I hear one of my kids say something like, "Dad, the sky looks like the color of our TV screen when it comes on," instead of "the TV screen is sky blue" or "that bug looks like the robots in that movie" rather than "those robots look like bugs." Such comments betray a vantage point lodged within media culture and looking out onto creation as something less familiar, perhaps even alien. A friend of mine just told me that he stepped outdoors one morning, heard birdsong, and immediately thought it was Angry Birds on his phone. A perspective so locked within the visual field of digital imagery and electronic acoustics renders us much more likely to be noticing the messages of banner ads and glowing bytes than the messages of the clouds.

CREATION HERMENEUTICS

Then again, cloud reading is not necessarily biblical. Observing the divine in creation can be as much pagan as Christian.

Interpreting natural phenomena as signs or omens has been the stock and trade of many a pagan priest, and the beauty of stars, moons, seas, and trees have so impressed humankind that they have become objects of worship (cf. Deut 4:15–19; Jer 2:26–27). As with any communicative art form, we have to develop some hermeneutical competence: how do we as Christians apprehend and construe the TheoMedia of God's material, visual, audible, and tactile creation?

The conviction that God's work and character are displayed in the beauty and mystery of the "natural" world is found throughout the Old Testament. The uncountable stars were a reminder that Abram had been promised a people without number (Gen 15:5). The girth and height of those Lebanese cedars were a reminder that God tended and nurtured the work of his hands (Ps 104:16). The sky above seemed noisy with worship (Ps 19:1). The untarnished beauty of a snow-draped landscape could evoke for the penitent a sense of God's willingness and power to cleanse from sin (Ps 51:7; Isa 1:18).

We hear Jesus saying in the New Testament, "consider the ravens" and "consider the lilies" (Luke 12:24, 27). He was calling his hearers to reflect on the TheoMedia of creation. There is much to learn from the divine provision for birds and from the beauty of flowers in fields. Writing to early Christians in Rome, Paul affirmed God's artistry in the natural world as a means of divine self-revelation: "Ever since the creation of the world his eternal power and divine nature, invisible though they are, have been understood and seen through the things he has made" (Rom 1:20). Much about God can be known through the cycle of the seasons, the sprouting of a seed, and the overhead flight of majestic clouds.

Furthermore, creation is a means not just of *revelation* (whereby aspects of God's character or attributes are manifested) but also of *direct communication* (whereby God relays a specific message).[7] A rainbow signified to Noah the promise of divine restraint in the future (Gen 8:13–17). A gentle, whispering breeze seemed to calm and redirect Elijah on Mount Horeb (1 Kgs 19:12–13). Lilies and ravens—the flora and fauna—place attributes of God on display. They can even serve as the medium of God's direct address, as when God spoke to Moses from a fiery bush (flora) and addressed Balaam through a donkey (fauna)!

CREATIONAL THEOMEDIA EVENTS

But the dazzling theater of creation cannot contain or convey the full brunt of divine revelation. Creation cannot entirely service the communicative needs of God, nor fully depict his divine identity. The flora and fauna in the Old Testament sometimes function not naturally but supernaturally (like Moses's bush and Balaam's beast of burden). The self-communication of God exceeds creation's capacities as a media form, so at critical moments in the Old Testament's story of Israel, we find God bending and upending creation to reveal more of himself than his handiwork's natural processes can withstand. Creation reveals much about God, but a "creational theophany" (the supernatural manifestation of God in nature) sometimes occurred to bring more direct, specific communication or more expansive revelation. These creational theophanies are divinely orchestrated "media events" that utilize yet stretch the natural world.

Some of these epic media events were horrifying. Before Noah saw the rainbow, God sent a flood that all but decimated humanity.

---

7. As noted in chapter 1, Nicholas Wolterstorff is careful to make the distinction between divine revelation and divine discourse/speaking. See *Divine Discourse*, 19–36.

Generations earlier, the mountain where Elijah felt God's gentle breeze and heard God's whispering voice had almost been splintered into smoldering shards by that same whispering, gentle-spoken God. That prior moment on Mount Horeb (a.k.a. Sinai) was probably the most definitive scene of God's divine revelation and self-communication in the Old Testament.

Before Elijah sought refuge in its crags, Sinai was the home of that shrub that had caught Moses's eye centuries earlier, ablaze with a fire that did not consume (Exod 3). Not long afterward, God reappeared on that mountain, but this time in a fiery tempest that would most certainly consume (Exod 19). The awful, holy ruckus at the giving of the Law was a visual and auditory spectacle the refugee nation of Israel was never to forget. When God offered his people the textual medium of the Ten Commandments, he appeared on the scene amidst terrifying scenery. The optical and acoustic TheoMedia in Exodus 19 included lightning strikes, trumpet blasts, swirling thick smoke, and a blood-chilling darkness. Sinai heaved and quaked under the weight of its Maker. At one point Moses tried to say something to God, and the response was thunder (Exod 19:19).

The heaving and quaking, thundering and trumpeting, all had a very specific purpose. "Do not be afraid," Moses told the trembling Israelites at the mountain's base, "for God has come only to test you and to put the fear of him upon you so that you do not sin" (Exod 20:20)—a strange exhortation: *do not fear . . . but fear.* The seeming contradiction bespeaks the inevitable tension of entering a relationship with a God both tender and terrifying. The boisterous, explosive TheoMedia event of Sinai was intended to convey the glorious ferocity and the exalted majesty of the One who was lovingly binding himself in intimate fellowship with Israel.

The manifestation of God on Sinai was the climactic culmination of a series of TheoMedia events that began a few months prior: the Exodus out of Egypt. Nine of the first ten plagues were nightmarish distortions of the natural world. In his standoff with Pharaoh, God sent no mysterious army with impressive war machinery across the Nile. No pyramids caved in and no palaces collapsed. The plagues were not *technological* disasters. They were almost entirely related to God's creation: the life-giving river became deathly blood, the sky vomited stones of ice, homes were swollen with rotting frog-flesh, darkness was permitted to go unchecked by the sun. God seemed ready to split apart the natural world as a protest against his people's oppression and Pharaoh's presumption. The last plague, however, involved less mediation. The firstborn in the homes of unbloodied lintels were struck by the hand of the angel of the Lord. Even the proud Egyptian king was found to be a grieving, broken father. He let the people go.

Israel's victorious God then made his presence visible in, and yet simultaneously hidden by, clouds and fire: "The LORD went in front of them in a pillar of cloud by day, to lead them along the way, and in a pillar of fire by night, to give them light, so that they might travel by day and by night" (Exod 13:21).

Creation was serving purposes beyond its normal capacities. Those plagues were awful disfigurations of the natural world that revealed God's wrath; and the pillars of cloud and fire were natural phenomena revealing—and yet concealing—God's gracious presence. The most dramatic element of the multifaceted TheoMedia event of the Exodus from Egypt came when Pharaoh, his brokenness morphing into an indomitable bitterness, changed his mind once more. From their seaside camp, the Israelites heard the rumbling of chariots and saw the flood of Egypt's army rushing toward them. There was nowhere to run . . . until the waters split open. Israel was brought into being as a nation through the birth canal of a ripped open sea.

The bending and upending of creation in Israel's Exodus is the Old Testament's most visual and aural revelation of God, the most spectacular media event in all history. The message? *The God of Israel is the one true King, his people belong to him alone, and come hell or high water he will do what it takes to rescue them.*

UNFORGETTABLE: HAUNTED BY THE THEOMEDIA OF SINAI AND THE EXODUS

The sights and sounds of the Exodus and Sinai were to brand the minds and hearts of each generation of God's people to come. These were media events staged "before your very eyes" (Deut 1:30; 4:34[8]), so that "you would acknowledge that the LORD is God; there is no other besides him" (Deut 4:35). The bellowing thunder and the rattling of the mountain were to echo permanently in their ears. The giving of the Law was a multi-TheoMedia event that left the Israelites reeling with a sensory overload of the holy. The use of creation throughout God's dramatic deliverance and

8. See also Deut 6:22; 7:19.

during the official designation of Israel as his own people afforded a range of searing sights and stentorian sounds to accompany the divine words.

We consider the ravens and the lilies. But we also consider the exodus plagues, the columns of cloud and fire, and the stone-crunching, thunderous sounds of a mountain summit nearly exploding. Creation and creational theophanies are TheoMedia relaying divine attributes and, at times, specific divine messages.

GOD AND NATURAL DISASTERS: THE INCURVATUS IN SE OF CREATION

This association of God's self-manifestation through creation, however, raises a host of sticky questions: What about natural disasters? Are rising seas, falling hail, and the seismic quaking of the earth forms of TheoMedia? Is the snarling face of God glaring through the hurricane's eye? Are tsunamis some form of divine communication?[9]

God spoke to Job out of the not-so-natural disaster of a visionary tornado (Job 38:1), and he brought crushing hail on Egyptian topography (Exod 9:18). But often the Lord is "not in the wind," "not in the earthquake," and "not in the fire" (1 Kgs 19:11–12). Creation can be a means by which God demonstrates the sweet beauty and terrifying splendor of his own character. But a creation suffering from the collateral damage of a mutiny against the Creator will reel and rock in the resulting state of a sin-induced sickness. Just as human beings as fallen image bearers are bound to yield fractured images, so a sin-struck world is bound to produce twisting winds and subterranean groans that do not derive from the One who made heaven and earth. As fallen image bearers, we humans need salvation. But salvation is not a need limited to human beings.

Creation needs salvation.

Though we see God using creation as TheoMedia in the Old Testament, we have to remember that, like image bearing humanity, creation is a media form impinged by sin's effects and, in its own way, curved in on itself. Job may have heard the voice of God amidst tornadic winds, but the fire and wind that earlier struck his household were from the hand of Satan (Job 1:16–19). Before the encouragement to consider ravens and

9. I have written on the topic of God and natural disasters on my blog and at The Ooze, critiquing the theological reflex of equating divine judgment with sudden calamity. See "I Believe in God . . . and Monsters."

lilies, Jesus rebuked and calmed a raging sea storm (Luke 8:22–25). He treated that maelstrom the way he had thus far treated demonic spirits and disease, as distortions of the divine intention that deserved not affirmation but severe rebuke (Luke 4:35, 39, 41).

Humankind and creation are corrupted forms of TheoMedia. They must be "read," that is, *interpreted*, with great care. Consider ravens and lilies, yes—but be wary of simplistic and judgmental interpretations. As Jesus himself once explained, not all that collapses or crumbles is strategically nudged by an invisible breath (Luke 13:1–5).[10]

The trees may clap their hands over God's deliverance (Isa 55:12); but sometimes the trees have their hands amputated from the shredding force of high winds. Creation may declare God's glory (Ps 19:1); but creation also groans for God's redemption (Rom 8:20–25). This dazzling theater was once an untainted means of divine communication, but when we human creatures rejected the Creator, we found ourselves malformed and perverted by sin (Rom 1:18–32). And we brought Creation into the darkness with us.

"Natural" disasters are indeed attributed to divine judgment at times in the Old Testament. Sometimes, "his way is in whirlwind and storm" (Nah 1:3). But a massive error in our interpretation of TheoMedia occurs when we fail to take into hermeneutical account the biblical reality that both humankind and Creation have been sabotaged by sin. Obviously, a cold-blooded murder is not a communicative act of God just because it was committed by someone made in God's image. The same reasoning can be applied to tornadoes and tsunamis, floods and earthquakes—not all winds blow from the mouth of God. Creation is a form of TheoMedia, but it needs salvation. We should allow the feral howls of thunderclouds and the pall of "dreadful and great darkness" (Gen 15:12) to remind us that God is mysteriously powerful; but we must also remember that those awful sounds may be the noise of Creation groaning for God's salvation (Rom 8:22), rather than the acoustics of Creation declaring God's praise (Ps 19:1).

Our Bibles are framed with creation accounts. "Behold, I am making all things new" (Rev 21:5) will one day sound forth from the throne of God as fallen Creation gives way to "a new heaven and a new earth" (Rev

---

10. Though I do not agree with all of his suppositions or conclusions, Terence Freitheim's book on natural disasters is an important contribution to how the church should respond theologically to calamity. See *Creation Untamed*.

21:1; cf. Isa 65:17). The Redeemer is coming one day over the horizon . . . and also *for* the horizon.

In the meantime, we still consider the ravens and lilies. We look to the bow in the sky and to stars uncountable and remember divine mercy. In spite of the violent *incurvatus in se* of Creation, beauty unspeakable speaks. The nearest star spurts its fiery hues into westward fleeing darkness every morning. Each dusk God stages a starset dripping into silvery blue silence.

But our eyes and ears have been so effectively trained to take in screen-displayed images and electronically amplified sound bites. What about birds and flowers, summits and streams? Are we watching? Are we listening?

Or are we complaining that bright golden rays are casting a glare on our screens?

Chapter 6

Physical Structures, Visionary Encounters, and the Media of the Absurd

Because the life-giving Creator Spirit is present wherever life flourishes, the Spirit's voice can conceivably resound through many media, including the media of our human culture. Because Spirit-induced human flourishing evokes cultural expression, we can anticipate in such expressions traces of the Creator Spirit's presence. Consequently, we should listen intently for the voice of the Spirit, who is present in all life and therefore who "precedes" us into the world, bubbling to the surface through the artifacts and symbols humans construct.

—Stanley Grenz and John Franke[1]

We worship a multimedia God. His multisensory modes of communication and self-revelation include more than just sights and sounds. Creation is not only filled with glorious vistas and the sweet acoustics of birdsong—We have acknowledged that the media of Creation is physical and therefore tangible. There are smells and tastes. The entire sensorium

---

1. Grenz and Franke, *Beyond Foundationalism*, 162.

can be engaged by what we find out of doors and beyond the horizon of our screens.

So there are other forms of TheoMedia including not only sights and sounds but also media requiring the senses of smell and touch. We now turn to the material elements of Israel's ritual worship, to direct mystical encounters with God, and to the media of divinely inspired visions and dreams. There is also an entire category of the downright bizarre.

TABERNACLE, TEMPLE, AND HOLY FURNITURE: THE AESTHETICS OF DIVINE PRESENCE

When we think of the word "holy," goats' hair and yarn do not normally come to mind. "Holy" is not usually a term that evokes images of tables, bowls, or embroidery. Neither do we associate "holy" with smells. The lack of such associations between holiness and our optical and olfactory senses might betray a tendency to conceive spirituality as perennially at odds with materiality, a conception quite foreign to the Old Testament.

The Tabernacle (and later the Temple modeled after it) supplied a sensory context of physical beauty central to Israel's worship. The twelve or so chapters in Exodus devoted to the Tabernacle and its accoutrements are laborious to work through. But reading those passages with our sense perceptions on heightened status might afford us with an extravagantly layered media experience! The descriptions are highly visual, almost even tactile in nature. What we find is that God has an eye for beauty, and not just the beauty of his created material in their natural form. He also has an eye for the aesthetic rendering of those materials into artwork *by human beings*. One could even say he has a *nose* for beauty, considering the many reports of God delighting in the "pleasing aroma" of incense and burning sacrifices. His resistance to having his image depicted by way of wood or metals does not translate into a rejection of visuality and materiality, *not even in the context of worship*.

The whole project of the Tabernacle is a technological undertaking the inspiration of which is presented as coming straight from God himself (Exod 25:9; 27:8).[2] We should not be surprised that the Creator of materiality is also a material Designer. The craft project of the Tabernacle is entirely God's brainchild. He himself provides the blueprints and casts

2. Dyer writes about God's divine "blueprints" for material projects in his chapter, "Redemption," *From the Garden to the City*, 98–114.

the aesthetic vision. Materials for the Tabernacle complex include fine linen, acacia wood, jewels, and spices. The sundry items also consisted of gold clasps and bronze pegs. There is lace and fancy needlework. The construction activities were engraving, weaving, carving, fastening, stone cutting, and even perfuming of all things. Blue, purple, and scarlet feature among the collage of colors, a collage that also comprises the gleaming of fine metals and the sparkling of various gems. Fragrances derive from the expert compounding of galbanum, stacte, salt, frankincense, and sweet-smelling cinnamon. The sort of designs etched, embroidered, or hammered into the artwork include celestial beings like the cherubim and terrestrial delights like pomegranates and almond blossoms.

All of this is for the pleasure of God, who is designing his dwelling place among his people. There is a divine interest here in *style*: God makes decisions about color, shape, and size. About the priestly garments, God expresses his desire that they be crafted "for glory and for beauty" (Exod 28:2, 40). I love that. God is not just interested in functionality. He is also interested in artistic "glory" and "beauty."

To be sure, these biblical descriptions of the Tabernacle (and eventually the Temple) and the vestments of priests are not grounds for a church to justify an exorbitant building program or for a shopper to justify an expanding wardrobe "for glory and for beauty." I recently found a website devoted to helping pastors set the pace in fashion—surely the aesthetics of the Tabernacle and the priestly garments were not intended to inspire a stylish look for preachers to appear well on screens. What we *do* find in the Tabernacle blueprints is that God possesses intense aesthetic interests. Beauty is not fanciful or dispensable for God. Nor need it be for us—when tempered by biblical teaching on avoiding vanity. As the Creator of a physical realm, God delights in the imaginative crafting of *things*. So can we—when safeguarded by biblical teaching on materialism.

The Tabernacle/Temple and its furniture do not just reveal God's artistic delights. Nor do they merely serve the purpose of supplying Israel's worship with a rich, sensory backdrop. God actually seems at times to mediate his presence and his holiness through the entire architectural complex.

We have seen already how the Ark of the Covenant served as God's earthly throne (see Exod 25:21–22). It was not uncommon to so closely associate that ornate box with the actual presence of God that seeing the ark was in some way like seeing him (Num 10:35–36; cf. Ps 24:7–10; 1 Sam 4:3–8). The Tabernacle and all its objects were so holy and so closely correlated to God that looking inside its embroidered walls could either cause death (Num 4:20) or even confer holiness by contact (Exod 29:37). Sighting the architectural complex of the Temple could be figuratively equated with beholding God (Ps 48:12–15).[3] The Jerusalem Temple was viewed as the locus where heaven and earth intersected.

Though it is regularly acknowledged that God cannot fit within a structure and that his presence cannot be architecturally confined, praying toward Jerusalem was in some sense like turning one's face toward God (1 Kgs 8:27–53). TheoMedia in the Old Testament include the physical—and very beautiful—structures, utensils, bowls, and tables of the Tabernacle/Temple with which God associated his presence. And the centrality of the Tabernacle amidst the camp (Num 2:2b)[4] and the elevated location of the Temple on Mount Zion established a visual form of TheoMedia saturation. The dwelling place of God occupied a dominant position in the public eye of God's people in contrast to the idols that occupied visual space among the surrounding nations.

GOD-SPONSORED TECHNOLOGY

We should make no mistake that the construction of God's dwelling place required a range of technologies. Setting gold filigree within a small jewel is undeniably technological. It should not be missed that God himself not only commissioned and designed this building program that necessitated so many diverse technological skills; he also filled with his Spirit the chief craftsmen and guided their use of the technology:

> Then Moses said to the people of Israel, "See, the LORD has called by name Bezalel the son of Uri, son of Hur, of the tribe of Judah; and he has filled him with the Spirit of God, with skill, with intelligence, with knowledge, and with all craftsmanship, to devise artistic designs, to work in gold and silver and bronze,

3. See the discussion in Anderson, "Towards a Theology of the Tabernacle and Its Furniture," 164–68.

4. The positioning of the Tabernacle in the camp also included the Levites' position encircling it as a perimeter "so that there may be no wrath on the congregation of the people of Israel" (Num 1:53b). This setup betokens a mediatorial role in the media. The medium is the message in this instance: the visual media of the Tabernacle (the "tent of meeting") occupied a mediated location within Israel. Both distance and closeness are conveyed—the former in that Levites served as an insular layer between the Tabernacle and the people, and the latter in that God and his Ten Commandments were centered in the midst of the people.

in cutting stones for setting, and in carving wood, for work in every skilled craft. And he has inspired him to teach, both him and Oholiab the son of Ahisamach of the tribe of Dan. He has filled them with skill to do every sort of work done by an engraver or by a designer or by an embroiderer in blue and purple and scarlet yarns and fine twined linen, or by a weaver—by any sort of workman or skilled designer. (Exod 35:30–35; cf. Exod 31:1–6; 36:1–2)

These technological skills are deemed as gifts directly supplied by God. We should acknowledge that the Tabernacle was not constructed in a mechanized age in which "technique," as Jacques Ellul put it, supplied society with its overriding "consciousness."[5] Israel lived in a tool-based culture that conceptualized technology quite unlike our own post-industrial, digitally ordered minds. Even so, it is worth noting that God is in no way squeamish here about the technologies he is calling to the aid of his Tabernacle project.

THEOMEDIA VERSUS IDOL MEDIA: A CONTRAST BETWEEN TWO TECHNOLOGICAL PROJECTS

Another striking point is that right in the midst of those twelve chapters in Exodus describing the Tabernacle, there is an interrupting account of another technological start-up project. It includes many of the same processes (carpentry[6] and metalworking), a shared material (gold), and was intended for similar functions (to receive sacrificial offerings). The project in question is the most notorious, most egregious of Israel's errors. It was the formation and worship of the golden calf and its altar (Exod 32). We read page after page of God's instructions about building and designing and crafting the visual TheoMedia of the Tabernacle and its elements, and then we abruptly find an unauthorized medium on which all Israelite eyes seem to be fixed.

Israel is choosing here an artistic rendering of God over God-inspired artistry.

---

5. "All-embracing technique is in fact the consciousness of the mechanized world." See Ellul, *The Technological Society*, 6. For Ellul, "technique" is the ubiquitous conceptuality, shaped by our use of machines and technology, that processes life on the basis of machine- and technology-related values (such as efficiency, utility, and speed).

6. I am assuming that the illicit altar Aaron built required woodwork.

The media contrast between the two projects is intentional. The same technology and raw materials were involved, though the purposes were vastly different. One media product consisted of *objects*—things and artwork that offered a worshiping context redolent of divine beauty. The other objectified God and encouraged worshiping him as a thing. Sometimes the gleaming of precious metal directs us to the Creator of all wonders. Sometimes it lures us into a spate of false worshiping.

Darkening even further this scene contrasting Israel's media preferences, we are told that Moses drops something on sighting the idolatrous worship. He drops from his arms the chief TheoMedium God has just produced for Moses to give to his people. The shattering of stone bearing the handwritten words of God is a soul-wrenching sound surely drowned out by the din of singing to a beastly statue. We will take a look at this tragic scene from a different angle in chapter 8, simply noting here that worldly media was chosen over TheoMedia even before the verbal TheoMedium of the Ten Commandments could be publicly presented.

In our brief study of the Tabernacle and its holy items we have found that God has aesthetic passions and interests. These sensibilities come to expression in the visual, tactile, and olfactory qualities of technologically produced wares. Israel's worship is enriched and strengthened by this non-verbal and non-textual apparatus.

It should be remembered, however, that the Tabernacle is not the first building project we have encountered in the biblical story. God supplied the blueprints in that case, too, yet functionality seemed to trump "glory" and "beauty" in Noah's construction of the ark. We must also recall the tower of Babel. The complexities of purpose and motivation have to be carefully weighed before we draw too fast a connection between the Tabernacle and our own artistic craftsmanship. Our bricks and mortar, gold and goats' hair could be used to honor our Creator and arch-Designer. They might also be used for presumptuous artifacts visually expressing our self-sufficiency (like Babel's tower), or even for idolatrous images from which we just cannot pry away our fixated eyes (like Aaron's calf).

MOSAIC MEDIATION AND THE UNEXPECTED VISITOR

The Book of Exodus can be understood as a long, mediated conversation. God is speaking to his people (and at times to Pharaoh) through the agency of Moses. Conversely, Israel also speaks to God through Moses, usually by grumbling and complaining, which God hears quite well without any help. Like an exasperated diplomat shuffling incessantly between two parties, Moses is seen as a divinely appointed mediator.

The first mediator of the Bible left God's people in perpetual need of mediation—failing to resist the serpent's temptation, human beings compromised their capacity to directly interact with God and were forced into exile. But there is a biblical *story*, an epic saga of redemption, because God deemed humanity's exiled distance intolerable to his holy sensibilities and determined that their incapacity to relate to him would be reversible. The serpent inserted his voice into the divine-human discourse and (temporarily) impeded it. In the great Exodus event, God staged his own interruption, inserting his voice through the lips of Moses to speak of rescue and salvation. Mosaic mediation is God's stretching out his arms to reestablish the divine-human fellowship.

There were moments, though, when God revealed himself in less mediated fashion, when he used no mortal go-between and no creational elements like cloud or fire:

> Then Moses and Aaron, Nadab and Abihu, and seventy of the elders of Israel went up, and *they saw the God of Israel*. Under his feet there was something like a pavement of sapphire stone, like the very heaven for clearness. God did not lay his hand on the chief men of the people of Israel; also they beheld God, and they ate and drank. (Exod 24:9–11; emphases added)

Eating a meal with God—this is unusually intimate and seems more fitting in Eden than on Sinai.

Perhaps that is the point.

By regularly allowing Moses and his cohorts the unique privilege of face-to-faceness, God seems to be following a redemptive movement that shoves hard against humanity's ebbing away from Eden's intimacy. Relational distance is still in force: the reports that Moses sees God face-to-face (Exod 33:11; cf. Gen 32:20; Num 12:8; 14:14; Deut 5:4; 34:10) are probably intended to be figurative since God himself is quite clear in Exodus 33:20 that "you cannot see my face; for no one shall see me and live."

This ambiguity of distance-yet-closeness is a significant feature of the TheoMedium of the mysterious, 'heavenly visitor'. God's ex-Eden engagement with individuals is often attended by a certain vagueness, by a poignant alteration between mediation and un-mediation. It is unclear whether the one appearing is God or some immortal representative. The three men who visited Abraham in Genesis 18 are understood as representing God himself. Jacob engaged an enigmatic stranger in physical combat and understood that later he had actually been wrestling with God (though surely he was a bit suspicious; Gen 32:22–32). Samson's parents were visited by a "man of God" who was later revealed to be the "angel of the LORD" (see Judg 13). It is guessed by Manoah, Samson's father-to-be, that they had been interacting with none other than the one and only God.

A sense of *remoteness* marks these scenes, even though less mediation is involved than the Israelites having to rely on Moses to relay messages back and forth. Those who wondered if the person with whom they had just spoken, wrestled, or hosted was God himself were left in a fog of mystery—they could not exactly (or accurately) put their fingers on what had just happened in the unexpected encounters.

In the narrative accounts of these encounters, the biblical writers are content to leave their readers/hearers just as confused as the biblical characters over what had just taken place. Was the figure an angel or God himself? If the account uses the term "angel" in reference to the curious person in question, why did the "angel" not correct the human interlocutor's unrestrained act of worshiping him (as in Josh 5:13–15)? We are hard pressed to know just what is happening in these accounts. And the physical descriptions of the Mystery Guest/Warrior/Opponent are quite sparse. These run-ins with the immortal are enshrouded in narrative and descriptive mystery not unlike how the cloud-column obscured God's glory in the wilderness. A haunting sense of person-to-Person *distance* is retained even though there is a recognition that the divine-human interaction underway is notably less mediated than usual.

VISIONARY EXPERIENCES AND GOD-HAUNTED DREAMS

This dual sense of relational distance bridged, yet not quite, is also found in the highly visual and aural descriptions of heavenly visions. Isaiah recounts, "I saw the Lord sitting on a throne, high and lofty; and the hem of his robe filled the temple" (Isa 6:1). Details are given about the mighty angelic beings hovering in the cosmic temple, about the sight of smoke and the sounds of voices (and surely the shaking of "the foundations of the threshold" was quite noisy; Isa 6:4 ESV). But the physical appearance of God himself, aside from the description of his posture ("sitting on a throne") and a terse observation about his clothing ("the hem of his robe"), is not supplied.

Daniel goes a bit further in the account of his vision when he tells us that the hair of the "Ancient of Days" was "like pure wool" (Dan 7:9). Little else is added. In Ezekiel's visionary call, the Being on the throne appeared in "something that seemed like a human form" (Ezek 1:26), yet the descriptors are rather non-humanly: "gleaming amber," "something that looked like fire," "a splendor all around" (1:27) which was "like the bow in a cloud on a rainy day" (1:28). Such reserve in offering anthropomorphic features to describe God honors the distinct aniconism of Israel's worship. As unmediated as God's presence seemed to be in these visions, the abstract nature of the prophet's visual descriptions ensures that a sense of distance obtains . . . in contrast to the open company God kept with humankind back in Eden.

All senses are on high alert, though, and functioning at top capacity for the recipients of these remarkable (and relatively rare) visionary experiences. Just as creation is incapable of bearing the full brunt of divine relation, it would seem from these visions that mortals are quite incapable of *receiving* the full brunt of divine revelation. No media form, it would seem, is elastic enough for fully communicating the unspeakable glory of the Person of God. One gets the impression that God wishes to reveal more of himself, but out of recognition of his interlocutor's mortality he maintains restraint. Mediation is required for the sake of protecting these human beings for whom such visions could incite the expectation of imminent death.

A bit less intimidating are those divinely inspired dreams we read about in which God revealed not so much his glorious presence but some bit of news or perhaps a hint of what awaits in the days to come. Dreams feature significantly in the accounts of Joseph and Daniel (their own dreams as well as those of others). Often puzzling and enigmatic by design, dreams are a form of TheoMedia that can come in the shape of a riddle. In his communication with us, God feels no obligation to be unambiguous.

ENCOUNTERS, VISIONS, AND DREAMS IN THE DIGITAL AGE? AFFIRMATIONS AND WARNINGS

Does God still speak in these media formats today? Should we expect encounters with a mysterious Stranger or fall asleep eager for dreamy revelations? Are visionary experiences of God's presence a regular part of today's economy of divine media?

The New Testament gives no reason to assume these TheoMedia have expired. Paul's unanticipated collision with Jesus while Damascus-bound has developed into somewhat of a standard conversion narrative for many Christians. The astonishing news that Gentiles are to be incorporated into the church was introduced to Peter through a dream. John the Seer's vista from Patmos was ripped open to expose the heavenly throne room of God and of the Lamb.

But we have seen already that a certain hermeneutical competence is required for "reading" TheoMedia. The need for interpretive wisdom is all the more necessary when it comes to visions, dreams, and numinous encounters. Like reading signs and omens in the heavens, heavenly experiences can just as well be pagan as biblical. When Nebuchadnezzar awoke from his nightly visions, those whom he immediately sought out as the dream-experts were naturally the "magicians," "enchanters," "sorcerers," and "astrologers" (Dan 2:2; 4:7).

Not all winds blow from God's breath. And not all dreams or visions come from heaven.

Dreams are so riddling that they often demand interpretation within the biblical accounts. Others were consulted for wisdom, implying the need for a *communal hermeneutic*. When it comes to visionary encounters with God's presence, we should note that the "star" of those experiences of God is God. I have heard a number of personal reports in which a Christian encounters God in some dramatic, visionary way. Suspicion is warranted, I think, when the vision is accompanied with an inflated sense of grandiosity and a subjective feeling of self-worth, usually related to a supposedly divine proclamation that the one having the vision will become great and perform countless marvels.[7]

---

7. Young Joseph's dreams about the sheaves and stars bowing before him seem a bit of an exception, but these were not visionary encounters with God, and Joseph's insensitive reports of those dreams to his brothers are not presented as commendable (Gen 37:5–11)!

In both Testaments of our Bibles, direct mystical encounters with God leave the encountered broken, unnerved, and eviscerated of pride and vanity. After seeing the Lord sitting on his throne, I doubt Isaiah would have thought, *now this will make a great status update on Facebook: "Saw God today and he gave me an important job to do. Awesome =)."* Actually, his response was to curse his existence ("woe is me"), and the "job" he was assigned was a futile vocation of proclaiming truth to unhearing, hostile audiences. Tradition has it that they one day sawed him in half.

In many circles today, "spiritual" encounters and weird dreams have become the means of authenticating spiritual maturity or of validating certain leading figures in the church. Some of these TheoMedia encounters may well be legitimate. Many of them are not. The careful discernment of a communal hermeneutic is required.[8]

THE ABRUPT IMMEDIACY OF GOD: A LESSON FOR THE DIGITAL AGE

In spite of the need for interpretive wariness, these sensory means of divine revelation and communication supply us this ominous (and exhilarating!) lesson about TheoMedia: *God can thrust himself into our lives at any moment.*

Our visual and aural space is always and ever apt to divine intrusion. At any moment, God may interrupt all other media in our lives to grasp our attention. The forms of TheoMedia we have just discussed—dreams, visions, and encounters—almost always seem to have come by surprise for the biblical characters who experienced them. They were not necessarily looking for God, and some were not even interested in God at all.

Then *boom.*

A relational God bent on communicating with us can get as loud as necessary. We can take courage in this: *our lives are not so media saturated that God cannot break through with his own media.* We are never too far out of reach from the communicative God of the Bible. Never.

---

8. On the dangers (and the actual benefits) of experiential spirituality, see my chapter "Experientialism" in *Faith Without Illusions*, 59–85.

THEOMEDIA ABSURDITIES: NEHUSHTAN, A DONKEY, AND A DISMEMBERED HAND

TheoMedia include the non-verbal and non-textual sights and sounds that God employs for revealing, communicating, and mediating his character, his messages, and his power. The Old Testament has a God-sponsored soundscape and a God-produced visual field for those with the eyes to see and the ears to hear.

The sights and sounds of media influence and give shape to our lives. What audiovisual media most occupies our senses today? There is much to hear, and lots to see throughout our daily grind. Are we straining our sight and attuning our ears to the potential forms of visual, aural, and even material TheoMedia? "Glory" and "beauty" abound all around us.

Sometimes that "glory" and "beauty" abound through the most unlikely of means. So we close this chapter looking at the absurd.

Near the end of their decades-long wilderness meandering, Israel complains directly to God (not just to Moses) about the shoddy provisions and the ridiculous itinerary of their journey (see Num 21:4–9). That is when the snakes appear. Slithering among the tens of thousands of Israelites are these venomous ("fiery" in the ESV) creatures in whose wake is death. The disturbing scene is one in which God uses the Theo-Media of Creation to bring judgment.

He also uses in that scene a visual, material artifact to bring life. God instructs Moses to "make" a bronze statue of a serpent by which divine healing is mediated for those reeling from snakebites. Relief only comes, however, to those individuals who will avail themselves of salvation through God's appointed means (by looking at this statuary symbol).

What are we to make of this?

The use of this serpent image, later identified as "Nehushtan," seems marked by superstition or magic. Yet God uses all sorts of oddities like this in scripture. The media of God boast a wide repertoire. He puts a mark on Cain as a public symbol of divine protection (Gen 4:15). God floats a "smoking fire pot" and a "flaming torch" between divided animal carcasses to signify covenant making with Abram (Gen 15). We have already touched on the oddity of both Balaam's donkey (Num 22) and the burning bush (Exod 3). We can add the "Umim and Thumim," perhaps some equivalent to holy dice one would cast to figure out God's will.

Some of these media forms just seem wacky. And don't forget Aaron's staff budding in Numbers 17. In Daniel we have the horrifying report that a set of fingers appear out of nowhere to write on a wall at a wild Chaldean party (Dan 5). God also communicated all throughout the Bible through signs and wonders, like moistening (then drying) Gideon's fleece (Judg 6:36–40) and causing a shadow to retreat for King Hezekiah (2 Kgs 20:8–11).

We should also mention that the sacrificial system endemic to Israel's worship included a vast range of sensory media: the sights and sounds of animal blood shedding, the smells of burning flesh and rising incense, the touch of a struggling lamb, heifer, or dove.

Again, what are we to make of these mysterious, sometimes bizarre means of God's communication and revelation?

It is always dangerous to build a theology on the exceptions. Sacrifices were commonplace, of course, but much of what we have listed was unusual, and it is appropriate for us to identify them as such. The exceptions are difficult to process because they often do not fit within a theological frame of reference constructed by the consistencies. Even so, God used that serpent-thing for the rescue of dying people—no small function for a physical object. So though we cannot build a theology on anomalies, we must certainly develop a theology large enough for the anomalous.

I think the lesson we can take from these absurd forms of TheoMedia is this: *God can use whatever he pleases when he communicates, reveals, or extends his power.* There are certain people in our lives for whom we have less affection than Balaam did for his beast of burden. You never know—that person might become the means by which God speaks to us. And there is a great deal of media out there that we find offensive: trashy novels, crass television shows, seedy films, and obscene music whose lyrics ring raucously in our ears. We need not normalize the pattern of looking for God in the bizarre, offensive, and absurd. But we do need to be ready to see and hear him amidst unexpected media . . . even media that disturb and unsettle.

One more thing: if God can use the absurd and the anomalous, then we can trust that he can even use something as absurd as the people of Israel. If he can use a bronze snake-thing on a pole, then he can even use you and me.

TheoMedia Note 4

Aaron and the Calf

Idolatry and Technological Determinism

In this brief note, I want to take a look at that awful scene in Exodus 32 when Aaron fashions the golden calf. The story has some lessons for the idea of technological determinism that we keep visiting throughout this book.

Though I have thus far taken what could be called a "soft" approach on technological determinism, the Bible is explicit that the ideology encoded within the technology of idolcraft is so overpowering that it is inescapable:

> The idols of the nations are silver and gold, the work of human hands. They have mouths, but they do not speak; they have eyes, but they do not see; they have ears, but they do not hear, and there is no breath in their mouths. *Those who make them and all who trust them shall become like them.* (Ps 135:15–18, emphases added)

According to scripture, no technology contorts, determines, and shapes the makers and users like idolatry.[1]

But the scene in Exodus 32 with the golden calf teaches us that we cannot just blame the deterministic capacities of our technologies when they go wrong.

Aaron refused to take responsibility for the technology of his idol-crafting, shifting blame to the technological processes themselves, as if they had a life of their own, over which he had no control:

1. For a theological and exegetical reading of idolatry as shaping the idolater, see Beale's *We Become What We Worship*.

> Moses said to Aaron, "What did this people do to you that you have brought so great a sin upon them?" And Aaron said, "Do not let the anger of my lord burn hot; you know the people, that they are bent on evil. They said to me, 'Make us gods, who shall go before us; as for this Moses, the man who brought us up out of the land of Egypt, we do not know what has become of him.' So I said to them, 'Whoever has gold, take it off'; *so they gave it to me, and I threw it into the fire, and out came this calf!*" (Exod 32:21–24, emphases added)

Aaron's alibi after being confronted over this grotesque offense is that he is simply offering the supply for the masses' demand. *And actually, I had no real involvement in the technological procedures—this thing just popped right out of the forge!* He blames both the consumer group and the technology behind the product, a move not unlike what we might find in the corporate world today: *we just threw some raw materials into the factory, and, what do ya know, look what came out the other end . . . .*

Now, the consuming crowds certainly share part of the blame. But we have to take ownership in how we are using technology. Though I do believe that technologies often possess inherent ideological inclinations that compel a certain usage, thereby yielding results that are loosely predetermined, this scene at the base of Sinai shows that human responsibility cannot be removed from the equation. The God who assigned us to exercise "dominion" in his creation expects us to own up to our technology production.

And even if a technology can service salutary ends, it does not automatically imply that it will always do so. Aaron's technical labors do not differ from the labors to which Bezalel and Oholiab are about to set themselves in the Tabernacle work. Both parties take into their hands engraving tools and a precious metal.

Yet look at the vast difference in the intent and function of the product. The Tabernacle and the tablets of stone are TheoMedia set at violent odds with that metallic calf.

PART 3

The Speech and Texts of Israel's God
Verbal TheoMedia in the Old Testament

Chapter 7

Word Anxieties and Word Theology

[T]he doctrine of Scripture must resist reducing the Bible to revelation, just as it must resist reducing revelation to either the merely propositional or the merely personal.

—Kevin Vanhoozer[1]

The Bible and preaching are rather *media* in which *summa vis et efficacia* [the highest force and efficacy] intrinsically and permanently reside.

—Karl Barth[2]

MENE, MENE, TEKEL, and PARSIN

—The Writing on the Wall, Daniel 5:25

1. Vanhoozer, *The Drama of Doctrine*, 48.
2. Barth, *Church Dogmatics*, 1/1:110. For the Latin translation I used the T & T Clark Study edition of *CD* (108, EN66).

Our task in this book is to identify God's media throughout the biblical story and discern the divine logic undergirding their use. Since God commissions and employs media throughout scripture, there are grounds for a theological framework by which we can appropriate and make sense of our own media culture today.

In the previous two chapters we focused on the aural, material, and visual means by which God revealed and communicated himself to Israel. Some of these TheoMedia were *ad hoc* in that God used sundry means at any given moment, depending on the situation at hand (e.g., Balaam's donkey). Some of these TheoMedia are more formal in that they were specifically marked as consistent means by which Israel was to recognize and perceive God (e.g., the visual symbolism of the Tabernacle). Already it can be said that the array of TheoMedia is wildly expansive.

We take up in this chapter the claim made earlier that, in the Old Testament, primacy is given to *verbal* TheoMedia, the media of God's words *spoken* and *written*. Accordingly, I suggested that the media to which God assigns priority determines the media we should excel in interpreting and using. If oral and textual TheoMedia are indeed prioritized, then it is incumbent on us to retain and strengthen the skills of *hearing* and *reading*. If the burden of the previous chapters on the sights and sounds of God was to argue that TheoMedia are various and multisensory, the burden of this chapter and the next is to show that they are subordinate to *logocentric* media, that is, the word-oriented media of prophetic discourse and holy texts.

But wait.

I want to acknowledge here from the onset of Part III that elevating verbal TheoMedia over acoustic, tangible, and optical TheoMedia might make some of us a bit nervous . . . and perhaps for good reason. So before making my case for the prioritization of textual and oral TheoMedia over other forms of God's media, I want to address some anticipated anxieties. In particular, I am concerned about the negative baggage associated today with print culture in many corners of both church and society. The chapter will eventually close with a 'propositional theology' of the Old Testament's word-media, but if the word 'propositional' makes you cringe, just bear with me as we address some of these verbal anxieties!

LITERARY SPIRITUALITY?

I mentioned earlier the anxiety incited by reading comprehension sections in compulsory exams. Those number 2 graphite pencils (okay, I know many exams are computer-based now) quiver in students' hands as the rating of their intellectual capacities hinges on how well they retain the data and logical flow of the most boring set of paragraphs one could ever imagine reading about socio-political crises in post-World War II Europe or medieval scientific developments in disease treatments (in case you are wondering, I made this sentence laborious on purpose).

Is God sitting at his holy lectern tapping his foot and holding out for us to pass his verbal exams so we can prove ourselves worthy of his affection? Does the Old Testament's emphasis on God's speech and texts demand a spirituality measurable by the literary portions of standardized tests?

Alan Jacobs points out that our first encounters with the written word are often tender and delightful, occurring in the lap of a parent who lovingly reads us stories.[3] Our earliest interactions with books come under the tutelage of a "lector," that is, a reader. Usually it is someone like mom, dad, or an older sibling. Our first books were highly visual with lots of bright illustrations, and we *looked* and *listened* rather than *read*. The textual medium of the printed page came to us first with a combination of visual and oral media.

Then our primary schools ushered us into the realm of the literate. Not only were books minus illustrations placed into our hand; Jacobs reminds us that we were also posed daunting questions like, "Which reading group are you in?"[4]

I am not saying that it is wrong to sequester children into reading groups. But we should recognize that doing so draws social lines and inadvertently tends to correlate self-worth to reading comprehension (later to be assayed by the SAT, ACT, or GRE in the States or GCSE tests if you live in the United Kingdom). Here is how Jacobs describes the anxious progress a child makes from illiteracy to literacy: "So reading, which starts for many of us in a warm cocoon of security, accompanied by an unassailable sense of being loved, gradually and inexorably . . . turns into

---

3. Jacobs, *The Pleasures of Reading in an Age of Distraction*, 147.
4. Ibid.

a site of stress. It becomes a contested environment in which we succeed or fail."[5]

If someone claims that the written words of God are given preference over other media forms when it comes to divine communication, then these reading anxieties begin to surface. Are better *readers* therefore better *Christians*? Is literacy an indispensable component of spirituality? Should Christians assess spiritual maturity on the basis of their reading competency?

What if you walked into a new church and someone asked, "Which reading group are you in: the 'Augustine/Barth/Calvin' section, the 'pop-Christian/Theology-lite' group, or are you one of those 'I just like TV' folks?" These (unlikely) questions highlight many of the tensions intrinsic to text-based media in the life of the church today. In church circles emphasizing the values of print culture, these tensions give rise to the haughty sentiment that we readers are more spiritual than those hands-on do-gooders and the charismatic visionaries. Bookishness can become an inadvertent means of ranking our own spirituality alongside the spirituality of others.

The process of an initial comfort gradually problematized with anxiety also occurs with the spoken word of direct address. When we were fresh out of the womb, most of the speech directed to our underdeveloped ears was—or should have been—quite pleasant (noting unfortunately that there are inevitable exceptions). When I have orally addressed each of my kids as newborns, it was with a mushy-gushy sweetness dripping with affirmation and delight.

Within six months, though, a new sound was regularly ringing in those cute little ears: "no-no." Later, there might come angry outbursts like, "Careful with that glass!" or, "Stop hitting your sister!" And to use the expression "we had words" implies an argumentative discussion took place.

Lectures and sermons—when some authoritative figure speaks a whole lot of words with little room for interruption—are sometimes understood as verbal events that, at worst, constitute oppressive acts of power wielding. In this perspective, lectures and sermons are just downright boring at best (and we all know that the great media sin of our culture is to be boring). "Preachy" is not a positive word. When a teenager quips about a parent's "lecture" or "sermon," the tone is usually accusatory.

5. Ibid., 148.

The negative connotations associated with long-winded verbalizing are thickest for those of us who just cannot follow along very well, for those of us who have been repeatedly caught whispering and note passing by the lecturer or preacher. Communication through words, spoken or written, has a complex personal history for each of us, with perhaps as many dark notes as bright (media are messy).

It should be admitted, though, that nonverbal and non-textual media forms are not without their own baggage today. Our earliest engagement of audiovisual media probably came in the form of entertainment (fun kid-songs, cartoons, animated films). But then we saw that horror film we were told to avoid, or we stared glassy-eyed at pornographic footage while at a friend's house. There is no media format—aural, oral, visual, tangible, visual, verbal, or textual—without some sort of negative connotation. As some of us react against the values of print culture, we should acknowledge what was examined in chapter 4: every media form and every instance of media use is marked by the dual dimensions of the beauty of the *imago Dei* and by the "incurvature" (sinfulness) of our souls.

WORD BAGGAGE

The sort of baggage with the written and spoken word I am most concerned about here is the theological association of "word" with austere, authoritative doctrine that squashes mystery, ignores narrative, and compresses truth into propositions.

Although words are undeniably used to convey mystery, tell stories, and offer imaginative renderings of truth, the claim that God prioritizes oral and textual media over other kinds will likely stoke anxieties pertaining to the growing reputation in the church for word-based media to be controlling and dogmatic. Evangelicals and many mainline Protestants with strong liturgical backgrounds may have little reason to wince when it is suggested that verbal TheoMedia are elevated over more sensory TheoMedia—to varying degrees, these traditions celebrate the precision and efficacy of word-based media in catechesis, in creedal affirmations, in corporate recitations of scripture passages, and in the regular act of preaching (namely of the "expository" variety).

Those hailing from Pentecostal, sacramental, or Emergent traditions might be inclined to raise some protests, however, and for very different reasons. The experientialism that features in more charismatic-style worship has sometimes been labeled as a neglect of "Word" in favor of "Spirit." Catholic and Orthodox emphases on the visual and tactile dynamics of the Eucharist, baptism, and other ritual practices have also been disparaged by the alleged iconoclastic tendencies of word-oriented tribes. For postmodern Christians, certain stripes of text-governed approaches to faith seem too beholden to dodgy power structures and more focused on parsing vocabulary than living out beauty.[6]

The concerns are valid.

I referred earlier to Leonard Sweet's recent book on social media, *Viral*. He contrasts two groups of Christians characterized by their media practices and media mindset: "Gutenbergers," those stuck in the print culture; and "Googlers," those whose impulses and perspectives are grounded in the philosophies and practices of the digital age. The groupings are overly caricatured, but he sums up well two stereotypical views of word-based media:

> I entered the world as a Gutenberger, and I share a deep devotion to the written and spoken word. But I wrestle with the Gutenberger Culture's use of words, and sometimes even its use of the Word. Gutenbergers proceed from a fixed point, which helps explain why they are drawn to objective facts, unimpeachable research, and hard statistics. For them, words serve much the same purpose as a mathematical proof. There is a feeling of certainty that comes with precise words and piercing definitions.
>
> Googlers are also big fans of words, but they approach them differently. To a Googler, words are important because they help a person express ideas, share news, and tell stories. Words can establish common ground and reveal shared interests. Instead of serving as a tether or anchor to a fixed point, for Googlers words are agents of change, experiments in conversation, small change in the coinage of the new realm of unmediated, interactive, unscripted connection.[7]

For Sweet, words can be used for asserting authority ("Gutenbergers") or for relating to others ("Googlers").

The contrast is between a propositional approach to media (the assertion of claims) and a personal approach (the intention to build

---

6. McLaren's chapter "Why I Am Mystical/Poetic" in *A Generous Orthodoxy* is a representative text for this perspective on more systematically text-based readings of Christianity (145–57). See also Jones, *The New Christians*, 152–57.

7. Sweet, *Viral*, 13.

relationships). Reducing the self-revelation of God through speech and texts to either of these categorizations is extremely unhelpful (note the epigraph by Kevin Vanhoozer opening this chapter). What I do find helpful in Sweet's quote above is that it demonstrates the array of associations and apprehensions with which various groups of people might receive the claim that God preferences words over other media forms for his self-revelation and divine communication.[8]

ANCIENT SCRIBES, EUROPEAN TYPESETTERS, AND TECH-SAVVY TWEETERS: DIFFERENT "WORD-VIEWS"

The rise of new media and the postmodern reevaluation of modernity's intellectual zeitgeist have coincided in such a way that print culture's unprecedented breakthroughs in a bygone era are getting some bad press. But we need to be careful not to make such direct connections between the word-media of Scripture and the conceptualizations of word-media in modernity and postmodernity. There are similarities, of course, but Hebrew and early Jewish understandings of word-media are not to be equated with the verbal ethos deriving from the print culture made possible by Gutenberg's fifteenth-century technology and utilized so readily in the Reformation and Counter-Reformation.

In addition, we cannot equate digital culture's use and understanding of words with how words were utilized in the Bible, as if casting off the typographic fetters of modernity will restore us to the pristine days of ancient oral societies.[9] Sweet claims, "Googlers tend to live by values that early Christians would recognize. They believe there is more truth in relationships than in propositions"[10] Yet the early church seemed to have

8. I would question the descriptors "unmediated" and "unscripted" when it comes to the "new realm" of social media enthusiasts; and the implication that "Gutenbergers" are self-assertive empiricists and not conversationalists when it comes to words seems unfair.

9. With this said, though, Robert Fowler offers a helpful overview of how we modern readers have misunderstood the Bible by perceiving it through the typographical perspective of inhabitants of a print culture: "Why Everything We Know About the Bible Is Wrong," 3–18. Though I learned much from this article and agree with many of Fowler's points, I would like to see his observations about the Bible *not being a book* in conversation with canonical theology, a conversation I acknowledge as perhaps beyond the scope of his essay.

10. Sweet, *Viral,* 15.

no qualms with expressing doctrine through carefully crafted hymns and creeds. The point here is simply to acknowledge that the cultures of the ancient Near East conceptualized words and word-based media in ways that are quite different from Western culture whether in the fifteenth, sixteenth or twenty-first century.[11]

In a culture of mass printing, and maybe even more so in a culture of digitization and pixelation, words are aplenty and perhaps less precious. They can be uttered, broadcasted, podcasted, penned, typed, or tweeted with relative ease. And with the technology of propagating so many words comes the technology of conveniently erasing them. The inhabitants of a print culture know what to do with unwanted words: smear them with white-out, black them out with one's bounteous supply of ink, or erase them with the other end of that number 2 graphite pencil.

In digital culture we just hit backspace, delete, or click on an "x" icon. For us, words are less binding, less reified, less irreversible than they were in the bygone days of Israel.

When it came to textual/written TheoMedia, ancient Israelite society was in some respects an *inscription* culture. What I mean by "inscription culture" is that the writing technology at the time was such that a word-limit of 140 characters might not have generated balking. Official writing-craft was laborious and required specialized training and skills. With words having to be engraved into stone or inscribed onto costly papyrus, they seemed to possess a certain durability and a binding power. Words published for public view were not cheap or cheaply rendered. Once etched or inscribed, they could take on both *mystical* (as in sacred or magical) and *monumental* (as in lasting and not to be forgotten) qualities, especially if the words on display were associated with a deity.[12]

---

11. The Hebrew and Greek words for "word" (*dabar* and *logos*) are slippery and versatile in meaning. In spite of the reputation of word-based media to be precise and clear, these old biblical words for "word" cannot be defined precisely with clarity. "Word, thing, action, matter, etc.," and "word, speech, message, book, volume, reason, logic, etc.," are stabs at their respective meanings. "Word" must therefore be defined on the basis of its context, not only in the sentence at hand, but its wider uses in all its nuances and complexities in the broader literary strokes of a culture's verbal/textual artifacts (and their underlying oral sources). For a concise yet in-depth summation of biblical concepts of word-media, see "Orality, Writing, and the Cultivation of Texts" in Horsley's *Scribes, Visionaries, and the Politics of Second Temple Judaism*, 89–108 (esp. 93). See also Carr's *Writing on the Tablet of the Heart*.

12. Horsley, *Scribes, Visionaries, and the Politics of Second Temple Judaism*, 94–95, 97.

Along with being an inscription culture, ancient Israelite society was an *oral* culture. Though we can to some degree claim that Israel practiced a "book religion,"[13] literacy may have been quite limited.[14] This meant that the individualism that widespread literacy has encouraged in the act of reading since the print culture's dawn would have been a bit odd for the folks of the Old Testament. Reading is regularly depicted in scripture as a massive communal event where a lector like Josiah or Ezra stands before the people with an open scroll. Some might associate such scenes of reading and hearing with lecturing or domineering preaching.

But perhaps it was more like a loving parent reading holy words to the children of God.

SOME REASONS WHY GOD'S WORD-MEDIA ARE PRIORITIZED IN THE OLD TESTAMENT

So on what grounds do I keep making this claim about the elevation of verbal TheoMedia over all other forms of divine media? We will pay more attention to this in the next chapter, but one reason to note here is that the aural/visual/tangible TheoMedia forms we have discussed in the previous chapters were either inspired by or sourced in oral and textual TheoMedia. Creation appeared because God *verbalized* it into being. The Tabernacle was constructed on the basis of *holy speech*. That gleaming, golden ark of the Tabernacle/Temple was a container for *scripture* (Deut 10:5).[15] And the prophets' visions, dreams, and visitations were the arresting, audiovisual context for a *divine message*.[16]

All forms of TheoMedia are important for the shaping of God's people. Though some Protestant strands have downplayed visual media in the life of faith, Jane Heath reminds us that there is such a thing as a

13. Van der Toorn, "The Iconic Book," 229–48.

14. Horsley, *Scribes, Visionaries, and the Politics of Second Temple Judaism*, 91. It should be noted, however, that there are vast degrees of literacy, from the basic ability to identify alphabet symbols with sounds to the capacity for reading lenghty, complex texts.

15. See Miller, *The Ten Commandments*, 3.

16. Though certainly the reception of God's words by the prophet was often inseparable from a visionary, ecstatic experience of beholding God in his heavenly court: "For who has stood in the council of the LORD so as to see and to hear his word?" (Jer 23:18; cf. the story of Micaiah in 1 Kgs 22:19–23 and of course Isaiah and Ezekiel in Isa 6 and Ezek 1–3, respectively). See also Horsley, *Scribes, Visionaries, and the Politics of Second Temple Judaism*, 105.

transformative "visual piety"—by looking on the wonders of God or his revealed-yet-concealed visionary presence, we are irrevocably altered.[17]

Even so, the *unmediated* sight of God is unsurvivable. Seeing him in his fullness is utterly beyond our ocular faculties, hence the need for communicative mediation. Though visuality is a significant complement to verbal TheoMedia, words are deemed more manageable media for those whose eyes cannot withstand the full visual brunt of divine revelation. So perhaps another reason word-media are prioritized is not because hearing and reading are fundamentally more important than seeing, but because we are too weak—too morally blemished—to behold God with our optic senses.[18] As God told Moses, "No one shall see me and live" (Exod 33:20).

So words have become critical media for God's self-revelation and self-communication. As he reminded the Israelites who stood as children around Sinai's base: "You heard the sound of words, but saw no form . . ." (Deut 4:12). At Sinai, God comes close to re-creating the sort of face-to-face relationship he enjoyed with Eve and Adam in Eden (Deut 5:4); and Moses seemed to converse "face to face" with God on the summit (Exod 33:11). Yet, tensions persist in these texts—in spite of Israel being "face to face" with God, Moses's intermediation between them is undeniable; and, as we have just seen above, God denied Moses a true face-to-face encounter in Exodus 33:20. We have discussed this distance-yet-closeness in chapter 6. It can be explained by drawing on the theological tradition about the fallen state of humanity: such direct, unmediated interaction with God is impossible due to our sin-enfeebled state. And because of sinful impulses and the ancient religious mindset, seeing something of God's form (if there even *is* a "form" for the God who is Spirit) would likely have tempted Israel to have tried crafting material depictions of him. Words spoken by God and inscribed at his inspiration are therefore the surest medium for understanding who he is.

17. Her new monograph on the Apostle Paul's use of visuality will likely be the definitive study on biblical visual piety for some time. Along with her focus on Paul, she reviews Jewish visual practices in the Old Testament as well as in the Greco-Roman and early Jewish context of the New Testament. See Heath, *Paul's Visual Piety*.

18. When copyediting my manuscript, my friend Rob O'Callaghan made this comment which I deemed insightful enough to include here: "It would seem words are a less direct experience—more mediated—than seeing with the eyes because of how languages work through the mental cognition process, where the phoneme 'cat' recalls the idea of a cat, which stands in for the actual presence of a cat. And that's before you even get to metaphors and poetic language."

WHEN WORD ANXIETY IS BIBLICAL . . . ?

Though I am sticking to the claim that verbal TheoMedia are prioritized over all others in the Old Testament, there are biblical grounds for serious concern regarding word-media.

We have already seen from the very first pages of the Bible that *God's words are distortable.* The following text from Genesis 3 compels us to hold word-media with some degree of apprehension:

> Now the serpent was more crafty than any other beast of the field that the LORD God had made. He said to the woman, "Did God actually say, 'You shall not eat of any tree in the garden'?" And the woman said to the serpent, "We may eat of the fruit of the trees in the garden, but God said, 'You shall not eat of the fruit of the tree that is in the midst of the garden, neither shall you touch it, lest you die.'" But the serpent said to the woman, "You will not surely die. For God knows that when you eat of it your eyes will be opened, and you will be like God, knowing good and evil." So when the woman saw that the tree was good for food, and that it was a delight to the eyes, and that the tree was to be desired to make one wise, she took of its fruit and ate, and she also gave some to her husband who was with her, and he ate. (Gen 3:1–6)

Words, even words from the mouth of God, can be easily co-opted and re-presented by evil. The serpent's twisting of words is so subtle. His perversion of holy speech is ever so slight. As with all other TheoMedia, careful hermeneutics are a necessity when it comes to the speech and texts of God.

We saw in chapter 1 that the first appearance of evil in the Bible is depicted in media terms. But Satan's initial activity does not occur by way of visual media, the sort of media some Christians today tend to associate with the devil. *The inaugural work of the forces of darkness is by way of word-media.* Sure, the fruit was "a delight to the eyes" and visually promised to be tasty on the lips. But the visual beauty of the fruit was God's doing and the nature of Satan's first move in scripture was not to pull off a visual stunt but a *verbal* stunt, corrupting words freshly reverberating in Eden from the mouth of God himself.

We should be wary of logocentric media not because sermons tend to bore us, not because we find lengthy texts laborious, not because we find cinemas more exciting than libraries, not because we find dogmatic

statements too stifling or dull. We should be wary about word-media because evil likes to fiddle with God's pristine voice. All throughout scripture we find the poisonous effects of false prophecy, of the declaration
"peace, peace, when there is no peace" (Jer 6:13) and the claim, "'Thus
says the Lord GOD,' when the LORD has not spoken" (Ezek 22:28). Every
false prophecy twisting God's words in scripture and in our own day is an
echo of that sinister voice in Eden: "Did God actually say, 'You shall not
. . . ?'" (Gen 3:1 ESV).

So some degree of concern over word-media is biblically warranted.
But let's be concerned for the right reasons.

By touting the prioritization of verbal TheoMedia, I am not claiming with a broad sweep that propositional statements are the best renderings of truth. I am not suggesting that the storied nature of the Bible is
to be demystified and reduced solely to tidy morals or systematized into
creeds. By emphasizing word-media, I am not arguing that expository-
style preaching is the only way to use a pulpit. But creeds, propositions,
and expositions need not be dichotomized vis-à-vis stories and narrative
theology. The Bible and its early Christian interpreters affirm a robust
combination of these approaches to understanding God and communicating him to others. It is unfortunate that we draw so many tribal lines
along borders that need not be . . . as if we enjoyed sequestering ourselves
into various reading groups.

A PROPOSITIONAL THEOLOGY OF OLD TESTAMENT WORD-MEDIA (AND DICHOTOMIES THAT DON'T WORK)

Satan's most ancient vocation is to incite social rifts over God's precious
words.

It happened in Eden. It is also happening today in the tensions between those of us steeped in postmodern word-anxieties and those of us
championing the word-centeredness of print culture. If we look carefully,
we will find that many of the tribal lines dividing Christians today are
drawn along certain dichotomies about words. The Old Testament's theology of verbal TheoMedia exposes many of these dichotomies as entirely
false.

For instance, in the citation above from Leonard Sweet there is a
polarization between two distinct uses of words: *propositional* versus

narratival. According to Sweet's caricature of Gutenbergers, words best express truth through dogmatic assertions or propositions. For Googlers, truth is best expressed through the words of storytelling.

The dichotomies between propositional and narratival do not apply to the Old Testament's theology of God's words.

Much of the Bible's theology of words is expressed by "narrative theology." In a "narrative theology," meaning is conveyed along the axis of a storyline. The plot of the exciting yet heart-rending story of God's relationship with his people in the Old Testament moves along Israel's attention or inattention to verbal TheoMedia (see the next chapter).

But the Bible's theology of words is also expressed through propositional theology. And that is exactly what I am doing here, "proposing" that the Old Testament's theology of words is expressed by both stories *and* propositions. Creating a dichotomy between the two is unhelpful, unfounded, and unnecessarily polarizing.

Here is another dichotomy with no warrant from the Old Testament that can be observed in Sweet's earlier quote polarizing Gutenbergers and Googlers: *authoritative* versus *relational*. Sweet portrays those stuck in print culture as using words authoritatively. Along with being propositional, Gutenbergers view words as the artillery of argumentation and as the vehicles of absolute truth. For the gentler Googlers, words are relational. They are the warm, loving means of building and maintaining friendships.

There is some truth in these stereotypes, but authority and relationality cannot be dichotomized when it comes to the words of God himself: they are intrinsic to one another. Certainly, holy speech wields authority: "Of the tree of the knowledge of good and evil you shall not eat" (Gen 2:17). But God's commanding voice also beckons us into fellowship: "Where are you?" (Gen 3:9). He uses words to express sovereign commands: "You shall have no other gods before me" (Exod 20:3); and after bowing to other deities God's words can decree punishment: "You shall become an object of horror" (Deut 28:37). Yet his words are also a means of drawing us back into fellowship: "I will now allure her and . . . speak tenderly to her" (Hos 2:14).

When it comes to God's words, spoken or inscribed, there is no dichotomy between authoritative and relational because for us to be in *relationship* with God, his *authority* must be respected; and even when that authority is rejected, God's words can become the means of relational reconciliation. The textual TheoMedia of the scriptures do not just indoctrinate or decree. They also express the imploring plea for intimacy renewed.

It follows that those of us responsible for teaching or preaching those holy texts from lecterns and pulpits should express the authority of God's words along with a personal warmth reflective of God's relationality. And if our words are relational but empty of authority, then whatever they may be, they are certainly not the words of God.

Another dichotomy that does not apply to the words of God in the Old Testament is *rational* versus *sensory*. We often understand words as media appealing solely to the intellect, not so much to the physical senses. Orality and textuality are therefore pitted against visuality and materiality, with the former understood as stuffy and erudite and the latter as lively and exciting.[19]

Print culture folks may indeed think of themselves as more rational than those who watch lots of TV and film. But, as hinted earlier, literacy is not a gauge of intellect. Nor is TV watching a sign of ignorance.[20] It is arrogantly presumptuous of us to think of words as exclusively rational media and to regard visual imagery as media that is dumbed down.

In the anti-intellectualism that flourishes in many corners of the church, it is easy to think of words as lifeless drips of ink on a page.[21] Sometimes they are, of course. And sometimes sermons and lectures really are dry, dull, and overly heady. But this dichotomizing of the rational versus the sensory does not work with the words of God.[22] In fact, word-media are often associated with nonverbal sights and sounds throughout the Old Testament:

> The word of the LORD came to me, saying, "Jeremiah, what do you *see*?" And I said, "I *see* a branch of an almond tree." Then the LORD said to me, "You have *seen* well, for I am *watching* over my word to perform it." The word of the LORD came to me a second time, saying, "What do you *see*?" And I said, "I *see* a

19. I am not insinuating that sensory media are less intellectual. On the contrary, I am simply trying to break down certain polarizing assumptions that could include the idea that images or tangible objects require less rationality to comprehend.

20. Though I do not agree with all his assessments, I was challenged by Steven Johnson's view that pop culture is making us smarter in *Everything Bad Is Good for You*.

21. See my chapter "Anti-Intellectualism," in *Faith Without Illusions*, 86–101.

22. In scholarly debates on ancient media studies, literacy/textuality is often dichotomized against orality. See Carr's critique of this dichotomy in *Writing on the Tablet of the Heart*, 6–7.

boiling pot, tilted away from the north." (Jer 1:11–13; emphases added; cf. also Jer 23:18)

In this passage, hearing God's words includes seeing visionary sights.

Think also of Ezekiel's prophetic call in which he "looked" and saw a scroll that he then heard God tell him to eat: the eyes, ears, and tongue are all necessary for this verbal experience! Think of that eerie scene mentioned earlier from Daniel 5 when a ghostly hand inscribed enigmatic words on the wall in King Belshazzar's sight. And the entire concept of a "text" requires visuality plus materiality—the sight of the letters' shape and the feel and weight of a paper scroll or a stone tablet accompany all ancient writing. The words of God entail a wide range of sense perception.

Most of the dichotomies over words along which we argue and stage ecclesial battles simply do not apply when it comes to the words of God.

A THEOLOGY OF VERBAL LIMITATIONS: THE NEW COVENANT AND THEOMEDIA IMPAIRMENT

We have seen that God is a multimedia God and that his words are also multimedia in nature. Like fire in the prophet's bones, they are hard to contain, bursting the limits of our dichotomies and bursting the limits of every media format that would communicate them. Verbal TheoMedia cannot be safely locked within ink or confined within chiseled inscriptions. They are living words, words that can be seen as well as heard, tasted as well as touched. These holy words are not lifeless or dull. They are "living and active," able to resurrect brittle bone piles and piece them into living armies (Heb 4:12; Ezek 37:1–14). They are our nourishment and lifeblood—we cannot live only by bread. We need "every word that comes from the mouth of the LORD" (Deut 8:3; 32:47).

But the Old Testament's theology of words acknowledges verbal limitations.

To be clear, God himself is not limited, and his words are effective and performative: "Then God said, 'Let there be light'; *and there was light*" (Gen 1:3, emphasis added). The word of God does something when uttered. His word "shall not return to me empty, but it shall accomplish that which I purpose, and succeed in the thing for which I sent it" (Isa 55:11).[23] The words of God are also durable: "The grass withers,

23. That words have power seems to be an intrinsic understanding in oral cultures;

the flower fades; but the word of our God will stand forever" (Isa 40:8; cf. Matt 5:18).[24] God's speech is intrinsic to his own identity, so the verbal limitations are not with the Speaker but with the accessibility and reception of the medium.

God's decision to enact a New Covenant is premised on the idea that some verbal TheoMedia are limited in their capacity to be received.

> The days are surely coming, says the LORD, when I will make a new covenant with the house of Israel and the house of Judah. It will not be like the covenant that I made with their ancestors when I took them by the hand to bring them out of the land of Egypt—a covenant that they broke, though I was their husband, says the LORD. But this is the covenant that I will make with the house of Israel after those days, says the LORD: *I will put my law within them, and I will write it on their hearts*; and I will be their God, and they shall be my people. No longer shall they teach one another, or say to each other, "Know the LORD," for they shall all know me, from the least of them to the greatest, says the LORD; for I will forgive their iniquity, and remember their sin no more. (Jer 31:31–34, emphases added)

At the time of Jeremiah's writing, the Sinai covenant ratified in stone-etched words had endured centuries of neglect. God acknowledges the poor reception of that covenant and, in an astonishing display of grace, reveals that he will yet forge a new covenant.

The means of covenant-making will, like the former covenant, include words. But they will be *heart*-etched. The textual TheoMedia of Torah that bound Israel to God as his people were spatially confined within and beside the Ark (Deut 31:24–26), with some scroll copies possibly spread about the land under the care of Levites or priests. The new covenant in Jeremiah 31 is marked by both a universality and an internalization of his words. These holy words will be more widely available because they will be engraved upon the individual hearts of every member of his re-formed people (cf. Deut 30:11–14).

---

see Ong, *Orality and Literacy*, 32. On words being performative "speech-acts," see the now-classic study of Austin, *How to Do Things with Words*.

24. And this: "Go now, write it before them on a tablet, and inscribe it in a book, so that it may be for the time to come as a witness forever" (Isa 30:8). From this verse we see that textuality serves the theological function of enacting this idea of durability—once written, the words are visually and materially there to stay. See also Proverbs 3:3; 7:3; Job 19:23; and Jeremiah 17:1.

Individual access to the corpus of holy texts was a luxury most Israelites would have lacked.[25] For instance, Moses commanded the Levitical priests and elders to make sure the Book of the Law (most likely Deuteronomy) was read publicly "before all Israel in their hearing." This was to happen *every seven years* (Deut 31:11; and 9–13). As we will find in the next chapter, the words of Deuteronomy were to infiltrate Israelite society via all sorts of domestic and private means (see Deut 6:4–9), but imagine only getting the full reading dosage of the whole book once every seven years. Well, okay, some of us may feel that that is quite as much Deuteronomy as one could stand, but remember that this was the charter document defining the identity of God's covenant people. Such public readings may have been retained better in the minds of those inhabiting an oral culture than they would in our minds today. Still, a seven-year gap in the corporate celebration of such a significant text as Deuteronomy bespeaks some degree of textual inaccessibility. In the new covenant, God will address this textual inaccessibility by inscribing his words on the hearts of his children.

Also, *less mediation* will be involved in that forthcoming covenant— "No longer shall they teach one another, or say to each other, 'Know the LORD,' for they shall all know me" (Jer 31:34). The new "text" of God will not be stored as a Temple archive, as if confined to the shelves of some elite theological library. There will be no more waiting every seven years to get the full text of Deuteronomy. New covenant textuality is not the domain of scribal experts or the purview of the powerful and the pedantic. We are to have unlimited access to God's words.

So God himself acknowledges certain types of textual limitations.

We know that St. Paul certainly did (though he was no "Googler," mind you!). The Apostle referred to the old covenant in negative textual terms, as a covenant "of the letter" that "kills" in contrast to the new covenant "of the Spirit" that "gives life" (2 Cor 3:6ff ESV; cf. Ezek 11:19; 36:26). This letter-based covenant had cast a "veil" (2 Cor 3:12–18) that darkened Israel's perception of TheoMedia.

To be clear, Paul is not calling for the end of reading or literary spirituality. He is not championing postmodern values as we know them or proposing a charismatic emphasis on the Spirit to the neglect of God's holy texts. But Paul does acknowledge the limitations of Old Testament

25. Scrolls were expensive, not very portable, and easily damaged. For more on the nature of a scroll as a media form, see Jacobs, "Christianity and the Future of the Book."

textuality, understanding the gospel in terms of Jeremiah's vision for a new covenant that would universalize and internalize God's words.

I suppose one could argue that the limitations of old covenant textuality came down to a technology problem—if the Israelites had the advantages of e-readers and smartphones with cutting-edge Bible apps, then access to holy texts would be granted to all (or at least to everyone with an e-reader or smartphone). Right?

Not exactly.

Though the new covenant vision of Jeremiah (and Ezekiel) promises a wider accessibility to God's words, the main problem is not technological but spiritual. The problem was not just media access, but media neglect and media impairment. The people to whom God revealed and communicated himself were often uninterested and also spiritually blind and deaf. They were TheoMedia impaired.

The most classic rendering of this can be found in the call of Isaiah:

> "Keep listening, but do not comprehend; keep looking, but do not understand." Make the mind of this people dull, and stop their ears, and shut their eyes, so that they may not look with their eyes, and listen with their ears, and comprehend with their minds, and turn and be healed. (Isa 6:9b–10).[26]

God himself seems to punish a neglect of his media by disabling his people's capacity for perceiving his media (see especially Isa 44:18). Then again, other places in Isaiah indicate that God wished to reverse TheoMedia impairment, repeatedly calling for a healing of blind eyes and deaf ears (Isa 32:3; 42:7, 16–20; 43:8).

Neglecting God's speech leads to a tragic impairment of our ability to receive his communication. The veil blinding and dampening Israel's perception of God was so very thick. Throughout the prophetic writings we find Israel in severe need of some media breakthrough, some divine intrusion into their desperate state of refusing to listen to words from above. Yet from beneath that thick veil some were shouting skyward this muffled cry: "O that you would tear open the heavens and come down"! (Isa 64:1).

And he would. Eventually.

---

26. This theme is common in Jeremiah as well; cf. 5:21; 6:10–11; 7:13, 25–29; 17:23 (impaired because they "stiffened their neck," ESV); 18:18; 19:15.

TheoMedia Note 5

Online Theology

When God Is Blogged

> Since the Christian life is consciously or unconsciously also a witness, the question of truth concerns not only the community but the individual Christian. He too is responsible for the quest for truth in this witness. Therefore, every Christian as such is also called to be a theologian.
>
> —KARL BARTH[1]

As noted in the opening chapter (with elaboration coming in the next chapter) the *Shema* in Deuteronomy 6:4–9 commands us to discuss the words of God in every setting and at all times: "Talk about them when you are at home and when you are away, when you lie down and when you rise" (Deut 6:7).[2] This is a call to *theological discourse*, an activity integral to the community of faith that should extend into every sphere of our lives . . . even the cybersphere. We should be doing theology online as well as offline.[3]

1. Barth, *Evangelical Theology*, 40.

2. I agree with Walter Moberly that the specific "words" to which Deuteronomy 6:6–9 refer are the words of 6:4–5. But since those words about loving the one God sum up the Law (as Jesus himself indicated), I think it is right to claim that theological discourse in general is something the *Shema* strongly implies. See "A Love Supreme" in Moberly's *Old Testament Theology* (forthcoming).

3. The most helpful material (in book format!) that I have found on doing theology online includes Bennet's *Aquinas on the Web?*, Bailey's "Welcome to the Blogosphere," and the section "Discernment: On Line versus In the Flesh" in Brock's *Christian Ethics*

But online theology is often set at odds with offline theology. Theologians heavily invested in print culture sometimes disparage the Internet as a suitable setting for serious thinking about God. Conversely, online enthusiasts praise the Internet as a media context intrinsically endowed with values and mechanisms superior to print culture's hegemonic and pedantic tendencies. According to Milton Bradley Penner and Hunter Barnes, the

> traditional academic form [of doing theology] does not breed conversation, but promotes monologue; it does not foster cross-fertilization of ideas, but reinforces one particular perspective on an issue; it is not open to other voices, but is designed precisely to close them off; and, finally any such discourse is not welcoming to all voices, but privileges a select group who have been properly vetted by the Western academy.[4]

These critiques have some validity. Theological discourse over God's words should not be solely the domain of academic professionals. It cannot be locked away in libraries or safely contained in lecture rooms. Like its subject matter, theology has a way of rupturing the walls and spilling out over the fences. If talking about God and his revelatory words is something that, according to the *Shema*, belongs in the living room, in the fields, and alongside the byways, then surely both ivory towers and Internet chat rooms also qualify as fitting contexts for the task.

Setting online theology at odds with offline theology is another one of our unhelpful and unnecessary dichotomizations. The church is best served when theology healthily spans a vast range of media formats that work in concert and complement one another (though I agree with Brian Brock that the formats available online will mean that the Internet cannot become "the primary locus of the church's theological thinking"[5]).

In this TheoMedia Note, I am just going to list some of the advantages of doing theology online, along with some of the limitations and dangers.

First, the advantages. The Internet allows nonprofessionals to do theology. For some, it may not seem very positive that the online practices of blogging and microblogging can amplify voices unsanctioned by standard academic protocol. But in the Bible, some of the greatest theological

---

in a Technological Age, 273–88.

4. Penner and Barnes, *A New Kind of Conversation,* 1.

5. Brock, *Christian Ethics in a Technological Age,* 286.

riches come from the untrained and the unordained. The disciples were conspicuously identified by the Sanhedrin's professional theologians and exegetes as "uneducated and ordinary men" (Acts 4:13). No one in their right mind would have accepted book proposals by the amateur disciples, even though a number of them were responsible for much of the New Testament. Some of the most prophetic voices have come out of the wilderness. Accordingly, those unsanctioned and unqualified often have a great deal to contribute, and the Internet grants them a public hearing.

A second advantage is that online theology offers a multimedia dimension that the book, the standard media format of offline theology, cannot provide. For instance, on my own theoblog I wrote not long ago about John the Baptist's ministry of pointing to Jesus and fading away (a topic I expand on in TheoMedia Note 7). To reinforce the written material in the blog post, I inserted an image of Matthias Grünewald's Isenheim altarpiece. Grasping the viewer's attention in this painting is the lanky, protruding finger of the Baptist that in turn redirects all eyes toward the crucified Christ (Barth had this image hanging in his study). Books can certainly include pictures, but they are costly for publishers. And in addition to images, theoblogians can add videos, music, and podcasts to their text. The multimedia capabilities honor the multimedia nature of God's communicative and self-revelatory work.

Online theology is also interactive. Social media allows us to share the theological articles and blog posts we find on the Internet. Comment streams permit contributions and corrections from other readers. Interactivity is often celebrated in the Bible (e.g., 1 Cor 14:29), with much of the New Testament comprising excerpts from the ongoing back and forth interactions of an epistle (an ancient form of social media). In his letters, Paul is sometimes in the midst of an ongoing, back and forth conversation with other Christians (given the communications technology of the day, however, the pace of interaction was quite slow).

Immediacy and accessibility are other virtues of online theology. The Internet allows an instant theological response to whatever happens to be newsworthy in our surrounding society. As helpful as a theological monograph might be on some contemporary situation, the church needs to be able to make more immediate theological responses while we wait for the printing presses to get cranked up. And the Internet can make such immediate responses accessible to a vast audience.

Many of these virtues and advantages, though, have a dark side. Again, media are messy. Accessibility, for instance, can be a bad thing, like when it comes to accessing theology that is superficial and distorted. The uninitiated online browser can be exposed to all sorts of twisted renderings of Christian faith. A thirty-second YouTube video chock full of skewed theology or a viral blog post appealing to pop-Christian sentiment can get to the masses almost instantaneously.

Immediacy can also be a vice for online theology. Many theobloggers rush into the discursive fray without reflection. Theological discourse on the Internet runs the risk of becoming no more than a "cottage industry of online indignation," as Timothy Dalrymple has put it.[6] Controversy generates traffic, so as soon as a hot-button issue hits the proverbial fan, online writers start typing and clicking "publish" with hopes of racking up the stats. Theology on the Internet is therefore often *impulsive*. And the interactivity can get downright virulent, spawning ugly verbal battles for all to witness on the web. Before we bash the highbrow mudslinging of print culture theology, let's just take a quick glance at the invective spilling out of those online comment streams.

Don't get me wrong: there is a lot of bad theology offline, and many professional theologians write with reactionary chips on their shoulders. But print culture does provide a number of mechanisms that can block emotionally charged theological outbursts. Editors do quality checks, and the time frame required for printed publishing allows more time for contemplation than that which is encouraged by WordPress or Blogger. Blow-ups among the professionals usually take place at academic conferences or in occasional journal articles that draw only a narrowly defined audience of specialists.

Another inevitable limitation theoblogians have to acknowledge is that the online format encourages oversimplification. Microblogging leaves little room for nuance, and blog posts over 700 words become tedious for most online readers to digest. Theology needs space. The subject matter ruptures not only the confines of lecture halls and libraries. It also exceeds the tightly bound digital architecture of social media.[7]

The advantage of the Internet for allowing voices unsanctioned by the academy can also be dangerous. Some voices are unsanctioned for good reason. Bad theology is a plague the Internet allows to go viral. Though the church needs unordained wilderness voices, we do not need

---

6. Dalrymple, "The Indignation Industry, or the Art of Blogging Controversies." This blog post is one of those must-reads for those of us with theoblogs.

7. On the limitations of the blog structure (along with all sorts of other helpful insights) see Jacobs, "Goodbye, Blog."

the cynical blasts of theobloggers exuding an elitism based on their self-appointed position outside church walls and/or academic halls. Though I am grateful for the Internet's capacity to amplify unlikely voices and to encourage interactivity, open-source theology is terribly risky. I adhere to Barth's sentiment in the epigraph that every Christian is called to be a theologian. But theology is not a flippant practice. It is sacred, precious work. The glory and radiance of the subject matter require disciplined speech and rigorous, worshipful thinking. Doing theology online does not permit us to be haphazard with the holy. So open-source away (it is a rather ancient biblical concept) . . . but with fear and trembling.

I will close this note with a few suggestions for those of us invested in doing theology online. The fear and trembling just mentioned is a good place to start. Also, online theologians should become experts in *redirection* (again, see TheoMedia Note 7). Because of the limitations of the blog and microblog format, let's utilize the hyperlink function to direct readers to thicker sources and richer material (the Tumblr format is really helpful for this sort of practice). Most importantly, our online content should function like that long, bony finger of Grünewald's John the Baptist, redirecting others to Christ.

One more thing. Any of us involved in theological discourse, online or offline, would do well to heed the wisdom literature's instructions on speech:

> Rash words are like sword thrusts, but the tongue of the wise brings healing (Prov 12:18).

> Those who guard their mouths preserve their lives; those who open wide their lips come to ruin (Prov 13:3).

> A soft answer turns away wrath, but a harsh word stirs up anger (Prov 15:1).

> A fool takes no pleasure in understanding, but only in expressing personal opinion (Prov 18:2).

The Epistle of James is an example of wisdom literature in the New Testament, and it warns us of the viral capacities of our speech: "The tongue is a fire" (3:6). And from the greatest sage of all: "I tell you, on the day of judgment you will have to give an account for every careless word you utter" (Matt 12:36).

So let's talk about the words of God—in the kitchen, in the café, along the path, and online. But with reverence and care.

Chapter 8

The Story of the Great King and the Lost Book

A Narrative Theology of God's Words

"There used to be something called God. . . ."

The Controller . . . had crossed to the other side of the room and was unlocking a large safe set into the wall between the bookshelves. The heavy door swung open. Rummaging in the darkness within, "It's a subject," he said, "that has always had a great interest for me." He pulled out a thick black volume. "You've never read this, for example."

The Savage took it. "*The Holy Bible, containing the Old and New Testaments*," he read aloud from the title page.

"Nor this." It was a small book and had lost its cover.

"*The Imitation of Christ*."

"Nor this." He handed out another volume.

"*The Varieties of Religious Experience*. By William James."

"And I've got plenty more . . . a whole collection of pornographic old books. God in the safe and Ford on the shelves." He pointed with a laugh to his avowed library—to the shelves of books, the rack full of reading-machine bobbins and sound-track rolls.

—FROM ALDOUS HUXLEY'S *BRAVE NEW WORLD*[1]

There once was an old kingdom that had forgotten its past. Century by century, founding laws vanished from memory. Ancient lore was rarely heard around the fires. Heroic tales of long ago had themselves begun to fade into the long ago. Families and villages took on new customs from outlying lands.

Kings had come and gone, but the rule of one still haunted every valley and hill. His name meant "forgetfulness," but the ugliness of his reign could not be forgotten. He had taken his counsels from the warlocks and witches. There were rumors he may have even consulted the dead. So entranced by the dark arts had he been that one day he slaked the thirst of a roaring god by burning a son on a forbidden altar. Surely the elders remembered that such things were once condemned.

The most visible vestige of the kingdom's bygone days was a temple. Standing as a visual memorial to prior devotions, it must have been wondrous in its time. But the king of forgetfulness placed new altars to sky-gods and star-gods in its sacred space. The clutter of these new deities littered the floors. Ritual prostitutes crowded the rooms. The gold had been scraped off the doors.

Then one day a little boy was crowned king of the land. At eight years of age he could barely swing the sword; but his arms grew stout, along with his heart. The old Temple must have caused him grief, because one day he began repairs. The new idols had been earlier removed, but stones were cracked, mortar joints were crumbling, and timbers were loose. At some point, amidst the comings and goings of masons and carpenters, a priest found something in the dust and debris that caught his eye, a timeworn relic from a different age. And so it was told to the king: "The priest has found a book."

It was Deuteronomy.

1. Huxley, *Brave New World*, 230–31.

THE BIBLICAL STORYLINE OF VERBAL THEOMEDIA

This Story of the Great King and the Lost Book, when the lost scroll of Deuteronomy was uncovered in the reign of King Josiah, is told in 2 Kings 22–23 and in 2 Chronicles 34–35. It is a story that illustrates what happens *when a culture realizes it has forgotten, then replaced, the media that were to shape and define its identity.*

The specific media Judah's populace had forgotten and replaced by the time Josiah took the throne were those of holy words once spoken by God and then inscribed in a sacred text.

In the previous chapter we considered potential anxieties over claiming that the Old Testament prioritizes God's words and texts over the panoply of all other TheoMedia. I then offered a brief "propositional theology" (the condensing of theological realities into concise statements or propositions) of God's words from the Old Testament, asserting that many of our word-media dichotomies do not apply to verbal TheoMedia. We closed looking at the idea of textual limitation—in spite of the high priority placed on verbal media, sacred documents were not that accessible, and Israel was plagued with a stiffened resistance to receiving God's words, whether penned, etched, or prophesied on the city streets.

In this chapter, we look to the Old Testament's narrative theology of textual and oral TheoMedia. Deuteronomy will serve as our grounding biblical document (with the prophetic voice of Jeremiah, who lived in Josiah's day, resounding in the backdrop). The grounding biblical text will be Deuteronomy 6:4–9. Our grounding biblical storyline, along which we can discern a narrative theology of word-media, is the gradual neglect of God's words detailed in the prophets and histories that led to a tragic era of destruction and exile (scholars might call this storyline the "Deuteronomistic History"[2]).

2. Since W. M. L. de Wette and later J. Wellhausen, Old Testament scholars have suspected that Deuteronomy was actually written under Josiah's reign, and other sections of the Hebrew Bible that are presented as earlier than Josiah bear the influence of "the Deuteronomist." For my purposes, I am content to side with McConville and observe a strand of Deuteronomic theology interwoven throughout the Old Testament. See his *Grace in the End.* With my emphasis on the tabernacle in the previous section, one could perhaps say that I am focusing on Deuteronomic material here and Priestly material in Part 2: "The Sights and Sounds of Israel's God." I am not entirely averse to what has come to be known as the JEDP theory, but my readings of scripture in this book are concerned with the Old Testament's canonical shape and storied theological themes.

We will begin in those dark latter days leading to Jerusalem's fall and then return to the earlier days of Israel's inception at Sinai and its journey through and out of the wilderness. The claim that God prioritizes verbal TheoMedia over all other divine media forms will be confirmed. What we will also find is that the Old Testament associates the rise and fall of God's people with their media preferences.

THE MEDIASCAPE OF DOWNFALL: ISRAEL AT A LOSS FOR (DIVINE) WORDS

The late Davidic kings in Judah could feel Babylonian breath on the backs of their necks. We enter our featured storyline in those waning years of the monarchial period, the time when God's people were governed by the kings who ruled from either Samaria (in Israel—the northern kingdom) or Jerusalem (in Judah—the southern kingdom).

The elevation of holy speech and texts over holy sights and sounds is most poignantly evident in the tragic tale that is nearing its denouement when Josiah is crowned king. When he took David's old throne in Jerusalem, Samaria had already fallen to Assyria, a disillusioning event tied to an embrace of idolatry and a disregard of the textual TheoMedia of the Law and of the oral TheoMedia of prophetic cries harkening them back to the Law. The northeastern power base eventually shifted from Assyria to the rising Babylonian empire. These Chaldeans would eventually force starvation and pestilence within Jerusalem's walls. And Nebuchadnezzar their king would put an end to the formal reign of David's line.

Down south in Judah, before the Babylonians parked themselves outside Jerusalem's gates, much of the optical/aural/material TheoMedia discussed in Part II was still available to the eyes, ears, and hands of God's people. There stood Solomon's Temple, a stationary reiteration of the old Tabernacle. That strange serpent of bronze had only recently been destroyed. Sacrifices were still taking place. The natural beauty of the clouds and stars, terebinths and seas, were no less visible in creation as sources of inspiration.[3] The prophets and seers had still been experiencing visions.

But God's people had begun misusing the nonverbal TheoMedia. The Temple had been housing pagan religious imagery, the bronze serpent had been worshiped as an idol, and certain elements of creation had

---

3. When I typed the word "terebinth" my word processing software recommended "terabits" instead. This former forestry major felt slightly offended.

been so divinized that sacrifices were being offered to gods of nature out on the hilltops.

Israel was saturated with visual and multisensory TheoMedia, but those media were misappropriated without the detailed guidance offered by the textual and verbal media of God's *words*, which they had been neglecting.

For the most part, a full-scale neglect or misuse of all TheoMedia forms was underway in the latter days of Judah's monarchy. To awaken his people to this reality, God sent prophetic words to call his people back to the inscribed words that warned them against such neglect or misuse in the first place. Without the governance of sacred texts and the direct address of oracular speech, the nonverbal sights and sounds of God were dangerously open to wildly deranged interpretations and uses. It is not that God's people entirely rejected word-media. It was that they rejected *God's* word-media. Unschooled in words of the Law, the ears of the people were easily deceived by the twisted words of false prophecy (cf. Jer 27:9).

There is no such thing as a media vacuum. Media are so intrinsic to society that when some fade away, others emerge.[4] Over time, Israel embraced and constructed an alien mediascape. Back at Sinai, "the LORD said to Moses: 'Write these words . . .'" (Exod 34:27). But those words were eventually lost by his people: the Hebrew title of Deuteronomy was eventually known as "These Words." The Old Testament's story of God's people after the reign of King Solomon is an epic saga of national schism and eventual collapse and dispersion that can be traced along Israel's media preferences, by how they allowed some media to fade into disuse ("These Words") and others to become dominant influences in their material culture.

More was at work in the gradual downfall than simply where the tradesmen, kings, farmers, and soldiers turned their eyes—there was injustice and economic exploitation. There was vain hoping in the political powers of other nations.[5] These factors are not ignored in the biblical accounts of why Israel and Judah fell. The chief sin of idolatry is much

4. In his perceptive essay "The Culture of the Word and the Culture of the Table," Borgmann writes that "culture . . . abhors a vacuum" (the context is the replacement of reading in the home by television viewing). See Borgmann, *Power Failure*, 120.

5. See Jeremiah, whose prophetic ministry began in the days of Josiah: "On your skirts is found the lifeblood of the innocent poor" (2:34) and "What then do you gain by going to Egypt, to drink the waters of the Nile? Or what do you gain by going to Assyria, to drink the waters of the Euphrates?" (2:18; cf. v. 36).

deeper than mere media usage, of course, yet we have to remember that idolatry itself is certainly a media format. And media language is employed throughout the histories and the prophetic writings to delineate the gradual decline of the nation into idolatrous practices. When the Bible offers summaries of what happened that led to the destruction of Samaria and Jerusalem (the most detailed of which is 2 Kings 17:7–23), those passages blatantly associate national demise with media choices. As the visual/aural/tangible TheoMedia of Creation ("every green hill" and "every green tree") were besmirched with the visual media of idolatry, God sent words "by every prophet and every seer" (2 Kgs 17:13), words intended to awaken his people and bring them back.

"But they would not listen" (2 Kgs 17:14).

The reason one of Israel's society-shaping texts could disappear into the dust of their Temple is because the command, "You shall read this law before all Israel" (Deut 31:11) was rarely obeyed. Josiah ripped his garments when the scroll was found because he realized that over the years verbal TheoMedia had been almost entirely neglected and displaced. God's people had spurned the words of his covenant and embraced the idolatrous mediascape of downfall.

DEUTERONOMY AND MOSES'S MEDIA LECTURES

Centuries before Josiah, Israel was positioned on the River Jordan's eastern shores, eyeing the land of legend: the land where old Abraham sojourned; the land where Jacob wrestled the angel of God in the dark; the land from which Joseph and his brothers first came to Egypt; the land that God was now granting them as a permanent home after forty years of refugee status in the wild. Rivulets of milk and honey were flowing beneath immense clusters of heavy grapes. There was some apprehension, though. Rumors had it that giants roamed that fair land. Reports indicated that all sorts of other strange folk were living in fortressed cities impenetrable to would-be invaders.

This was the setting in which Moses began speaking the words that we now know as the text of Deuteronomy. It was his farewell address, the collection of his final few lectures/sermons to the newly formed people of God.

In his opening remarks, Moses placed emphasis on visuality. Israel was not to forget this "great and terrifying wilderness *that you saw*"

(1:19).[6] They were to trust that God would rescue them "just as he did for you in Egypt *before your very eyes*" (1:30). This emphasis on the faculty of sight continued—

> *See*, the LORD your God has given the land to you; go up, take possession, as the LORD, the God of your ancestors, has promised you; do not fear or be dismayed (1:21).

> . . . *You saw* how the LORD your God carried you, just as one carries a child . . . (1:31).

> . . . *Your own eyes have seen* everything that the LORD your God has done . . . (3:21).

> *You have seen* for yourselves what the LORD did . . . (4:3).

> But take care and watch yourselves closely, so as neither to forget the things *that your eyes have seen* nor to let them slip from your mind all the days of your life . . . (4:9).[7]

Moses was making it clear that the highly visual TheoMedia events of Israel's recent past were to haunt and shape every generation to come.

But the call to heed visual TheoMedia then transitioned into a call to heed verbal TheoMedia. The boisterous scene at Sinai and the awful plagues on Egypt were surely you-had-to-be-there type events. How could God expect his people to be shaped by unrepeatable incidents in the distant past no one would remember having seen and heard once the eyewitnesses had died off?

No matter how loud the splitting of that sea or the thundering on the mountain, no matter how astonishing the sight of those water-walls closing onto Pharaoh's army or how disturbing the sight of smoke billowing black on Sinai's crest, these were memories the Israelite eyewitnesses would take with them to their graves in that new land, with the threat that those events would be eternally forgotten. They had observed those formative spectacles as trembling children peeking from behind their parents' dusty cloaks.

The nature of a media *event* is that it happens, and then it is over. Religious festivals (Deut 16) and commemorative songs (Deut 32) were ritual religious media forms that would help serve as reminders. But as Moses's sermon by the river proceeded, the Israelites, now with their

---

6. All italicized emphases in the scripture citations here and immediately following are mine.

7. See also Exodus 34:10 and Deuteronomy 6:22; 7:19; 10:21; 29:2–3.

own little kids clutching their cloaks, were called not only to remember what they "saw" God do. They were also called to "hear" and "listen" to the voice of God speaking afresh words that could be recorded, written down, memorized, and passed on:

> And now, O Israel, *listen* to the statutes and the rules that I am teaching you. (4:1 ESV)

> Assemble the people for me, and I will let them *hear my words*, so that they may learn to fear me as long as they live on the earth, and may teach their children so. (4:10)

> Then the LORD *spoke* to you out of the fire. *You heard the sound of words* but saw no form; there was only a *voice*. (4:12)

> Has any people ever *heard the voice* of a god *speaking* out of a fire, as you have *heard*, and lived? (4:33)

> From heaven he made you *hear his voice* to discipline you. On earth he showed you his great fire, while you *heard his words* coming out of the fire. (4:36)

> Moses convened all Israel, and said to them: "*Hear, O Israel*, the statutes and ordinances that I am addressing to you today; you shall learn them and observe them diligently." (5:1)

So on the cusp of a settled life in Canaan, Moses's audience was not only to recall what their eyes had seen, but also to listen and hear the words of God. Most ancient societies had idolatrous imagery erected that sustained a sense of continuity and shared social identity down through the generations. For Israel, it was events of rescue and covenant-making that shaped who they were, and these had to be collected and passed down through the word-media of storytelling and writing.

THE CONQUEST OF CANAAN AS MEDIA DISPLACEMENT

The emphasis on word-media did not mean that Israel was to eschew a material culture. It meant that the current material culture of Canaan, the land of promise so precious to God himself (Deut 11:12), was to undergo a wholesale reconfiguration. The idolatrous media landscaping those hills and plains were to be utterly demolished.

We found earlier in chapter 4 that Israel was commanded to "break," "dash," "chop down," and "burn" the artifacts of idol media (Deut 7:5; 12:2–3). And the inaugural event marking the Canaan invasion was to be the establishment of a new type of material culture, a logocentric mediascape that would distinguish the culture of the new settlers from that of the land's former inhabitants:

> On the day that you cross over the Jordan into the land that the LORD your God is giving you, you shall set up large stones and cover them with plaster. You shall write on them all the words of this law when you have crossed over, to enter the land that the LORD your God is giving you, a land flowing with milk and honey, as the LORD, the God of your ancestors, promised you. So when you have crossed over the Jordan, you shall set up these stones, about which I am commanding you today, on Mount Ebal, and you shall cover them with plaster. And you shall build an altar there to the LORD your God, an altar of stones on which you have not used an iron tool. You must build the altar of the LORD your God of unhewn stones. Then offer up burnt offerings on it to the LORD your God, make sacrifices of well-being, and eat them there, rejoicing before the LORD your God. You shall write on the stones all the words of this law very clearly. (Deut 27:2–8)

Stones covered in scripture were to memorialize Israel's entry into a new life in this new place. The "conquest of Canaan" is as much a *media* conquest as a military one. The altars, idols, poles, and pillars were to be blotted out from the land's memory. The media of Canaan were to be replaced by the media of God.

MEDIA DUST: THE STORY OF THE STONE WORDS AND THE METAL BEAST

As he is preparing God's people for their entrance into Canaan, Moses brings up old wounds by recalling what may well be the darkest scene in the Old Testament's storyline of word-media: that awful moment on Sinai when they opted for Canaan-style and Egypt-like religious media over the sort of media God himself was endorsing in front of their impatient eyes. So before Moses allows Israel to enter Canaan's mediascape of idolatry, he drags a nasty skeleton out of the closet and reminds them of

Aaron's golden calf. We have given this story some previous attention, but we need to revisit the scene from a different angle.

In the way the story is told in both Exodus 32 and Deuteronomy 9 there is an intentional contrasting of media forms. We previously noted that the raw materials and technical skills so richly described and so enthusiastically conscripted by God for the work of the Tabernacle are the same by which Aaron fashions the calf idol. This contrast is repeated later on in 1 Kings. Solomon's Temple construction (which was modeled after the Tabernacle and incorporated many of its furniture pieces) is juxtaposed with Jeroboam's offensive fashioning of his own version of golden calves. The "sins of Jereboam" repeat as if on a broken record throughout the saga of the monarchy, largely referring to those calves, products of material culture whose infamy knew no end until Assyria destroyed Israel generations later (cf. 1 Kgs 5–8; 12:25–33).

The other media contrast underway in Exodus 32 and Deuteronomy 9 is between the visual media of idolatry and the textual media of God's words. The Ten Commandments were reified in the form of a technological product from the hands of God himself. Just as he fashioned human beings, God crafted the first text of scripture. The actual tablets seemed to have come directly from God's hand, the inscribed words the work of his "finger" (Deut 9:10; cf. Exod 31:18; Deut 4:13; 5:22). Both God and Aaron were at work on the mountain: the former crafting a text, the latter crafting an idol.

So there were two media products: God's stone texts, Aaron's metal calf. When these two products were brought onto the stage at the same time in the biblical account, both were violently destroyed. It is a scene that ends with the dust of stone and the dust of metal. The calf is pulverized into shiny powder, and Moses will have to retrieve a duplicate copy of the Decalogue. Before he returns to the summit for the new tablets, however, there is bloodshed. As the dust of stone and metal settle, disloyal Israelites are put to death ("to dust you shall return"—Gen 3:19).

The hurling of those brittle tablets onto the hard surface of Sinai was more than just the impulsive protest of an incensed prophet. Powerful theological realities are being vividly displayed in this scene. For one, the media of God cannot coincide with the media of idolatry. And here is another: that to which we choose to affix our vision has tremendous power for "orientating the whole person."[8] Choosing God's words crafts

8. Heath, *Paul's Visual Piety* (forthcoming).

us into a certain type of person. Choosing idolatry turns us into a vastly different sort of person.

Media preferences alter who we are.

Moses finds this painful story of the stone words and the metal calf to be gravely instructive for the Israelites who are about to make their fateful river crossing. They are a people shaped by certain media that cannot abide certain other types of media. The program of Canaan's media displacement must therefore begin immediately. Hence the charge to physically mark their entry into Canaan with those plastered rocks. Think of the contrast in media form and content that will instantly take place once God's people set foot onto their new land. Rather than images carefully crafted through metallurgy and woodworking, Israel will pile up twelve rocks and cover them with script.

Stone words.

THE CALL OF THE SHEMA TO MEDIA SATURATION

We now come to one of the most grounding biblical passages for this entire book. It is also one of the most prominently weighted passages of the entire Bible. Not many biblical passages have a name. This one does: the *Shema*, a title that comes from the Hebrew verb "to hear."[9] Here is how it begins: "Hear, O Israel: The LORD is our God, the LORD alone. You shall love the LORD your God with all your heart, and with all your soul, and with all your might" (Deut 6:4–5).

These first two verses of the passage will ring a familiar bell, even if we are not prone to thumbing through Deuteronomy in our quiet times. We probably recall seeing them in the red-letter font of Mark or Matthew. When asked which commandment was to be singled out as the highest of all—the one divine exhortation to be exalted above all others—Jesus cited Deuteronomy 6:4–5 (Mark 12:29–30; Matt 22:37; cf. Luke 10:27–28).

In contrast to God's people in Judah's final days as a kingdom, Jesus quoted Deuteronomy quite a bit—more than from any other Old Testament book, in fact.[10]

While working on this chapter, I read to my kids from Jesus's temptation scene in Luke's Gospel and tried to inspire them with this: "When Jesus was attacked by evil, he quoted Deuteronomy." For children who

9. Moberly, "Toward an Interpretation of the Shema," 125–28.
10. McConville, *Grace in the End*, 9.

regularly battle fairy tale beasts in their imaginations with toy swords and homemade archery kits, they did not seem very inspired. An old book whose name they can hardly pronounce and probably cannot spell seems like shoddy weaponry should a dragon draw nigh.

My wife and I have explained to our children that there are dark spiritual forces out there tempting us to do wrong. But the confrontation between Jesus and Satan in Luke 4 seemed a bit absurd: "Dad, if Jesus had not eaten in forty days, then why would it have been a sin to turn a stone into bread?"

The second temptation caused less consternation. Gaining the kingdoms of the world in exchange for worshiping the devil was recognized as clearly wrong. My oldest son perceptively suggested that Satan may have been guilty of false advertising. He knows the serpent of old is a renowned trickster, so maybe he did not control all those kingdoms like he made out. My son smelled something suspicious, like when a friend promises a candy bar she does not actually have on her person.

The final temptation as Luke has it (Matthew follows a slightly different order) made no sense whatsoever to my kids. They could not quite figure out why jumping off the Temple heights would be a temptation. Surely Jesus would not fall for something that dumb. Only a fool would purposely hurl oneself off a bike or out of a tree, much less off a building onto stone pavement. As far as my kids were concerned, there was nothing notably heroic in Jesus's valiant refusal. He was just using the sort of common sense they had learned as toddlers: don't jump from heights.

I almost explained that Jesus was actually resisting the temptation to pull off a spectacular stunt in the most public and religiously significant place in Palestine. Such a grandstanding media event would have resulted in a supernatural display of angelic powers (as Satan suggested) guaranteeing instant celebrity status for Jesus.

But I just stuck with a simple summary of one of the scene's main points: *Though Israel forgot Deuteronomy, Jesus did not.*[11]

Like Josiah, Jesus is a Davidic king who is not at a loss for Deuteronomic words. After he found the Lost Book, it was said of the Great King that "before him there was no king like him, who turned to the LORD *with all his heart, with all his soul, and with all his might,* according to all the law of Moses" (2 Kgs 23:25; emphases added). This description directly quotes from the *Shema* to describe Josiah. And the last and final

11. The temptation scene recapitulates Adam's fall to temptation in Eden and Israel's fall to temptation in the wilderness.

Davidic king, Jesus, quoted from Deuteronomy to fend off the word-twisting assault of Satan; and he later exalted the *Shema* as the highest demand on our lives (Matt 22:35–38; Mark 12:28–30; Luke 10:25–27).

I mentioned in the introductory chapter that though we may be familiar with the first couple of verses of the *Shema*, we are less so with the rest of it. And the rest of this magisterial passage *calls us to media saturation with the words and texts of God*:

> Hear, O Israel: The LORD is our God, the LORD alone. You shall love the LORD your God with all your heart, and with all your soul, and with all your might. Keep *these words* that I am commanding you today in your heart. Recite them to your children and talk about them when you are at home and when you are away, when you lie down and when you rise. Bind them as a sign on your hand, fix them as an emblem on your forehead, and write them on the doorposts of your house and on your gates. (Deut 6:4–9; emphasis added)

"Keep," "recite," and "talk about" these words (*oral* media practices). "Bind," "fix," and "write" them (*textual* media practices).[12] Which words? Most specifically, the words of the first two verses of the *Shema*.[13] The call to love this unique and only ("one," ESV) God with every fiber of one's being is the most elemental call on the lives of God's people. Since the first two verses of the *Shema* serve as a summation of all the covenant obligations placed on Israel and spoken by Moses, "these words" generally refer to all the words of the covenant binding Israel to God.

When and where are the hearers to keep, recite, and talk about these words? Always, anywhere, and everywhere: when home and not at home, when lying down in bed and rising up for the day, when out and about, and when walking along the way. The *Shema* confirms the

---

12. The references to oral TheoMedia are right at home in an oral culture. But the textual elements of words written on amulets, hands, doorposts, and gates seems more at home in a literary culture. Since the inhabitants of oral cultures retain verbal media so competently, it may well be that the letters of the *Shema* could have been visually associated with the memorized, recited, and talked about words of the passage. And some members of local villages may have possessed elementary writing skills. Richard Horsley suggests that these written texts served as a sort of literary iconography: "Such inscriptions on the doorposts were iconic talismans completely embedded in and reflective of a world of oral communication." See Horsely, *Scribes, Visionaries, and the Politics of Second Temple Judaism*, 95.

13. See the chapter "A Love Supreme" in Moberly's *Old Testament Theology* (forthcoming).

observation in the previous chapter that the words of God are multisensory in that "these words" are to be affixed unavoidably in every Israelite's visual space: bound to the hands, dangling between the eyes, emblazoned on the entranceways and exits of houses and gardens. No time of day, no physical space, and no sphere of life ("home" or "away"—public or private) are to be removed from the verbal TheoMedia of Deuteronomy 6:4–5 and the words of the wider covenant texts they represent.

Israel's faith has been described as a "book religion." What other religions in the ancient Near East did with their images, the Israelites sometimes did with their texts, prominently displaying them within their visual range and at times wearing them the way devotees of other gods would wear amulets or charms.[14] The logocentric material culture of Israel was not limited to the plastered stones by Jordan's riverbanks. The *Shema* prescribed a word-oriented materiality and visuality that was to infiltrate every shred of everyday life.

The greatest commandment in scripture—the highest demand on our lives—encourages a set of media practices by which our lives are saturated with verbal TheoMedia. The *Shema* should be recognized as a central text as the church negotiates twenty-first-century media. It is a passage that reminds Christians in the digital age and every age that we are called to media saturation, but the media that are to so thoroughly permeate every dimension of our lives are the media of God.

Yet Christians have historically read the first two verses of the *Shema* without giving much heed to verses 6–9.

Walter Moberly points out that Jewish readers of this passage have been keen to embrace its prescribed media practices, while Christians have focused almost exclusively on the love command in 6:5 and on the notion of divine oneness in 6:4. The following media practices in 6:6–9 are largely ignored at best or, at worst, used to negatively caricature Jewish piety.[15]

Why have we broken up the passage of the *Shema*, heeding its call to love the one God, but barely noticing its call to media saturation with God's words?

Professor Moberly suggests that we have replaced the *Shema*'s media practices with the regular recitation of the Lord's Prayer and with the

14. For a comparison of these practices, see Van der Toorn's essay "The Iconic Book."

15. Again, see Moberly's chapter "A Love Supreme" in *Old Testament Theology* (forthcoming).

visuality of the cross symbol. We will soon begin studying the "new media" of the New Testament, which certainly include the imagery of Jesus's cross.

What I want to emphasize here is that the highest command of the entire Bible is inseparable from the command of verbal TheoMedia saturation. Loving the one God with all of one's heart, soul, and might is intrinsically bound to knowing him according to his words and living out the ethical vision those words supply. It is a call embraced by Josiah, the last great Davidic king in Jerusalem, and reasserted by the final Davidic King whose reign knows no end.

AT A LOSS FOR (DIVINE) WORDS TODAY?

It is worth asking if we are in danger of gradually displacing verbal Theo-Media with the various media of our own day.

It is unlikely that some embittered citizen of Jerusalem took that old scroll, buried it secretly in the Temple cupboards, and then engineered a propaganda campaign convincing the populace that Deuteronomy simply did not exist. That book collected dust because of gradual disuse. It was "lost" not because it was destroyed, captured, or burned, but because folks just slowly lost interest over time.

The people of God have never had such access to their sacred texts as we do today—Bibles are selling quite well, and we can instantly access Deuteronomy through a range of media formats like e-readers, smartphones, and laptops (there is no need to heave around bulky scrolls). But those living in Judah during the monarchy *still* had some degree of access to Deuteronomy. It was right there in the Temple all along. If you lose a sacred book in the ancient world and you really want to find it, the first place one would look would surely have been the Temple, the center of all religious life and devotion, right?

We have seen that large texts were not very accessible artifacts for most ancient people; we have also seen that the primary problem of not heeding them is more related to interest than to access. In the case of Deuteronomy's tragic media displacement, the issue was indeed lack of interest rather than lack of access. And along with the lack of interest, there was an enthralling curiosity in the media of other societies.

Though he enacted dramatic reforms after discovering the lost Law book, Josiah's noble efforts were simply too late. Manasseh, the king of "forgetfulness"[16] (and Josiah's grandfather), had irreversibly locked Judah into a trajectory of collapse (Jer 15:4). Exile and destruction awaited Jerusalem just as it had already come to Samaria, the capital of what was once called Israel in the north. When Josiah tore his robes at the hearing of those ancient words from Deuteronomy, the people of God had already exchanged their media preferences, opting for the mediascape of downfall. They chose to heed verbal media that were plausible but unauthorized. They chose sensory religious media that were either misconstrued without the guidance of verbal TheoMedia, or just outright pagan, which verbal TheoMedia vehemently condemned. The Assyrian war machinery crunched through Samaria's gates and the Babylonian banners waved high in Jerusalem because the leaders of God's people failed to heed the words of God.

What followed? Babel-style exile . . . and even destruction:

> Why is the land ruined and laid waste like a wilderness, so that no one passes through? And the LORD says: Because they have forsaken my law that I set before them, and have not obeyed my voice, or walked in accordance with it, but have stubbornly followed their own hearts and have gone after the Baals, as their ancestors taught them. Therefore thus says the LORD of hosts, the God of Israel: I am feeding this people with wormwood, and giving them poisonous water to drink. I will scatter them among nations that neither they nor their ancestors have known; and I will send the sword after them, until I have consumed them. (Jer 9:12c–16)

Note the juxtaposition between the religious media: "law" (textual) and "my voice" (verbal) versus "the Baals" whose images and altars peppered the land. As mentioned earlier, Jeremiah was preaching in the days when Deuteronomy, the covenant text that recorded God's "law" and "voice," was found under a heap of dust.

If he showed up on the streets of our own twenty-first-century cities and byways, Jeremiah would not have to worry about the proliferation of Baal imagery or about sacrifices offered to the "queen of heaven." But his brutal years of ministry had so trained his senses to detect distracting media with distracting messages that if he did make such an appearance today, he might still be known as the "weeping prophet."

---

16. On Manasseh's name meaning forgetfulness, see Leithart, *1 and 2 Kings*, 261–65.

CONCLUSION: POST-EXILIC ISRAEL

As a testimony to God's mercy, the biblical story of Israel does not end in 586 BC when Nebuchadnezzar finalized his siege of Jerusalem and deported hordes of Judah's residents all throughout Babylon. Fresh new words came from prophets like Ezekiel who saw God's Spirit resuscitate fallen Israel out of a corpse-strewn valley. Eventually, many of the exiles returned to Judah and began resurrecting Jerusalem out of its rubble. Under the leadership of Ezra and Nehemiah, the national revival of Israel was associated with more than just rebuilt walls and re-plastered homes: there was also a spiritual revival, evidenced in the mass public gatherings for the reading of Torah. For the Old Testament, Israel's national revivals corresponded to a return to verbal TheoMedia. That was the case in Ezra's day. Corporate confessions accompanied the readings and certain feasts and celebrations were reinstituted. The Temple was rebuilt, and God demonstrated his willingness to forgive past sins.

Some still found reason to weep, though. If you strained your ears and listened carefully enough, you could hear it through the din of celebration when the foundations were laid for the new Temple. The cries came from the old men, those who had seen that holy building as boys in its larger, grander version, its timbers strengthened by long-dead Josiah (see Ezra 3:12–13). The new building did not do justice to the vision of King David and the extravagant blueprints of King Solomon. "David," "Solomon"—legendary names from long, long ago.

For many, the new dawn of post-exilic Israel seemed a bit dimmed, not quite as bright and shiny as hoped for. Prophets like Haggai and Zechariah reinforced the wild hopes, voicing words of a new era, a forthcoming age of triumph and restoration. Yet David's throne never quite got a solid occupant, in spite of that covenant made to him centuries ago. The promises seemed awkwardly unfulfilled. The strange, confusing din of sobbing plus rejoicing canonically lingers at the closing margin of the Old Testament. A haunting sound it is, faint but discernible . . . a sound of hoping commingled with the sound of hopes dashed. Something had to happen. Eyes glanced longingly at the horizons.

No one came.

Except Gentile king after Gentile king.

TheoMedia Note 6

"Weighting" Media

The *Shema* in Our Twenty-first-Century Homes

It is common to hear parents today talk of their children as born naturals when it comes to the devices and apps of our media saturated culture. When grandparents visit, they often call on their primary school grandchildren to help them figure out the three or four remote controls to the multimedia apparatus occupying a central position in our living rooms. When we go to the kitchen to refill our coffee mug, we might return to find a toddler holding the electronic tablet we left on the sofa. Taking a sneak peak over his shoulder we find him effectively destroying green pigs with a red ball-bird on the screen, hardly hindered at all by the stickiness of his fingertips. We wonder if perhaps this is evidence of some evolutionary development, if maybe there is such a thing as a techno-gene that has been added to our DNA strands.

The truth is, our children are simply developing competence in the media technologies we encourage and allow in our homes.

Unlike Israel in the Book of Deuteronomy, most of us are not poised as refugees on the edge of a riverbank, mustering up courage to enter a new land bristling with enemies. For most readers of this book, whatever hills may be in sight are not topped with the ritual accoutrements of exotic gods and goddesses. Our lives are radically different from those of the families straining to hear what old Moses was saying while they camped "in the Arabah opposite Suph, between Paran and Tophel, Laban, Hazeroth, and Dizahab" (Deut 1:1b ESV).

We do not milk cows or goats, hunt down wayward sheep at sunset, or sacrifice the firstborn from our flock. And many of us love bacon. We have not misplaced Deuteronomy in some cobwebbed corner of a church building. I admit it is hard to see how a strange document from the alien sands of antiquity relates to family life in the twenty-first century.

My wife and I are trying to sort through the implications of the *Shema* for our home. Deuteronomy is the covenant text that was to govern the family and national life of God's people as they embraced the settled life. It *must* have something to say to us. Since Jesus harkened to the *Shema* as the pinnacle summation of God's ethical commands, and since its original context is about TheoMedia saturation with God's words, then Deuteronomy 6:4–9 should hold appreciable sway over my home life and media life.

I am pretty sure that we are not called to vandalize our suburbs and city streets by breaking, dashing, chopping, and burning the billboards, cinemas, and jumbotrons. God called Israel to destroy the public media of Canaan, but that sort of program is not legally possible, and certainly not advisable in our current context.

But the *Shema* certainly casts vision for what media we allow to most influence our lives. Repeatedly throughout this book we are finding that media as a concept is not of casual interest to God. He is not passive about our media practices. Bound to the command to love God with all our being is the persistent promotion of verbal and textual TheoMedia at the table, around the hearth, and at the bedside.

Children are treated with great importance in Deuteronomy. They are the ones who will carry the religious heritage into the future and pass down the stories and texts that reveal YHWH. As we have mentioned, the great media events of the plagues, the exodus, and Sinai were to be collectively remembered by Israel through storytelling in the home (Deut 4:9–10; 6:2; 6:20–21; 11:19; 32:46; cf. Exod 10:2; 12:26) and through the texts preserved in the Ark (the Ten Commandments), those placed beside the Ark (other legal material, like Deuteronomy), and the text of the *Shema* inscribed and recited in the home (Deut 10:4; 31:24–26).

Whatever we make of this, we can at least say that verbal TheoMedia should feature in our homes.

Does this mean that every conversation around the dinner table has to be about Old Testament legal material? Does this mean that the kids should be discussing those old inheritance rights for the firstborn when they load into the minivan?

In the opening of chapter 2, I shared about the daily media medley of my home. Obviously, I am somewhat comfortable with my children watching certain films and kids' shows. They hum the score from *Star Wars* and dance around to a couple of pop music hits. In all honesty, my oldest kids are reading more of J. K. Rowling and Roald Dahl than of Moses. My younger children are more familiar with Elmo and the Octonauts than they are with Zephaniah and Jeremiah. Now, in spite of that Beyoncé song, we *are* quite selective about what they see, hear, and read (and already they lodge complaints because many of their little peers seem to be allowed wider access to rougher material). But to a limited degree Miranda (my wife) and I are encouraging them, like young Daniel, to learn "the literature and language of the Chaldeans" (Dan 1:4). We want them to learn and even enjoy certain offerings of our Western culture (we do try to provide more than just the pop cultural offerings!).

This exposure to culture is tricky to manage and negotiate, and I sometimes cringe with self-disappointment when I think of how much exposure they are getting to outside media sources. If the minutes and hours were counted, then I know the Bible would rank below Pixar and DreamWorks on a domestic media chart.

Teaching the Bible in the twenty-first-century home can be an immense challenge, and not just because children ask hard questions, like when my son wonders why Jesus would be tempted to jump off the Temple or when my daughter asks why God used to permit such a grievous injustice as letting the inheritance pass to a younger brother when the oldest child in the family was a daughter. One reason teaching the Bible is so challenging for my wife and me is because our four kids are all at different levels of understanding and reading comprehension. There are also the extracurricular demands of their young lives: homework assignments, gymnastics sessions, birthday parties, play dates with friends, church commitments, etc. And not to be forgotten is a toddler who doesn't mind interrupting all of it at any hour of the day (or night). Finding time to teach Deuteronomy amidst all the hustle and bustle can be a defeating exercise.

Some parents catechize their children and encourage scripture memorization. Some home school their kids and devote hours each week to biblical and theological lessons. For me, what I have determined as most important at this stage in my parenting is to ensure that my children understand the Bible's overall narrative story of redemption. And I encourage them to make that story the frame of reference through which they read, hear, and assess all other media and every other story.

In other words, I am teaching them the biblical story and prioritizing it as their hermeneutical lens.

As I just mentioned, if I were to measure my children's media influences (watching TV/film versus reading scripture), the stats would be depressing. I have thought about making this rule: *you can only watch TV for as long as you have read scripture*. My wife has kindly helped me realize that rules of that sort are not very feasible for four kids at different learning levels, two of whom are still unable to read.

But we can *weight* the Bible with heavier significance than all the other media in our home. Even if other media sources quantitatively triumph over the media source of scripture, I am engaged in a perennial exercise of qualitatively prioritizing scripture over all other influences.

This involves helping my daughter to understand the Christological themes surfacing in *Harry Potter*. It involves critiquing films that misrepresent violence as something silly and harmless (which may well include *Harry Potter* flicks). I am always pleased to find my oldest son snuggled up in the top bunk with a "chapter book" in hand. But I will frequently pat him on the head and gently say something like "enjoy that book, son . . . but remember, the Bible's story of God's rescuing love is the strongest story of all."

I am not justifying giving secular media a quantitative superiority to TheoMedia in the home. In suggesting the practice of weighting the former qualitatively, this is just one struggling dad stumbling around in the digital age and trying to do something right. It's a start.

PART 4

Media Christology
Jesus, Media Legacies, and Focal Media Practices

Chapter 9

The Page-Splitting God Who Rips Sky and Veil

An Interlude

The grace of being in the image was sufficient to know God the Word, and through him the Father. But knowing the weakness of human beings, God anticipated also their carelessness, so if they cared not to recognize God through themselves, through the works of creation they might not be ignorant of the Creator. But since the negligence of humans descended gradually to lower things, God again anticipated such weakness of theirs, sending the law and the prophets, known to them, so that if they shrank from looking up to the heavens and knowing the Creator, they might have instruction from those close by . . . nevertheless human beings, beaten by the pleasures of the moment and the illusions and deceits of the demons, did not raise their gaze to the truth.

—ST. ATHANASIUS, *ON THE INCARNATION*[1]

"Where are you?"

1. Athanasius, *On the Incarnation*, 75–76.

This is the sound of relational distance, the sound of intimacy lost, the sound of a communications disaster of cosmic proportions. That primordial question from Genesis 3:9 is ringing faintly in the obscuring mist from a pained Voice almost out of range. Why the distance? Because the voice of another was heeded ("did God actually say . . . ?"). And so naked eyes now gleam with fear from the shadows of a dark wood. We are exiled. Exiled from Eden.

"Here am I."

That is the sound of response, the sound of a refugee answering from "among the trees" the divine summons.

East of Eden, the Voice of God kept calling out in the darkness, like a bereft parent coaxing lost children from their hiding places. Every now and then comes a "Here am I," heard somewhere three days away from Moriah, then from out of Haran, and centuries later from the slopes of Sinai.[2] With this call and response, divine-human distance began to be closed. God cried out into the night, and on the reply "Here am I" he built a nation, the nation of Israel.

It was a nation that proved eager to keep heeding other voices, other sounds, other sights. Other *media*.

We have seen throughout this book that the company of God and human beings throughout the Old Testament was kept through a complex matrix of divinely appointed media. The terrifying scene at Mt. Sinai made unforgettable the fact that, although God yearns for relationship, it is a relationship marked by mediation: "The people stood at a distance, while Moses drew near to the thick darkness where God was" (Exod 20:21). This was a distance God *demanded* they keep. The sheer holiness of the divine presence could not commingle with mortals as in Eden. As the canonical storyline of Christian scripture makes clear, the covenant made at Sinai could only bridge the relational divide between God and humankind in part. But a Tabernacle and eventually a Temple provided space where the two parties could meet, a thick veil shielding the created from the Creator.

Over the centuries, prophetic cries were lifted and inspired speech was etched and inked. Even so, the media of God was rarely heeded for long. Heaven and earth seemed destined for this distanced relationship, the alienation permanently signified by the sky as an impenetrable ceiling.

---

2. These references are to Abraham (Gen 22:1; cf. v. 11), Jacob (Gen 30:11), and Moses (Exod 3:4), respectively.

THE YEARS OF THE BLANK PAGE

My Bible has a blank page. You can find it between Malachi and Matthew. The wordlessness on that white sheet of thin paper does not represent nothingness. A lot was happening during the Years of the Blank Page.[3] For the Jewish people, some of it was nightmarish as the chariots of new Gentile kings and their regional appointees wheeled across Judean soil. In the wake of those chariots came a new language and a new culture. "Hellenization," the program of acculturating the eastern Mediterranean world and beyond with Greek language, Greek aesthetics, and Greek religion, was sometimes conducted gently and slowly. But it was a rigorous campaign of media displacement.

At times, that program was forcibly shoved down choking throats.

This was certainly the case with many Jews for whom cultural blending meant the loss of their identity as the unique people of God. Hebrew had already become a revered but archaic tongue.[4] Aramaic was the language flourishing in Palestine, but the people of God had been dispersed throughout the known world—the conversations in their homes and on Gentile streets were often in Greek. The old sacred texts discussed in our previous chapters were eventually translated into this lingua franca. Otherwise, normal Jewish folks throughout the Mediterranean world could hardly have understood the textual media of their religious heritage.[5]

---

3. The Old Testament ends its chronological record of Israel's history with Ezra and the restoration of Jerusalem and the Temple. Other historical events after this period may well be reflected in later writings like Daniel, Joel, and Zechariah, but the events during the Years of the Blank Page were recast within an earlier historical framework (e.g., anxieties and eschatological hopes during Hellenization may be reframed and presented within the Persian context of Daniel). Curiously, the biblical story remains parked in postexilic Jerusalem . . . until the Christian canonical addition of the New Testament resumes that history with the birth of Jesus and the emergence of John the Baptist. See the brief discussion in Childs, *Biblical Theology of the Old and New Testaments*, 164–65.

4. It seems that Hebrew had already begun to fade into disuse during the Babylonian exilic period. When Ezra read and interpreted the Law in Nehemiah 8, translation from Hebrew into Aramaic may well have been involved. See Carr, "Literacy and Reading," 888–89.

5. The story of the Septuagint (Greek translations of the Old Testament literature) is told in the *Letter of Aristeas* (cf. also Josephus, *Antiquities of the Jews*, 12:1–118). Though the translation work of the Septuagint is attributed to the behest and patronage of King Ptolemy II (285–247 BCE) in Alexandria, it is likely that the work was understood to be serviceable for the Diaspora Jews for whom Greek was the primary language. See Hunt, "Letter of Aristeas," 2:7–11.

In this period talk arose of an "age to come."[6] The present evil age seemed beyond salvaging. Surely there would be a Day, a Day of the Lord, that would end this era of Gentile governance and cultural oppression. Surely a new era would dawn, an age in which the extravagant promises of the prophets of old would become reality. Rumors were whispered, sometimes shouted, that David's heir would surface from the ashes and rubble of Israel's darkened history.

During these Years of the Blank Page, many Jews learned to adjust to their marginalized status. Synagogues where their scriptures could be read and prayers prayed emerged among the Diaspora Jews (those scattered abroad) as well as in Judea and Galilee. Sabbath keeping, circumcision, and a kosher diet became identity markers in Gentile societies. Some, however, adjusted so thoroughly that it was hard to tell a Jew from a Greek. Some resisted Hellenization violently, meeting death for their zeal. Others staged uprisings, some of which incurred merciless retaliations. There was quite a bit of excitement in the 160s BCE, though, when the sons of old Mattathias fought David-like from the clefts and caves of the wilds. When these Maccabees and their descendants took over in Jerusalem, however, the reign of their dynasty fell short of the profiles pictured in those bold prophetic promises.

> Rejoice greatly, O daughter Zion!
> Shout aloud, O daughter Jerusalem!
> Lo, your king comes to you.

That was from Zechariah (9:9). But when would such a king come? And from where?

"Where are you?" was not just the cry of God to humanity. At times it was also the cry of humanity to God. Israel's worship was often marked by gut-wrenched, bare-knuckled prayers slamming the silent heavens with pleas unanswered. The spluttering moans and panicked cries of the biblical laments pounded "Where are you?"[7] against an ironclad sky. The petition we have already seen in Isaiah captures the angst well: "O that you would tear open the heavens and come down" (Isa 64:1).

6. This language of a present evil age and an age to come surfaces in multiple New Testament texts: Matt 12:32; 13:49; 24:3; 28:20; Luke 18:30; Rom 12:2; 1 Cor 1:20; 2:6–8; 3:18; 10:11; 2 Cor 4:4; Gal 1:4; Eph 1:21; 5:16; 6:13; Heb 9:9, 26; cf. also 2 Cor 5:17; 1 Cor 7:31.

7. Many an Israelite heard from their enemies while lying face down in the mire, "Where is your God?" (Ps 42:3; 10; 79:10; 115:2). For the biblical lament poetry, see my chapter "The Way of the Tragic Poet" in *Faith Without Illusions*, 157–78.

He would. And now we come to the point in the Bible's salvation-history when the sky gets ripped apart.

STRIPS OF FABRIC AND SHARDS OF SKY

The Bible opens with what appears to be a calm, peaceful scene: "The Spirit of God was hovering over the face of the waters" (Gen 1:2). The Gospel of Mark opens in similar fashion. The Spirit is portrayed as a dove hovering above the waters of the River Jordan.

But the scene is not calm or peaceful in Mark 1. Before the Spirit's dove-like descent, something harsh and violent happens, something that is sudden, striking, and permanently damaging. As a man bursts out from the surface of those baptismal waters, there is a silent explosion overhead in the cosmic curtain. The Spirit's descent is through a punctured hole in the heavens, through the shredded edges of a ripped open sky: "In those days Jesus came from Nazareth of Galilee and was baptized by John in the Jordan. And just as he was coming up out of the water, he saw the heavens torn apart and the Spirit descending like a dove on him" (Mark 1:9–10). The Greek word behind "torn apart" is *schizō*. It is the etymological ancestor of our English word "schism." The idea of the Greek verb is to split open or tear asunder.

This violent puncturing of the sky is a decisive moment in the biblical plot of redemption for Mark. It is the moment when it becomes clear that our God will tolerate no longer the divine-human alienation, when he will content himself no more with the mediation of prior centuries: "In Mark, then, God has ripped the heavens irrevocably apart at Jesus' baptism, never to shut them again. Through this gracious gash in the universe, he has poured forth his Spirit into the earthly realm."[8]

This is a God who will suffer no more barriers between himself and his people. This is a God who commits violence against the obstructing boundaries. This is a God who will tear heaven apart to get to his children.

It is not just the sky that gets torn in Mark. The verb *schizō* reappears at the end of the Gospel, forming what biblical scholars call an *inclusio*, the dual use of a word or theme that encloses or bookends a larger body of text to serve as an interpretive frame. Mark is to be read within the frame of divine-human boundaries being torn and ripped apart: "Then

8. Marcus, *Mark 1–8*, 165.

Jesus gave a loud cry and breathed his last. And the curtain of the temple was torn in two, from top to bottom" (Mark 15:37–38).

God rent the heavens and came down, leaving a gaping gash overhead, its edges dangling with tattered sky. And then the fabric of the Temple veil that screened the divine presence from the rest of the world came suddenly unstitched. Our God is a sky-ripping, curtain-tearing God. No divine-human barrier is safe from him. In the New Testament, God is answering his own question "Where are you?" with this: *Wherever you are, I am coming for you. And I will find you.*

With the sound of tearing, our study on the media of God now turns to Jesus. And strips of fabric and shards of sky are falling to the ground.

TheoMedia Note 7

Fading Away from the Scene and into the Church

Celebrity Culture, Christian Leaders, and John the Baptist

And the LORD said to me: Proclaim all these words in the cities of Judah, and in the streets of Jerusalem.

—JEREMIAH 11:6

One who is more powerful than I is coming; I am not worthy to untie the thong of his sandals.

—JOHN THE BAPTIST, LUKE 3:16

For those who had a public message to air in the ancient world, there was a range of accepted mechanisms already in place for engaging a crowd. Jeremiah could go to the Temple steps, and Paul could take his stand on Athens's Areopagus.

It was not uncommon in those days for public personas to enter the marketplace with hopes of gaining a following. The sort of mass communication activities of prophets and apostles often resembled the stratagems of ancient world celebrities.[1] Paul took pains to distinguish himself from the audience-craving Sophists, itinerant speakers who used their rhetorical skills to wow the crowds and secure an income.[2] "Woe to me if I do not proclaim the gospel" declared Paul (1 Cor 9:16), yet the public squares were filled with the voices of others clamoring for a hearing. The words of God burned like fire in Jeremiah's bones, but false prophets were engaged with what appeared to be the same line of work.

So how can the leaders of God's people be faithful to their calling without slipping into worldly techniques governed by unwholesome motives?

The media channels of contemporary life have made the kitsch and swagger of celebrity culture virtually ubiquitous in Western society.[3] It has most certainly seeped into the church. On some of the biggest screens in the land are the faces of pastors preaching to satellite congregations. Twitter started paying attention to Christian leaders because some of them have racked up more followers than pop icons.[4]

So is preaching via satellite wrong? Is a large Twitter following evidence of a Christian leader's compromising bow to our media culture?

Maybe. Maybe not. The point is that Christian leaders must carefully negotiate a range of means for getting a message into the public sphere, something faced by Christian leaders in biblical times as well. In spite of how beholden to shallow self-promotion some media outlets seem, God is still putting fire in prophets' bones. The Spirit still calls us to quill and ink (or to keypad and pixelated text, as it were). How can church leaders whom God has assigned a public message be faithful to our calling without being corroded by the influences of celebrity culture? How can we responsibly use social media encoded with values that promote popularity?

1. Though I use the term "celebrities" here, it should be noted that the mass media apparatus of our own day exponentiates this concept radically. For the most part, fame in the ancient world would have been regionally and locally confined. See Schwartz, "What Difference Does the Medium Make?" 228–29. Some type of celebrity status did, however, accompany certain leaders of the church. See 2 Corinthians 8:18: "With him we are sending the brother who is famous among all the churches for his proclaiming the good news."

2. See Paul's comments in 1 Corinthians 1:18—2:16.

3. See Ward's study on celebrity culture and religious meaning, *Gods Behaving Badly*.

4. Bailey, "Twitter Reaches Out to Christian Leaders at Catalyst's 'Be Present' Conference."

Another factor complicating the issue is that the messages of many Christian leaders are materialized in purchasable products (like books, for example!) that can be immediately accessed and bought by following a well-placed link. To a frightening extent, this means that our public messages have to be buy-able to be received. So consumer culture intertwines with celebrity culture when it comes to the church's public voice. Sadly, the Christian publishing industry is beholden to both: to exist, it must sell products; to sell products, the authors must have a following.[5]

We should be wary when the words of our (allegedly) inspired messages are so often hyperlinked to webpages that ask for a credit card number.

I am not sure anything Jeremiah had to say to the Jerusalem populace would have sold like hotcakes on the Temple steps. But we also know that Paul had to clarify his distance from the Sophists because their rhetorical antics and his own verbal activities seemed to share some parallels. How do we navigate the murky waters of voicing divine wisdom and prophetic speech in a culture that worships fame and loves to buy and sell media products? How can we serve as TheoMedia in our media culture?

Enter: John the Baptist.

THE MINISTRY OF CHRISTOLOGICAL REDIRECTION

The forerunner of Christ was somewhat of an off-the-charts celebrity in the ancient world. Hordes flocked to him from a broad geographical range. His following was immense. But before we begin making assumptions that John the Baptist would be identified as @Jbap had he lived in our own day,[6] let's acknowledge that his ministry launch base was quite counterintuitive (the wilderness) and his clothing was a far cry from designer jeans (camel's hair). Jesus pointed out that John's ministry did not conform to the expectations of his own day (Matt 11:7), so we should be careful assuming he would have conformed to the protocols of platform building in our own.

I am not very keen on character studies in Sunday school curricula, but I am quite pleased for focus to be directed to the Baptist. After

---

5. I am thankful that the publisher of this book has developed in-house printing capabilities to reduce their dependence on both celebrity culture and consumerism.

6. In case you are wondering, I could not find anyone using the Twitter handle @ Jbap as of the week I submitted my manuscript to the publisher.

all, Jesus called him the greatest man born of a woman (Luke 7:28; Matt 11:11). It makes good sense to give a little attention to the man Jesus himself called the greatest. But what we find when we look to John is that the all-consuming vocation of the greatest man born of woman was *to point to someone greater, and then fade away*: "He must increase, but I must decrease" (John 3:30).

In all four Gospels, John appears like a bolt out of the blue only to recede into the backstage shadows. The fourth evangelist, however, having had more time to process John the Baptist's influence in the early church, has made explicitly clear that the ultimate function of his public persona was *redirection*.

There was absolutely no self-orientation to John's celebrity status in the fourth Gospel (or in the other Gospels, for that matter): "In order that he may not be in any sense the object of his own preaching and action, he disowns every kind of movement towards himself."[7] At one point John's disciples are disturbed when word got out that Jesus's ministry was overshadowing their own. This is a case of ministerial territorialism—the ministry of Jesus was getting a bigger piece of the populist pie. For John, this was the sign of his own ministry's success. There is no question that he had a divinely mandated public persona. The man had a message, and he kept preaching as the crowds grew larger. But his calling was to highlight another and then slip offstage.

THE MINISTRY OF ECCLESIAL ASSIMILATION

When he does slip offstage, though, his voice is not obliterated. In the Gospel of John, there is no record of the Baptist's death. What we do find is that his voice becomes indistinguishable from the voice of the church. Biblical translators have a hard time figuring out where to place the quotation marks signifying John the Baptist's voice in 1:16–18 and in 3:31–36.[8] His words bleed into the words of the community or into the words of the narrator who is understood as a community member.

---

7. Hoskyns, *The Fourth Gospel*, 169.

8. Many of the fourth Gospel's earliest interpreters believed that the Baptist's voice extended beyond 1:15, joining in the confession of the believing community. See Harris, *Prologue and Gospel*, 31–34.

Moreover, certain roles and designations that belong to John in the Gospel become the roles and designations of Jesus's community of disciples.[9]

So as a first-century "celebrity," John the Baptist redirected to Jesus and he also assimilated into the church.

The fourth Gospel takes John's renown and baptizes it into proper Christological and ecclesiological functionality. His voice is uplifted to testify to Jesus, and yet his voice is not permitted to stand over and against the voice of the church. To the extent that the people of God follow John's redirecting gaze, his own ministry dissolves into the wider ministry of the faith community. So a two-dimensional trajectory marks the Baptist's celebrity status: he is always pointing to another while simultaneously fading into the collective voice of the church.

Many of our celebrities today are notoriously averse to redirection and to the fading of their voices. Integral to the idea of celebrity status is that the status must be maintained. Pointing elsewhere and blurring the lines distinguishing fans from the famous are radically counterintuitive. While celebrity culture emphasizes the individuality of the celebrity, the fourth Gospel calls for such an intensive identification of the Christian leader with the faith community that the two share the same platform.

Modern-day celebs stereotypically love the stage and resist being absorbed into the audience. But the stage presence of Christian leaders is only legitimated by voice fading and redirection. Increases in church attendance, satellite campuses, book sales, blog stats, retweets, or online followership ratchets up the degree to which we are responsible for pointing away from ourselves while being absorbed into our hearers, viewers, readers, and followers.

But what is interesting is that social media allows public figures opportunity to practice redirection and assimilation in ways perhaps unprecedented. The new media technology at our fingertips is well disposed for directing online readers elsewhere and for allowing the celebrity/fan divide to soften and blur. We can send direct tweets to prominent pastors and offer constructive critiques to their blog posts.[10] Christian members with an impressive online presence, however, must learn how to utilize

9. John is sent by God (John 1:6, 33), and the disciples will be sent by Jesus (20:21). Just as John is the "friend" of the bridegroom (3:29), Jesus will call the disciples his "friends" (15:14). John bears witness to Jesus (1:7 et al.), but so will the faithful members of the newly formed community (15:26).

10. I am thankful for Dr. Tim Hutchings comments over coffee that helped shape the observations in this paragraph.

new media formats for these practices of Christological redirection and ecclesial assimilation. Like John the Baptist, many of us have a message that needs some public airing.[11] Faithful proclamation in John's day and in our own is marked by pointing to Someone greater while identifying ourselves with the faith community following our gaze.

11. To be clear, I do think John the Baptist's ministry was quite unique and to some degree unrepeatable. His voice serves as a canonical hinge, if you will, extending the prophetic speech of the Old Testament into the new reality created by the Gospel of Jesus Christ. In spite of his singularity, however, John the Baptist's disposition toward himself can be understood as paradigmatic for Christian leaders. According to Wink in his seminal study on the Baptist, John has been "made the normative image of the Christian preacher, apostle, missionary, the perfect prototype of the true evangelist, whose one goal is self-effacement before Christ . . . His whole function is to 'witness,' that others might believe through him . . ." (*John the Baptist*, 105).

Chapter 10

Gospel and Incarnation
Jesus as the Ultimate TheoMedium

We believe in one Lord Jesus Christ, the only Son of God, eternally begotten of the Father, Light from Light, true God from true God, begotten, not made, of one Being with the Father. Through him all things were made. For us and for our salvation he came down from heaven: by the power of the Holy Spirit he became incarnate from the Virgin Mary, and was made man.

—FROM THE NICENE CREED[1]

Once the mind of human beings descended to perceptible things, the Word himself submitted to appear through a body, so that as a human he might bring humans to himself and return their sense perception to himself.

—ATHANASIUS, *ON THE INCARNATION*[2]

Remember, the purpose of this book is to discern in Christian scripture a theological framework for understanding the use and concept of media in the twenty-first century. The underlying conviction is that God himself

1. Excerpt taken from Holy Eucharist service II in *The Book of Common Prayer*.
2. Athanasius, *On the Incarnation*, 16.

employs media (means of revelation and communication), so there must be a divine logic that can inform our own use and understanding of media in the digital age. Also, the media God employs and prioritizes determines what media forms Christians must gain (or retain) competence in interpreting and engaging.

As we cross the canonical threshold of the Years of the Blank Page into the New Testament,[3] we will find that the TheoMedia we have studied thus far are about to be reconfigured. Jesus's arrival forever altered TheoMedia and the way God had related to human beings since the Fall. When "Jesus came into Galilee, proclaiming the gospel" (Mark 1:14 ESV), the sights and sounds, words and texts of Israel's God—all his means of relating to humanity—were about to be fulfilled, replaced, and expanded.

Since we are crafting a theological framework for appropriating and understanding media today by studying God's own means of revelation and communication, we consider now a "media Christology." In other words, we want to understand the concept of media through Christ. How does Jesus alter the means of communication and divine self-revelation in the God-to-human fellowship?

We are hoping to learn how his entry into our world informs how we should use media. Throughout these chapters on media Christology, we are looking for "media legacies." By this phrase, I am referring to ideas about or attitudes toward media deriving from the work and life of Jesus. These legacies often give way to "focal media practices," that is, media practices that orient and shape our lives.[4]

"GOSPEL": THE VERBAL MEDIA OF EUCATASTROPHE

First, we should note that the word *gospel* is a media term. When the gospel is discussed in church, the concern is usually with its *content* rather than with its *genre*. The term refers not just to a particular message, but also to a specific *type* of message. *Gospel* is a term from the ancient world

3. I am not suggesting that the actual blank page between the Old Testament and the New Testament in many Bibles should be literally canonized; I am just figuratively recalling that there is an historical gap between the testaments.

4. I am adapting the idea of a focal practice from philosopher Albert Borgmann, whose ideas have been recently fleshed out in Boers's *Living Into Focus*. See Boers's chapter, "Finding and Funding Focal Fundamentals," 177–201. Also helpful is the chapter "Do We and Our Churches Live by Our Focal Concerns?," in Dawn's *Unfettered Hope*, 79–107.

labeling a particular communications category, the genre of shockingly glorious newsflash. As a media form, gospel is the oral pronouncement of indescribably "good news."

Gospel is a term deriving from ancient military and political imagery. Think of a scene in which two armies are waging fierce battle over the hillside while hapless citizens wring their hands and pray for deliverance from the invading force. And then, someone from the unguarded city wall makes out a moving shape on the horizon, the shape of a man racing from the scene of war. This is the "runner," the swift-footed messenger who dashes from the quieted battle tumult to announce the awaiting fate of those who have sent their husbands, fathers, and sons bearing sticks and swords in service to their embattled king. Gospel is the news cried out through the heaving breaths, pounding heart, and trembling lips of the runner that our king has triumphed and that our enemies have been defeated.

An even more fitting scenario may be that of a nation enslaved to the iron-fisted rule of an unconquerable empire. To the dizzying shock of all, on what might appear to be a normal day, an emissary from some mythic foreign kingdom appears at the gates and pronounces unimaginable news: *the tyranny is over; the oppressor has been decisively defeated; a new King has come and you are forever free.* This breathless relief of deliverance beyond all expectation and hope is portrayed here in Isaiah 40:

> Get you up to a high mountain,
>   O Zion, herald of good tidings;
> lift up your voice with strength,
>   O Jerusalem, herald of good tidings,
> lift it up, do not fear;
>   say to the cities of Judah,
> "Here is your God!"
>   See, the Lord GOD comes with might,
> and his arm rules for him;
>   his reward is with him,
> and his recompense before him. (Isa 40:9–10)

The twice-used phrase "herald of good tidings" is a translation of one word in the Greek Septuagint version of Isaiah, a participial form of the verb *euangelizō*, meaning "to proclaim good news" (notice the similarity to our English word *evangelize*). In the passage above, the exiled children of Israel are being exhorted to rejoice and open their eyes to see that their one true King, the Creator Lord, is rushing to their rescue.

In Isaiah 52 the same word appears twice in the phrase "[him] who brings good news," drawing from the imagery of the runner from the battlefield:

> How beautiful upon the mountains
>   are the feet of him who brings good news,
> who publishes peace, who brings good news of happiness,
>   who publishes salvation,
> who says to Zion, "Your God reigns." (Isa 52:7 ESV)

The noun form of *euangelizō* is *euangelion*, translated into English as "gospel." In Greek, the word *angelia* means "message" and the prefix *eu-* means "good."

By the time of the New Testament, "gospel" could refer to the announcement to Roman citizens that the Emperor or one of his generals had just defeated some foreign army; but the Christian use of the term derives mainly from the ideas found in Isaiah 40–55.[5] The gospel is the public announcement—a loud, street-level outcry—that God has come to save and to establish his reign. The gospel is the "hear ye, hear ye" in the town square announcing the arrival of the rescuing King. The gospel is the drum-banging, bell-clanging media announcement that a new reign and a new age have dawned. The gospel is the trumpeted clarion blast signaling the end of all other reigns and consigning the present evil age to the fading past.

As mentioned in this book's opening chapter, J. R. R. Tolkien coined the term *eucatastrophe* to refer to a surprise event of catastrophically good ("eu-") proportions. Here is his definition: "It is a sudden and miraculous grace: never to be counted on to recur. . . . It denies (in the face of much evidence, if you will) universal final defeat and in so far is *evangelium*, giving a fleeting glimpse of Joy, Joy beyond the walls of the world, poignant as grief."[6]

The verbalized gospel cracks into the soundscape of a fallen world to give news of what Tolkien called the "Great Eucatastrophe"[7]: Christ became Incarnate and, though crucified, was resurrected.

---

5. Bauckham, "God Crucified," 34.

6. Tolkien, "On Fairy-Stories," 153. Tolkien is writing about the genre of the fairy-tale, of which a climactic eucatastrophe is a defining feature.

7. Ibid., 156. "The Birth of Christ is the eucatastrophe of Man's history. The Resurrection is the eucatastrophe of the story of the Incarnation. This story begins and ends with joy."

Hear ye, hear ye: some lordly figure has risen from an ancient line of kings to challenge the occupying forces of Sin, Disease, Death, and the Devil. Through cross and emptied tomb, the foundation walls of Evil's fortress have rumbled and fissured. The dungeon gates have been blown open. Prisoners are clambering through the debris toward daylight as the Risen King ascends from his tomb with a death grip on the throat of Death itself. Nothing can ever be the same again, because "if the Son makes you free, you will be free indeed" (John 8:36).

THE GOSPEL AS A MEDIA LEGACY FOR THE CHURCH

Many of us within the church lament the power of media today in our world. But no mediated message—no matter the technological genius, no matter the sweeping influence—is as powerful as the gospel. Paul has called it "the power of God for salvation" (Rom 1:16). In spite of Jacques Ellul's conviction that technology's systemic integration into our society and hearts was thoroughly binding and inescapable, he also held the conviction that the gospel is powerful enough to make possible "the *spiritual disintegration* of complexes and systems."[8] The church has been entrusted with the most earth-moving, sky-exploding medium in the history of communications. So "get you up on a high mountain," O church of Jesus, for "your God reigns."

This gospel is one of the chief media legacies of the church, the defining *oral* medium of the redeemed people of God. Not only are we entrusted with the content of the gospel—that God's reign is breaking into our sphere through Jesus and his Spirit—but also with the *genre* of the gospel, with the media announcement of news so catastrophically good that it is beyond register.

This message and its exultant urgency should mark our media practices as a people. Obviously, the gospel directly encourages the focal media practice of Christ-centered preaching in the life of the church. Another focal media practice is Christ-centered *writing*—our four canonical "Gospels" indicate that the "gospel" can be presented textually as well as orally. As the message of Jesus's rescuing reign spills out into multiple media formats, our use of contemporary communications technology should somehow be redolent with the life-giving power of this message of eucatastrophe. Underpinning and infusing our lives in a media culture

8. Ellul, "Technology and the Gospel," 117.

must be the most powerful and shockingly wondrous message and media form of "gospel."

How can our online media practices become focal media practices infused with the gospel?

First, let's note that the gospel does not simply announce the end of divine-human alienation. The work of God through Jesus and his Spirit addresses the full scope of the Fall in Genesis 3. Nothing less will save. We are in need of a rescue operation as extensive as the damage, and that damage entails not only our vertical interrelations with God but also our horizontal interrelations with one another. In our introductory chapter it was observed that the very first effect of sin recorded in Genesis 3 is a communications breach between human beings: Adam and Eve stitched together makeshift clothing to screen themselves from one another. The perfect transparency and vulnerability symbolized by unashamed naked-ness was damaged and lost.

The gospel is horizontal as well as vertical. To proclaim the gospel vision of humankind's restored fellowship with God without proclaiming the gospel vision of human beings' restoration to one another is to preach a half gospel.

The portrayal of Jesus according to St. Luke is most energetically de-voted to this horizontal dimension: when Jesus arrives on the scene, hu-man society gets reordered. Drawing from Isaiah 61:1, Jesus uses the verb *euangelizō* and directly relates his gospel proclamation to the destruc-tion of societal structures that bar and limit human interactions (Luke 4:18–19). Paul explained to the (mostly Gentile) Corinthians that their financial gifts to the Jewish Christians in Judea would demonstrate their "confession of the Gospel of Christ" (2 Cor 9:13). When Paul accused Peter and his cohorts of "not acting consistently with the truth of the Gospel" (Gal 2:14), it is not because they had failed to preach the vertical redemption of the human-divine fellowship; it is because of where they were sitting at the dinner table in Antioch. By refusing to eat with Gen-tiles, Peter and other Jewish believers were doing violence to the gospel that announces not only the tearing of the Temple veil but also the tearing down of "the dividing wall" between alienated people groups (Eph 2:14[9]).

To be marked by the media legacy of the gospel, our modern-day media practices should reflect this horizontal movement from alienation

---

9. See also Ephesians 2:17 and 3:6. Though it is not very clear in the English trans-lations, in 2:17 where we read "So he came and proclaimed peace to you who were far off and peace to those who were near," the word for proclaimed is from *euangelizō*.

to fellowship among our fellow human beings and should in some way attract others to the vertical restoration available between God and us. I argued in TheoMedia Note 2 that screens can be screens, as in thin veils that hide. Social media do not guarantee relationality. If we are not careful, all this "sharing" we are doing with tweets, emails, blog posts, status updates, and online comments might amount to nothing more than being "alone together," as Sherry Turkle has recently put it. The point of her recent book is that communications technology can actually isolate more than it binds us together.[10]

The media legacy of the restorative gospel includes a vigorous resistance to screening ourselves with our screens. Our online interactions should bridge rather than replace or obscure interpersonal relationships. If the gospel is a media legacy marking who we are as God's people, then our social media practices should ultimately be grounded in the gospel-shaped motivation to draw toward others (not away from them) and to draw others toward the God who cries out into the forests—and into cyberspace—"Where are you?"

INCARNATION: JESUS AS THE "MULTIMEDIUM" OF GOD'S EMBODIED PRESENCE

We have seen that a gashed sky and a torn veil together form an *inclusio* in Mark's Gospel. Matthew has an *inclusio* as well. Drawing from Isaiah 7:14, the first evangelist records "Immanuel" as an alternative name for Jesus, a name meaning "God with us" (Matt 1:23). This idea of God's intimate proximity is echoed in the final line of Matthew's Gospel, with Jesus claiming, "I am with you always" (28:20).

So Mark's presentation of Jesus is framed with God's destruction of barriers between him and us. Matthew's presentation of Jesus frames his narrative with the assurance that God is ever with us in and through Christ. With such *inclusios*, these sacred Gospel texts are notifying their hearers and readers that the mediation between God and humanity is being reconfigured through Jesus.

The classic statement of Christ's Incarnation is found in John 1:14— "The Word became flesh." We have seen that God's word can generate galaxies, suns, and oceans. We have affirmed that the word of God is authoritative, but also relational—the humans called into being by his

10. Turkle, *Alone Together*.

authoritative speech are also personally addressed by that same speech. In Jesus, the star-forming, authoritative, and relational utterance of God was embodied in flesh and blood. The Apostle Paul writes about the work of Christ as unprecedented and beyond all imagination: "what no eye has seen, nor ear heard, nor the human heart conceived" (1 Cor 2:9; cf. Isa 64:4). Perhaps most inconceivable of all is that our God entered the human realm assuming the vulnerability of human flesh so that eyes *could* indeed see and ears hear:

> what we have *heard*, what we *have seen with our eyes*, what we have *looked at* and *touched with our hands*, concerning the word of life—this life was revealed, and we have *seen it* and testify to it, and declare to you the eternal life that was with the Father and was revealed to us—we declare to you what we have *seen* and *heard*. (1 John 1:1–3a; emphases added)

The Word of God was not just orally spoken or textually preserved in some ancient document; that Word was also tangibly, visually, and materially present.

In all his flesh and blood reality, we could say that Jesus is the "Multimedium of God." We could also understand Jesus—speaking, touching, imaging, embodying—as the most significant and the most multisensory TheoMedium of all.

There is a hole in the sky, and all heaven has broken loose at the arrival of God the Son. Though other TheoMedia we have studied have offered powerful glimpses of the identity of God the Father, in their revelatory and communicative capacities they pale in comparison to the TheoMedium of the Incarnate Christ: "No one has ever seen God. It is God the only Son, who is close to the Father's heart, who has made him known" (John 1:18). And the face-to-face immediacy of Jesus signaled the possibility of *un*-mediation in the divine-human fellowship.

In embodying the full revelation of Israel's God, the TheoMedia we have examined from the Old Testament have been fulfilled, expanded, or replaced by Jesus. Creation: Jesus is the co-author of God's "dazzling theater"[11] who entered its realm to bring the salvation for which it groans. Words: Jesus is the ultimate Word who took on flesh. Visions and dreams: Jesus haunted the dreams of Pilate's wife (Matt 27:19) and he is the ladder Jacob saw centuries earlier in that night vision (John 1:51). Tabernacle:

---

11. As mentioned earlier in chapter 5, this phrase is from Calvin, *Institutes*, 61.

Jesus himself has now come and "tabernacled"[12] among us (John 1:14). Temple: his resurrected body has become the new nexus between heaven and earth (John 2:20–21). The sacrificial system: Jesus offered himself as the "once for all" sacrifice that removed all sins (Heb 10:10; cf. John 1:29). That bronze serpent had been lifted up for dying eyes to behold for salvation, but "as Moses lifted up the serpent in the wilderness, so must the Son of Man be lifted up, that whoever believes in him may have eternal life" (John 3:14). As Moses and the elders ate and drank with the living God on Sinai (Exod 24:9–11), so the disciples ate and drank with Jesus whose body was given up as true food, whose blood was offered as true drink (Matt 26:2–5; Mark 14:12–21; Luke 22:7–13; John 6:52–58).

Creation, God's Word, Tabernacle, Temple, visions and dreams (even the bronze serpent!)—as the Incarnate Word of God, Jesus has fulfilled all these media forms in their verbal, visual, visionary, material, acoustic, and tangible capacities. As the Multimedium of God, and the ultimate TheoMedium, Jesus demonstrates that God engages our entire sensorium.

Think of his media practices. Those of us with red-letter versions of the Gospels are quite visually aware that Jesus was strongly invested in the oral media practices of preaching and teaching. Yet he also communicated through touch:

> . . . He had cured many, so that all who had diseases pressed upon him to touch him (Mark 3:10).

> . . . She said, "If I but touch his clothes, I will be made well." (Mark 5:28).

> People were bringing even infants to him that he might touch them (Luke 18:15).

Though Jesus "never wrote a word of his teaching, nor did he ever command anyone else to do so"[13] (at least as far as we know!), there is an account of Jesus writing or scribbling in the dirt (John 8:6);[14] and it certainly seems as though he was literate ("He stood up to read . . ."—Luke 4:16;

12. The Greek word *skēnoō* in John 1:14 (rendered "lived" in the NRSV) draws from to the imagery of the Tabernacle, the Greek for which is *skēnē*. See Anderson, "Towards a Theology of the Tabernacle and Its Furniture," and Lincoln, *The Gospel According to Saint John*, 104.

13. Fowler, "Why Everything We Know About the Bible Is Wrong," 7.

14. Though I should note that this account in John 8 is not found in the earliest manuscripts of the Gospel.

"How does this man know his letters, having never been taught?"—John 7:15[15]).[16] Jesus also communicated through gestures, the most haunting of which had to have been the silent turning of his eyes to Peter after the rooster's crow (Luke 22:61); and the most enduring of which was the extending of bread and wine over an intimate supper.

We also know that he engages the entire sensorium because so many of his miracles included healings of sensory impairment. Indeed, the fact that the deaf could now hear and the blind now see were understood by Jesus himself as central elements of his messianic mission (Luke 7:22). As far as smell and taste, remember the fragrance of ointment spilled out for his death-coronation, and the commands to take and eat the bread and to raise the cup of new life to your lips.

The four canonical Gospel narratives are dense with this sort of multisensory language. Luke describes the sound of angel choirs on a not-so-silent night. Matthew pictures the brightness of a star that caught the Magi's eye, then forces our ears to hear the raucous sobs of mothers lamenting the execution of their little boys. Mark would have us hear the shriek of demons in flight and the sudden hush of howling winds. John helps us hear the tinkling of coins smattering across the stone Temple floor as sheep bleat and cattle groan at the fury of overturning tables. Also in John, see the emerging silhouette of a dead man called forth from his grave. Hear the threefold "I AM" that sends an armed posse tumbling in Gethsemane. Feel the warmth of a charcoal fire, lift your ear to detect that rooster crowing in the distance, then hear the bitter sounds of a grown man weeping in the night. See the placard nailed to a vertical crossbeam scripted with "Jesus of Nazareth, the King of the Jews." Mark would have our vision dimmed by the swarming clouds blocking noonday sun. Our ears are to be filled with the weeping of women on the hill. And never forget—how could it be forgotten?—that haunting plea of "*Eloi, eloi, lema sabachthani?*" Then—if we can bear it—let us lift our wearied ears to that awful death cry in the daytime darkness.

15. This is my translation. The Greek makes specific reference to what probably amounts to alphabet letters, though the NRSV reads, "How does this man have such learning, when he has never been taught?"

16. Fowler seems to believe that Jesus was illiterate, quickly pointing out that scribbling in the dirt does not necessarily amount to writing and suggesting that Luke's portrayal of Jesus reading may be a projection of Luke's own literacy ("Why Everything We Know About the Bible Is Wrong," 7). I really appreciate Fowler's essay, but I wonder if his understanding of Jesus as illiterate is a projection of his criticisms of print culture.

But let us also notice the dawn's light stretching the shadow of a rolled away stone as another voice is heard nearby: "He has been raised; he is not here."

The sights, sounds, tastes, materiality, and smells of the Gospels are produced by a collision of the holy with the earthly as the Word became flesh. "Where are you?" God has called out. And then in Jesus he himself announced to the world, "Here am *I*."

THE INCARNATION AS A MEDIA LEGACY FOR THE CHURCH

Just as the medium and message of the gospel informs our media practices, so also does the Incarnation of Christ. As argued above, the gospel is (for the most part) a verbal communications medium. The Incarnation is a *material*—"corporeal," to be more specific—means of communications by which God makes himself so immediate and tangible that mediation seems virtually eliminated. And this movement of the Incarnation from distance to relational nearness is paradigmatic for the church. Here is how.

For one, the embodiment of God places communicative emphasis on the multisensory experience of physical presence. If God himself puts such stock in face-to-face physicality, then surely this emphasis is to be reflected in Christian communication habits. The proximity of physical presence is preferable over distanced communication via social media. Now, this claim requires nuance and clarification—undeniably, there are times when face-to-face interaction is simply not possible for human communication partners. It can even be unhelpful. As we will find in the upcoming TheoMedia Note "St. Paul and Canonized Social Media," the great Apostle once avoided a face-to-face meeting with the Corinthians because he knew it would threaten rather than help their mutual fellowship! Some social media interactions can become dangerous or scandalous when they become face-to-face, as when online flirtation leads to abuse or to an affair when conducted offline. But in the big picture of the church's media practices, the Incarnation suggests that embodied presence is better than physical distance when it comes to our communication with one another.

But the Incarnation also encourages the church's presence in the (seemingly) disembodied realm of the Internet.

The Incarnation is about God reaching to the furthest extent possible by the most unsuspecting means to establish and sustain relationships. This surely means that the church should infiltrate the sphere of the Internet. I am not saying that all Christians should go online. Collectively, however, if the church is to embrace "incarnational ministry," that means we will be willing to relationally extend ourselves into any and all realms for the sake of the gospel.

The phrase "incarnational ministry" has to be used carefully so as not to detract from the singularity and uniqueness of the Incarnation (capital "I") of Christ. Obviously, none of us can perform "Incarnational ministry" with the capital "I"—we will not graciously opt to take on flesh as gods reaching out to our hapless subjects. It is not the *function* of the Incarnation that is paradigmatic for Christians, but its *disposition*.[17] All of us can *embody*, so to speak, the incarnational disposition of reaching out to the furthest extent possible to secure face-to-face intimacy. Just as God sent Jesus, so he sends us (John 20:21). Though God's embodied presence within the thick and muck of human reality was unique, it establishes a certain pattern and perspective to be emulated by Christians in "incarnational ministry" (lower case "i"). I have friends for whom this pattern and perspective of the Incarnation have led them into dark and foreboding places to embrace the hardship, pain, and joys of fellow human beings trapped in poverty.

All of us, however, can learn from the Incarnation when it comes to how we use the media of our digital age. God was willing to take on flesh to reach us. Some of us (though perhaps not all!) should be willing to take on Twitter handles to reach others. Yet there is also something important about this movement from distance to physical nearness; the horizontal dimensions of the gospel of an Incarnate Lord certainly call for social media practices marked by a willingness to enter the cyberworld, but also a willingness to see those online interactions develop into offline, face-to-face friendships when possible.

17. Even though I am arguing that the Christological function of the Incarnation is unique and singular, I would certainly want to affirm the patristic teaching that the Incarnation is fundamentally *participatory*—Jesus participates in our flesh that we might participate in his divine life. In this sense, there is indeed a "reverse paradigm" at work, one can say, in that Jesus enters our life and we enter his. The space or scope required for satisfactory nuancing is simply not available in this chapter (or in this footnote!).

WHEN THE INCARNATION AND COMMUNICATIONS TECHNOLOGY MEET

I began thinking of my own media practices in light of these incarnational principles when I re-entered university student ministry in 2008. I was not very keen on signing up for Facebook (I like to impress people by not being impressed with fads and trends). But I did so because I knew this would help me engage students, meeting them "where they are," if you will, in the world of social media.

I was also averse to texting. It seemed highly impersonal. Email and phone calls, however, just did not work anymore. Being out of campus ministry for just a couple years, I was finding that my emails seemed to disappear into thin cyber-air and my calls were consigned to slow deaths in voicemail inboxes. However, if I sent a text I would get an instant reply (not only is texting cheap, but you can do it in class—two plusses for university students). I would also hear back quite soon if I posted on someone's Facebook page.

I did not want to send texts and post Facebook comments. Neither communication forms felt very conducive for sharing about Christ's work in our lives. At first, I resisted using the media preferences of those under my pastoral care.

God demonstrates a different perspective in the Incarnation. He was willing to meet us on our own communicative level, sending Jesus as the Word made flesh.

I began using these less intimate media forms, but with a loose strategy based on the incarnational movement from distance to physical presence. I tried to use my texts and Facebook comments not as substitutes for face-to-face communication, but as means of maintaining friendship and ensuring eventual face-to-face interaction. Me: "Jordan! Hope that test went well. Coffee tomorrow at Primavera? 11 am?" Or maybe, "Leah, are you coming to the service tonight? Let's catch up!"

So the Incarnation pushes me to extend my relational reach even into the realm of digital communications. Simultaneously, it also encourages me to be always moving in a relational direction from distance to nearness, ultimately hoping to engage my friends in face-to-face interaction over coffee or a meal.

In spite of the relational direction pressured by the Incarnation, we have to acknowledge that physical presence in our relationships is something that is becoming increasingly more difficult to manage. Families and friends are becoming more and more geographically dispersed all over the globe. Media technology helpfully affords us the opportunity to practice the horizontal dimension of the gospel and maintain these relationships in our society's constant state of diaspora. (Now that my wife and I live across an ocean from our families, the face-to-face experience my kids get with their grandparents is usually *virtual*, not physical, as we sit in front of the webcam). Along with geographical distance, disability and illness can limit our interaction with others. Those who are unable to attend worship services or travel to a nearby coffee shop can experience Christian fellowship through social media.

It is problematic, though, when our technologies excuse those of who can get out of the house from building new friendships in our immediate physical locale. Not all social media interactions require a movement from online to offline. Part of the beauty of online communication is that it enables relational interaction without geographical or physical proximity. There is no way we can have face-to-face meetings with all our Twitter followers, blog readers, or Facebook "friends"; but when it comes to the folks in our neighborhood, local churches, schools, and workplaces, our interactions through media technologies could enact a trajectory moving from disembodied online interaction toward physical nearness. Generally speaking (again, see the TheoMedia Note on Paul for legitimate impracticalities of "face-to-faceness"), we should honor Christ's Incarnation by infiltrating multiple communications realms but with a high valuation of embodied presence, refusing to treat social media as a fitting replacement for face-to-face interaction, but enjoying its capabilities for enabling interaction with those who are not across the table or in our living room.

TheoMedia Note 8

Paul and Canonized Social Media

Two Lessons

"The biblical material is surprisingly unselfconscious about the tying together of a church by something so fragile as letter writing. . . . Christianity is an epistolary faith, based on writings to and from friends who know each other in the flesh and others who do not—yet are not for that reason any less part of the body of Christ."

—JASON BYASSEE[1]

In the last TheoMedia Note we learned from John the Baptist about modern-day celebrity culture. Here we look to Paul to learn about modern-day social media. The point here is not to argue that the great Apostle would have had a Facebook account or that he would have maintained a theoblog. It is probably obvious by this point that I find those conclusions tenuous. We can, however, find in Paul's prolific ministry of correspondence some principles that can govern our use of new media.

We probably learn more about Paul's writing ministry from 2 Corinthians than from anywhere else because he openly states some of his communications strategies. The situation into which he is writing is tense. His relationship with the Corinthians has been on the brink of collapse. Since Paul lacks the eloquence of a true "influencer" and looks bad

---

1. Byassee, "Practicing Virtue with Social Media."

on stage, some high-flying celebrity types ("super-apostles") have turned the congregation in Corinth against him (2 Cor 10:10; 11:5).

Here is the first lesson we can take from this situation: face-to-face interaction is not always best. For some readers this claim may seem a bit audacious. We are repeatedly warned (even in this book!) that social media can be used as an excuse for avoiding real intimacy. We find elsewhere in the New Testament that the ancient social media format of the epistle was regarded as inferior to actually seeing someone up close and personal: "Although I have much to write to you, I would rather not use paper and ink; instead I hope to come to you and talk with you face to face, so that our joy may be complete" (2 John 12).[2]

But Paul did not just send letters because they were practical. On at least one occasion in his relationship with the Corinthians, he deliberately sent a letter rather than showing up in person. The reason? The strain between him and this beloved congregation was so volatile that he knew a face-to-face encounter would do more harm than good: "I made up my mind not to make you another painful visit" (2 Cor 2:1). Had he done so, things could have gotten ugly: "it was to spare you that I did not come again to Corinth" (1:23).

Paul was not being evasive. He was not trying to avoid the inconvenience of dealing with real flesh and blood folks. His decision to write a letter rather than make an appearance was because he knew that a face-to-face encounter could have burned all his relational bridges with the Corinthian church. This letter is now lost to us, but it was penned "out of much distress and anguish of heart and with many tears, not to cause you pain, but to let you know the abundant love that I have for you" (2 Cor 2:4). So Paul employed social media not to get out of sticky situations, but to preserve the sort of face-to-face fellowship he hoped to continue enjoying. All of Paul's media practices have to be understood within the context of his "ministry of reconciliation" (5:18). His use of communications technology was entirely devoted to bridging relationships, not distancing them even if that meant delaying a visit.

The second lesson about social media from Paul's communication practices is that our identity must be consistent, whether we are interacting face-to-face or online. We have seen in TheoMedia Note 3 that screen-based communication offers the temptation to be someone we are not. One of the perennial struggles in social media is the inconsistency

2. See also 3 John 14 and 1 Thess 2:17; 3:10.

of our online persona with our offline selves. Paul's celebrity detractors actually accuse Paul of this sort of duplicity: "His letters are weighty and strong, but his bodily presence is weak, and his speech contemptible" (2 Cor 10:10; cf. 10:1). Here is how Paul responds—"Let such people understand that what we say by letter when absent, we will also do when present" (10:11).

There was no misrepresentation in Paul's use of ancient social media. He did not put on a fake, sugary smile after having bashed someone in a letter. His mediated presence was consistent with his face-to-face presence.

Let's go and do likewise.

Chapter 11

Crucifixion
Cross-visuality and the Eucharist

For our sake he was crucified under Pontius Pilate; he suffered death and was buried . . . .

—FROM THE NICENE CREED

For the Master of the Universe, whose suffering world I do not comprehend. For dreams of horror, for nights of waiting, for memories of death, for the love I have for you, for all the things I remember, and for all the things I should remember but have forgotten, for all these I created this painting—an observant Jew working on a crucifixion because there was no aesthetic mold in his own religious tradition into which he could pour a painting of ultimate anguish and torment.

—FROM CHAIM POTOK'S *MY NAME IS ASHER LEV*[1]

Throughout this book I keep referring to the multimedia theophany at Sinai. The visual spectacle and aural cacophony of God at the giving of the Law was seared into the collective memory of Israel's senses. No one

1. Potok, *My Name Is Asher Lev*, 287–88.

present that day around the mountain's base could forget such a scene: swirling clouds, exploding lightning, the thundering voice of the Deity. The mist and dreadful darkness obscured the full sight of his being, but there was no mistaking that the booming voice was the Lord's. As Moses reminded them later: "You heard the sound of words but saw no form; there was only a voice" (Deut 4:12).

It is the most definitive scene of divine self-revelation in the Old Testament.

God had communicated with Moses on that same mountain not long beforehand through the eye-catching wonder of a burning bush. Mount Sinai was also where God revealed himself in quite a different way to Elijah, through the thinness of a "still small voice" (1 Kgs 19:12 ASV).

Other heights deserve mention as important locations for the multimedia self-revelation of God's identity. Before Elijah heard that striking quietness of God's voice on Sinai, he had just witnessed God's holy fire consuming his offering on Mount Carmel. There was also Mount Zion where the gleaming Temple was built and then rebuilt. In the New Testament, Matthew gives us the Sermon on the Mount where Jesus, Moses-like, delivered a fresh interpretation of the Law. On the Mount of Transfiguration Moses and Elijah shockingly made cameo appearances, yet as subordinates to the radiant Christ.

There is another height important for the multimedia revelation of God: a low hill called "The Place of a Skull."

THE SIGHTS AND SOUNDS OF THE CRUCIFIED GOD

The locals knew that place by the Aramaic title, "Golgotha." And on this site of divine self-revelation what we *see* is a man dying naked and nailed to a wooden post. What we *hear* is the coarse yell of his dying shout. The sights and sounds from Golgotha differ starkly from those on Sinai in Exodus 19.

They are nonetheless the sights and sounds of Israel's God.

On Sinai, Israel "saw no form" but heard the "sound of words." But on Calvary, there was a form visible to the eye. This form was not enclosed within the swirling darkness but visible below the cloud cover. It was the form of God crucified. And there was the sound of words:

> *Eloi, eloi, lema sabachthani?* (Mark 15:34; cf. Matt 27:46).

Father, into your hands I commend my spirit (Luke 23:46).

It is finished (John 19:30).

Sounds are events. They happen, and then they are gone.[2] According to theologian Stephen Webb, since "speech leaves no trace in space . . . it is the perfect medium for a God who does not want to be seen."[3] But in the Gospels, we find that God *does* want to be seen. On Calvary, he is seen as the epitome of abject misery and humiliation. With that "cry of dereliction" ("My God, my God, why have you forsaken me?"), it may well be that Mark and Matthew portray Jesus dying as the Son of God who cannot see or hear his Father. Perhaps a divine media silence is underway. Though God spoke to Jesus at his baptism and thundered an affectionate endorsement of Jesus on the Mount of Transfiguration, the heavens were deathly quiet during the Crucifixion.

Was Jesus himself crying out "Where are you?" to a God now hiding among the trees . . . or, as it were, among the clouds?

The second evangelist would have us look and listen with the Roman centurion who stood at the foot of the cross. His eyes and ears were fixed not on the clouds above but on Jesus's final cry and ghastly sight.[4] In the face of heaven's ironclad silence, we stare into the dying face of the One who has entered our fog among the trees, the One who has embraced the divine-human distance in order to restore it forever.

That's when the sound of ripping could be heard in the Temple.

We cannot recapture the sounds from that day. No high tech recording equipment was near at hand. We can, however, hear the voice of the Crucified in the church's reading of the Passion Narratives.

And we can be visually haunted by the image of the cross.

The visual emblem of our faith comprises two perpendicular bars. Various denominations and traditions throughout church history have appropriated this imagery in different ways. I am not endorsing or condemning here the Orthodox use of crucifixion scenes in iconography or the Catholic use of the crucifix. My point is simply that, for Christians, permanently anchored within our field of vision is the symbol of the cross encompassing meaning of unfathomable breadth, height, and depth, and

2. Ong, *Orality and Literacy*, 32.

3. Webb, *The Divine Voice*, 45.

4. In Matthew's account, the centurion is specifically focused on the earthquake and other goings-on (cf. Matt 27:54 and Mark 15:39).

representing the character of a God who can rumble and crush mountains with his weight, yet allows the physical weight of his own incarnate flesh to droop from nails hammered into a beam.

Is this the same God? Are Jesus and the God of the Old Testament compatible?

Along with the holy majesty of the Sinai scene—so poignantly unlike the holy misery of Golgotha—remember the face-to-face wrestling match with Jacob (Gen 32:22–32), recall the tender imagery of a shepherd cradling a baby lamb in his bosom (Isa 40:11), and consider the maternal imagery portraying God as a mother looking with compassion on her nursing infant (Isa 49:15). We see throughout the Old Testament that God has this impulse to reach out to us, to touch us, to get into our lives. He can be just as tender as a lovesick mother and can even make his presence approachable through the mysterious mediation of an angelic figure. And let us not forget that although Jesus dies the death of a lowly slave, his transfiguration occasioned fear, and from his face fled demon and storm. The theophany of Sinai and the death on Calvary are manifestations of the same tender and terrifying Triune God: "The identity of God—who God is—is revealed as much in self-abasement and service as it is in exaltation and rule. The God who is high can also be low, because God is God not in seeking his own advantage but in self-giving."[5]

MEDIA LEGACIES OF THE CRUCIFIXION: CROSS-VISUALITY AND CRUCIFORM MEDIA PRACTICES

This self-giving nature of our exalted Creator, so vividly depicted in the emblem of the cross, is to mark our own lives. Like the Incarnation, Christ's crucifixion is paradigmatic for Christians. There are limitations to the degree that we can emulate Christ's death, of course—just as we do not take on flesh and enter the created realm as a glorious deity, we cannot die the one death that liberates sin-shackled humanity. These singular Christological events in history cannot be and need not be repeated, though we most certainly *participate* in the Incarnation and crucifixion of Jesus. As we embrace the disposition of the Incarnation, extending ourselves as far as possible to penetrate relational boundaries, so also can we embrace the crucifixion's disposition of self-giving and self-emptying.

---

5. Bauckham, "God Crucified," 45.

The great Christological hymn in Philippians 2:6–11 that describes Jesus's debasement through crucifixion and then subsequent exaltation is provided by Paul to encourage humility and self-sacrifice on behalf of the church. Note the preceding verse: "Let the same mind be in you that was in Christ Jesus" (Phil 2:5). In other words, adopt the mentality of the One who deserved the highest of praise yet died for others like a wanton fool. The cross of Jesus's crucifixion is an image that represents a way of life.[6]

The gospel pronouncement is a *verbal* media legacy for the church and the Incarnation a *material/corporeal* media legacy for the church. The symbol of the cross is a *visual* media legacy for the church. We proclaim orally the vertical and horizontal good news of the gospel message, that a new King has come and died on vertical and horizontal beams to invalidate the media legacy of Satan's word twisting in Eden. The visual symbol of the cross, however, is so intertwined with the verbal message of the gospel that Paul understood his preaching as the "word of the cross" (1 Cor 1:18 ESV): "When I came to you, brothers and sisters, I did not come proclaiming the mystery of God to you in lofty words or wisdom. For I decided to know nothing among you except Jesus Christ, and him crucified" (1 Cor 2:1–2).

This cross-infused message must shape our media practices and interactions in the digital age. As we look to the Incarnation that urges our relational extension into the lives of others, we also take up a figurative cross, a visual symbol emblematic of a self-giving God. This image reminds us that our media practices are to be selfless and shaped by self-giving interactions. Our media ethic should be describable by the term "cruciform"—cross-shaped.[7]

What would it mean for us to embrace a "cruciform" media ethic? For starters, we can certainly say this: no more embittered remarks in the comment streams; no more self-centered blog posts promoting our online significance; no more vain status updates; no more tricky stratagems for beefing up our pool of followers simply for the sake of augmenting our self-importance.

6. I know that there has been heated debate over whether or not this Christological hymn is provided as a way of demonstrating the uniqueness of Jesus or as a way of presenting Jesus as a model to be emulated. Philippians 2:5 certainly seems to confirm the latter. I side with those who find both purposes at play.

7. On the concept of Christians embracing a crucifixion-shaped life, see Gorman's study *Cruciformity*.

Look, I know the lines are fuzzy. I am just wanting to convey that our activity online with social media is subject to the same ethical standards as our offline interactions. The cross of Christ opposes self-orientation in any and every setting, online or offline. The motivations behind my status updates are often suspect. My heart vainly flutters a bit when there is a sudden spike in the traffic on my blog. At times I resonate a bit too happily with that exclamation mark when Twitter informs me, "You were mentioned in a Tweet!" The point here is that Christ's call to selflessness, visually depicted in the cross, extends to any and all realms, even the new realm of the Internet. We need to carry the determinative force of the optical medium of the cross symbol into that realm and comport our media practices accordingly.

Throughout this large section on Media Christology, I am suggesting that the church understand media through the person of Jesus and through the ancient media practices his saving work encourages. Our verbal interactions are to be informed by the verbal proclamation of the gospel. And if we are going to inhabit a visual culture, then we should draw on the visual media legacies of the cross.

Should we actually visualize Jesus's death as represented in the cross symbol? Unlike the highly graphic rendering on offer in films like Mel Gibson's *The Passion of the Christ*, the written Gospel accounts give sparse visual details about Jesus' torture and execution.[8] And curiously, early Christians did not produce art directly depicting the awful scene on Golgotha.[9] So to what extent does scripture actually warrant a visual piety of the cross?

Some sort of cross-visuality is affirmed when Paul writes to the Galatians that "it was before your eyes that Jesus Christ was publicly exhibited as crucified" (Gal 3:1 ESV). Now, the Galatians were not present at Golgotha on that fateful day. But Paul's prior preaching ministry had

8. See the balanced and thoughtful reflections of biblical scholars on the film in Corley and Webb, eds., *Jesus and Mel Gibson's The Passion of the Christ*.

9. Besides a rough, secondy-century graffito (apparently from the hand of a pagan mocking Christianity) and two engraved gems from the fourth century, "the earliest known representations of Jesus crucified date to the early fifth century, and are extremely rare until the seventh"—Jensen, *Understanding Early Christian Art*, 131. It is likely, however, that early images of a lamb and of Abraham's offering of Isaac were intended to metaphorically depict Christ's death. See Jensen's entire chapter "Images of the Suffering Redeemer" for an intensive overview of the reasons scholars have offered as to why the crucifixion, so prominent in early Christian texts, was largely absent in Christian material culture until the early medieval period (130–55).

presented such a "vivid, verbal portrait of the event of Jesus' crucifixion"[10] that the scene could be understood as having occurred "before your eyes."[11] The imagery is orally produced. Yet the visuality of the cross is so important for Paul that he correlates the Galatians' forsaking of the gospel with their forgetfulness of this imagery.

Attending to the visuality of the cross also seems affirmed by the repeated calls in John's Gospel to "Behold" Jesus as the Crucified: "Behold the Lamb of God who takes away the sin of the world!" (John 1:29; cf. 1:36). The same visual command is echoed by Pilate with "Behold the man!" and "Behold your King!" at the moment when the Passover lambs were being sacrificed in the Temple (John 19:5, 14). The fourth evangelist seems to be calling out to us, "Look! Look at the Crucified who is Lamb, Man, and divine King." And we should not forget that when John the Seer saw Jesus in his vision on Patmos, the description provided is that of "a Lamb standing, as though it had been slain" (Rev 5:6). These images are constructed verbally, but the death of Jesus is certainly being presented in visual terms.

Crosses dangle around our necks. They are positioned in prominent sight in our churches and engraved into pulpits and altars. Sometimes they adorn the walls of our homes. Every day, my walk into work requires that I pass by an eleventh-century cathedral, its foundation walls laid out in cruciform outline. The imagery of the cross has historically saturated the visual space of most Christians, in worship, art, and architecture. Are our eyes trained to notice this optical medium today? Have we the faith and courage to comport our lives to its message?

THE FOCAL MEDIA PRACTICE OF THE EUCHARIST

The cross of Christ is not just to be appropriated visually. Jesus actually demanded that we practice a multisensory engagement of his crucifixion when he said, "Do this in remembrance of me" (Luke 22:19).

---

10. De Boer, *Galatians*, 171.

11. The verb translated "publicly exhibited" is actually chirographic (referring to handwriting) and textual in scope: *prographō*. Literally, it means "to write before" (with "before" meaning physically "in front of" or meaning temporally as in "earlier"—see De Boer, *Galatians,* 171). The meaning may well be both, but some sort of physical "in front of"—and thus an emphasis on visuality—is clearly implied by the phrase "before your eyes." Again, for other images used by Paul, see Heath, *Paul's Visual Piety.*

Though the perpendicular bars of the cross are not the primary optical focus in the Eucharist, the snapping and crumbling of unleavened bread and the outpouring of wine depict before our eyes the death of Christ's incarnate body and the flow of his life-giving blood. The Lord's Supper as practiced in Christian worship is a tactile, olfactory, optical, oral, aural, and material celebration of the most radical communications move on behalf of God. Through the Incarnation of Christ, God became seeable, hearable, touchable . . . and therefore also *killable*. That death is paradigmatic in terms of ethics (how we live), but also effective in terms of salvation. The multimedia experience of administering and receiving the bread and cup honors the multisensory way in which Christ arrived on the scene and died on our behalf. Church traditions vary in how this sacrament is understood and practiced, but looking to Jesus as the crucified and participating in the meal commemorating his death and its effects are ritual media practices that shape and define the identity of all Christians.[12]

To conclude this chapter, let's recall that Jesus appeared and upended the TheoMedia of the Old Testament. Divinity came among us and engaged the full range of human senses with the fullness of God. Seeing the imagery of the cross and experiencing the multimedia event of the Lord's Supper remind us that God entered our realm and walked, talked, dined, and suffered with us.

Then they buried him.

12. On the concept of ritual media, see Carey's essay "A Cultural Approach to Communication," 13–36.

Chapter 12

Resurrection & Ascension
Word-media, Baptism, and Christ as Mediator

... On the third day he rose again in accordance with the Scriptures; he
ascended into heaven and is seated at the right hand of the Father ....

—FROM THE NICENE CREED

Long ago God spoke to our ancestors in many and various ways by the prophets, but in these last days he has spoken to us by a Son, whom he appointed
heir of all things, through whom he also created the worlds. He is the reflection of God's glory and the exact imprint of God's very being, and he sustains
all things by his powerful word. When he had made purification for sins, he sat
down at the right hand of the Majesty on high.

—HEBREWS 1:1–3

There is no media silence like the silence of death. Nothing is quieter.
No communicative breach is more definitive. Death is the ultimate act of
relational closure.

While serving as a pastor, I once helped dig a grave in our church's cemetery for someone's urn. After the family members placed the remains of their loved one in the hole, we filled the empty space with earth. When the prayer and scripture reading were finished, I slammed the back end of the shovel to pack down the loose red dirt. Dust to dust, ashes to ashes. Finality. No relational distance is wider than that which is symbolized by a dirt-filled grave.[1]

Or a sealed up tomb.

And that is precisely why no sound is more disruptive in a sin-plagued cosmos than the voice of a man once dead. No sound is more volatile in a death-governed world than the sound of man recently buried and now speaking. No sound is more eucatastrophic than the living speech of a death-silenced loved one.

Yet you never know what sort of thing an escapee from the tomb might say . . .

THE SIGHTS AND SOUNDS OF THE RISEN LORD

"Do not hold on to me."

This is what the risen Jesus tells the first eyewitness of his resurrection in John's Gospel (20:17). In a curious case of mistaken identity, Mary Magdalene assumes he is the gardener. Recognition comes when she hears him call out her name. Surely the most natural reaction to the shivering, explosive joy of eucatastrophe is to grasp the feet of the King you thought dead. Just the other day Mary had heard his final breath. She had seen with her own wet eyes the blood and water spill out of his corpse onto Golgotha's dirt. And now there he stood alive and well. His inhaling and exhaling, the pumping of his heart, the warmth of his skin—they collectively served as a damning protest against the reign of Death.

"Do not hold on to me."

Something is different. Before his death, the Incarnate Christ was so tangibly accessible. In these post-resurrection scenes, Jesus can still be touched, but not in a way that will confine and therefore threaten the impending event of his Ascension (as John's Gospel takes particular care to highlight). The explanation given for the command "Do not hold on

1. Dr. Tim Hutchings has pointed out to me, however, that some communicative connection with lost loved ones is maintained through a variety of means such as visiting a gravesite. There are also online means of staying connected to the deceased. See Hutchings, "Wiring Death."

to me" is that "I have not yet ascended to the Father" (20:17). Jesus is indicating to Mary that his bodily presence is temporary. So, to honor the imminent departure: "Do not hold on to me."

Had Mary ignored that command and gripped the risen Christ with all her might, keeping him within grasp would have been tricky. On this side of the tomb, Jesus's bodily existence was hard to keep up with and, as his tomb could attest, hard to contain. Locked doors did not keep him out any more than a sealed grave could keep him in.

The Incarnation affirmed God's inclination toward physical, tangible means of interaction and communication. Since Jesus did not return from his grave as a disembodied ghost (see Luke 24:29), this emphasis on corporeality is verified in the resurrection. To convince them of his physicality, Jesus had the disciples place their hands on his wounds and he even ate food before their eyes (everyone knows that ghosts do not eat broiled fish).

He could also vanish and reappear without warning. Richard Hays puts it succinctly when he writes that the Risen Christ is "both palpable and elusive."[2] As we are about to see, this palpability and elusiveness signaled a new era of TheoMedia.

THE SENSORY DEMANDS OF THOMAS: THE MEDIA OF BELIEF . . . ?

Have you ever had that experience of non-experience, when something extraordinary happened among your friends the one moment you were not around? That is what happened to the disciple named Thomas. Pretty much the best thing that has ever happened in human history took place one evening among his friends, and he missed it.

The other disciples were hiding in a room with the doors barred shut when Jesus was suddenly found in their midst (where there is an empty tomb, there is no point in a locked room). The cross-wounds were placed on visible display for the disciples and then Jesus did something rather awkward. He breathed on them (John 20:22). But this was no social blunder. This was nothing less than the formation of a new humanity.

After breathing on them, Jesus said, "Receive the Holy Spirit." It is not the first time in Scripture God breathed onto someone: "Then the LORD God formed man from the dust of the ground, and breathed into

2. Hays, "Reading Scripture in Light of the Resurrection," 236.

his nostrils the breath of life; and the man became a living being" (Gen 2:7). In John 20, the resurrected Christ is reenacting Creation. A new genesis is underway with the regeneration of a brand new race of human beings (see also Ezek 37:1–14).

Jesus had exhaled his final breath on the cross. Water and blood spilled onto the ground from the spear hole in the side of his corpse. Just as God formed Eve from the "side" of Adam, the church is formed from the life-giving water and blood flowing from the "side" of Jesus.[3] In a garden on the first day of the week (an echo of Eden and Genesis 1–2?), those dead lungs sucked in air once more, and then the Co-Creator Christ exhaled his Spirit into the disciples.

Thomas missed the whole thing.

No matter how energetically the disciples tried to convince their comrade that Jesus was alive, had stood among them, had breathed into them, Thomas refused to believe. Their oral testimony was not enough for him. Thomas demanded visual and tactile proof: "Unless I *see* the mark of the nails in his hands, and *put my finger* in the mark of the nails and *my hand* in his side, I will not believe" (John 20:25, emphases added). For Thomas, hearing is not believing. The media of belief for this "doubting" disciple are *seeing* and *feeling*.

My children feel as though they got the short end of the chronological stick by being born after Jesus's resurrection and Ascension. They want to see Jesus visibly, to feel his hugging arms, to hear his voice telling them at night while Daddy is asleep that there is no reason to worry about that creepy noise coming from under the bed. They envy those lucky little kids in the Gospel accounts that got to sit on his knee to receive his blessing. Forget the Roman tax system, the hard agrarian lifestyle, and the absence of protective child labor laws—my children would take Galilee, 23 AD, over our home in England, 2013, any day of the week. Like Thomas, they insist on having the Incarnate Christ front and center, touchable, seeable, hearable.

My kids have not had their sensory demands granted. Thomas did. He was soon standing face-to-face with his resurrected Lord. Opportunity was given for Thomas to see and even to touch the death wounds when Jesus reappeared and offered him the multisensory experience he had deemed requisite for belief. After Thomas made the climactic confession of John's Gospel—"my Lord and my God!" (20:28)—Jesus then shifted

3. For this scene in John 20, see Thompson, "The Breath of Life," 69–78. For the Eden imagery in John 20, see Hoskyns, "Genesis I-III and St John's Gospel," 210–18.

emphasis away from sensory experience: "Blessed are those *who have not seen* and yet have come to believe" (John 20:29; emphasis added).

Anticipating how his bodily absence would affect his disciples, Jesus had explained the night before his death that his departure would actually be to their favor: "It is to your advantage that I go away, for if I do not go away, the Advocate will not come to you; but if I go, I will send him to you" (John 16:7). The vacuum of Jesus's bodily absence will be filled by the indwelling presence of his Spirit (the "Advocate"), whom Jesus breathed into his disciples that evening when Thomas was elsewhere. Contrary to how my children sometimes feel about missing out on Jesus's bodily life on earth, I tell them we live in advantageous times because now we can enjoy the indwelling company of Christ's Spirit. And when we believe without the multisensory experiences Thomas demanded for himself, we are "blessed."

Seeing and touching are not necessarily the Christ–sanctioned media of belief.

WORD AND SPIRIT: THE REPRIORITIZATION OF SPEECH AND TEXTS

Immediately after Jesus designates as "blessed" those who believe without sensory experience, the narrator of the fourth Gospel suddenly jumps from behind the literary curtain into the center stage spotlight to speak to us.

His special message is that although many signs have been performed by Jesus, "these are written so that you may come to believe that Jesus is the Messiah, the Son of God, and that through believing you may have life in his name" (John 20:31). "These are written"—this is the language of textuality. It is also the language of the work of the Spirit, because Jesus told his disciples that when the Advocate comes he "will teach you everything, and remind you of all that I have said to you" (John 14:26).[4]

John's account of the sending of the Spirit, the doubting of Thomas, and the narrator's personal note to the Gospel's hearers/readers collectively affirm that oral proclamation and textual testimony are once more to be recognized as the governing TheoMedia for the newly formed

4. And also: "The Spirit of truth, who proceeds from the Father, he will bear witness about me" (John 15:26 ESV).

people of God. And this verbal media would derive from the inspiration of the Spirit (John 16:12–15).

As the embodiment of God—seeable, hearable, touchable—Jesus is the definitive manifestation of the divine identity: "Long ago God spoke to our ancestors in many and various ways by the prophets, but in these last days he has spoken to us by a Son . . ." (Heb 1:1). But this same passage from Hebrews also reminds us that "he sat down at the right hand of the Majesty on high" (1:3).

The Ascension of Jesus to the right hand of God has compelled a re-prioritization of verbal TheoMedia. He is now known *orally* through the gospel preached[5] and *textually* through Gospels penned. A multiplicity of other media forms convey the identity of Jesus, but they are introduced to us and governed by word-media.[6] The palpability and elusiveness of the resurrected Christ prepared his disciples for a new chapter in the Bible's ongoing storyline of humanity's redemption. After the days when Jesus walked among us with his own two legs, we must rely on holy speech and Spirit-inspired texts as the prioritized TheoMedia of the church.[7]

This prioritization of word-media is affirmed all throughout the New Testament. Jesus himself, the *Word* made flesh, emphasized textual media in his earthly ministry, and not only in his preaching. He repeatedly used phrases like "It is written,"[8] and one of his most common re-

5. The early preaching of the Apostles is often referred to as the "kerygma" based on the Greek word for preaching. See Bultmann, *Theology of the New Testament,* 1:33–62; cf. also Dodd, *The Apostolic Preaching and Its Developments.*

6. Watson, *Text and Truth,* 1–2.

7. This is not to say with Rudolf Bultmann that Jesus was not raised *bodily* but only *verbally* in the gospel preaching of the early church: "Christ meets us in the preaching as one crucified and risen. He meets us in the word of preaching and nowhere else." Bultmann did not believe that the resurrection was an actual historical event. Jesus transcends history and appears eschatologically in the oral proclamation of preaching. See Bultmann, "New Testament and Mythology" (for the citation, see 41; for his specific treatment of the resurrection, see 38–43). Neither am I claiming that Jesus is now embodied in the pages and script of an ancient codex or scroll: the Word became flesh, not text (see the discussion by Watson in *Text, Church, and World,* 223–31). The claim here, rather, is that since the resurrection and the Ascension created a situation in which Jesus, the ultimate TheoMedium, is now bodily absent, the prioritized Theo-Media available to us now are *verbal.*

8. Matt 4:4, 7, 10; 11:10; 21:13; 26:24, 31; Mark 7:6; 9:13; 14:21, 27; Luke 4:4, 8; 7:27; 16:31; 19:46; 21:22; 22:37; 24:46; John 6:31, 45; 8:17; 15:25. As this phrase "It is written" attests, Jesus squarely located his identity and mission within the language and hope of Israel's scriptures. He did not enter a "text-free vacuum" (Watson, *Text and Truth,* 2).

plies to his questioners was "Have you not read?" (Mark 12:10, 26; Matt 12:3, 5; 19:4; 22:31; Luke 6:3). Though Paul urged the Galatians to recall the visuality of the crucifixion (Gal 3:1), he then placed emphasis on "hearing with faith" (Gal 3:5).[9] After reminding his readers that he was an eyewitness to Jesus and actually heard the heavenly voice of God at the Transfiguration, Peter assures early Christians that they have an even more reliable medium for belief, "something even more sure." He is referring to the oral media of "the prophetic word," which visually shines like a lamp "in a dark place." Textuality is included because Peter implies that these words of prophecy are connected to Spirit-inspired scripture (2 Pet 1:16–21).

Along with Peter, the Johannine eyewitnesses persistently cherished the visual, material, and aural dimensions of the Incarnation. But in the situation of Jesus's bodily absence they, too, emphasized the verbal media of oral proclamation and textuality. In the passage below, my added italics depict material/visual media and the boldface highlights verbal media:

> We declare to you what was from the beginning, what we have heard, what we have *seen with our eyes*, what we have *looked at* and *touched with our hands*, concerning the word of life—this life was revealed, and we have *seen it* and **testify to it**, and **declare to you** the eternal life that was with the Father and was revealed to us—we **declare to you** *what we have seen* and heard so that you also may have fellowship with us; and truly our fellowship is with the Father and with his Son Jesus Christ. **We are writing** these things so that our joy may be complete. (1 John 1:1–4; emphases added)

What was "seen," "looked at," and "touched" (material/visual Theo-Media) is now *testified/declared* (oral TheoMedia) and *written* (textual TheoMedia) to the Johannine Christians . . . and also to us. Seeing, hearing, touching, writing, reading—these media practices are all integral to the life of the church, complementing one another. But in the bodily absence of Jesus, who cannot now be physically seen or touched, verbal TheoMedia are naturally weighted. From Francis Watson: "For Christian faith, Jesus is not encountered directly but is mediated through texts. Not only through texts, but also through community, through the neighbor,

---

9. See Martyn, *Galatians*, 283.

through bread and wine. Yet it is the texts themselves that specify these nontextual mediations."[10]

In the earliest days of the church after the Ascension, knowledge about Jesus was given through the oral proclamation of the Apostles. Their testimonies are now available to us via written documents. We have emphasized cross-visuality and the multisensory experience of the Eucharist. Yet the Crucifixion and the Institution of the Lord's Supper are communicated to us through the pages of our New Testament writings: "Access to the reality of Jesus is textually mediated."[11]

RESURRECTION MEDIA LEGACIES AND PRACTICES: CHRISTOLOGICAL HERMENEUTICS AND BAPTISM

Throughout these chapters on "Media Christology," we are considering how Jesus's life and work establish certain "media legacies," patterns and concepts that should mark how Christians use and understand media today. The verbal proclamation of the gospel announcement, the textual testimony of the written Gospels, the visual imagery of the cross, and the relational extension through all communicative boundaries as seen in the Incarnation—these are media legacies that shape who we are as followers of Christ and give shape to our media practices. The purpose is not to think of Jesus in terms of our current media culture, but to think about our media culture on the basis of Jesus's identity. To go a step further, Jesus is the interpretive key through whom we understand all TheoMedia.

And a Christological lens for perceiving reality through Christ is one of the media legacies of the resurrection. Without what Richard Hays calls a "hermeneutic of resurrection,"[12] we will not understand the means by which God has revealed himself in Israel's past or how he reveals himself today in and through the church. Apart from a Christological hermeneutic shaped by the resurrection, we are TheoMedia impaired.

10. Watson, "Are There Still Four Gospels?," 96.

11. Watson, *Text, Church, and World,* 223. This clarification may be helpful: "I argued . . . for an *intratextual realism* which would understand the biblical text as referring beyond itself to extra-textual theological reality, while at the same time regarding that reality as accessible to us only in textual form, in principle and not only in practice." And a bit later: " . . . it is necessary to speak of the text as *mediating* the reality of Jesus rather than as *constructing* it" (224–25).

12. This phrase appears throughout Hays's "Reading Scripture in Light of the Resurrection."

When Paul critiqued textuality in 2 Corinthians 3, it was a critique of a hermeneutic that fails to take Jesus into interpretive account.

Though the Incarnation provided a multisensory experience of God, seeing, hearing, and touching Jesus did not guarantee knowing and understanding Jesus. If we lament with my children that our own eyes and ears have never physically seen the Lord's face, we should do so with the reminder of what we have just learned, that multisensory experiences were not necessarily the media of understanding or believing. The Gospel accounts are clear that not all have eyes to see. And the oral TheoMedia of Christ's own words often fell on deaf ears.[13] This was true even of the disciples.

In fact, the opening of their senses seems to correspond with the opening of Christ's tomb.

Luke recounts the journey two disciples made to Emmaus. Their prior hopefulness had been eviscerated by the crucifixion, and they were not in the mood for chitchat. Yet a stranger butted into their cynical conversation: "Beginning with Moses and all the prophets, he interpreted to them the things about himself in all the scriptures" (Luke 24:27).[14] They did not recognize Jesus until later, when he performed that familiar visual act of breaking bread. At that point, "their eyes were opened" (v. 31). Also "opened" to them in this scene were the "Scriptures" (v. 32). When Jesus reappeared later in the passage amidst the wider group of his disciples, "he opened their minds to understand the Scriptures" (v. 45). Hays writes, "The disciples' faculties of perception are opened by God in such a way that they now recognize not only Jesus but also that the Scriptures have been opened by Jesus' interpretations."[15]

Christ is the ultimate TheoMedium who opens up the verbal Theo-Media of our sacred texts. As word-media were reprioritized, the Resurrection supplied a new hermeneutic for hearing and reading them.

The power that emptied the tomb of the great King enables our "faculties of perception" to interpret not only our scriptures, but also the entire world with all its media and media forms. The cracked open tomb has cracked open our dulled senses to see, hear, taste, and understand life from the perspective of life rather than death. My wife and I

13. Note the phrase from Jesus, "ears to hear" (Mark 4:9, 23; Luke 8:8; 14:35; cf. Mark 8:18).

14. I am borrowing language here from my retelling of this scene in the final chapter of my *Faith Without Illusions*, 199–203.

15. Hays, "Reading Scripture in Light of the Resurrection," 231.

call this perspective "hopeful realism,"[16] a disposition that rereads and reinterprets the tragedies and glories of our age through a "hermeneutic of resurrection." When a supposed dead man interrupts our cynical conversations with his life-giving words, as Jesus did on the Emmaus road, then we can never view the world the same again. Our senses have been baptized into this Christological hermeneutic. The media of God are now opened to us, and our worldview is irreversibly altered.

Speaking of baptism—this ritual is a focal media practice deriving from the resurrection.

The multisensory ritual of the Eucharist reminds us of Christ's Incarnation and crucifixion. The multisensory ritual of baptism also reminds us of Christ's crucifixion, but places dramatic emphasis on the resurrection:

> Do you not know that all of us who have been baptized into Christ Jesus were baptized into his death? Therefore we have been buried with him by baptism into death, so that, just as Christ was raised from the dead by the glory of the Father, so we too might walk in newness of life. For if we have been united with him in a death like his, we will certainly be united with him in a resurrection like his. (Rom 6:3–5)

Though a ritual practice, the act of baptism is also a media form, a highly visual and public depiction of our participation not only in Jesus's death, but also in his resurrected life.

Like the Eucharist, there is a rich, multimedia quality to baptism. Consider the sound of water displaced and dripping (or perhaps pouring, depending on the mode of baptism practiced). Think of the sound of liturgical confession and ministerial pronouncement, the touch of soaked robes and wet floors, the sight of a saint dripping wet with the watery glory of a life yanked out of a spiritual grave. All of these elements convey together that Christ has penetrated that ultimate boundary wall of death itself and pulled us through the rent veil into the realm of life.

When we experience or witness this special media form, have we eyes to see and ears to hear? Along with the visual imagery of the cross, are we also being shaped by the dripping, pouring, soaking, sloshing, or splashing of the baptismal waters?

---

16. During my research for this book, I was pleased to discover that Marva Dawn uses the phrase "hopeful realist," defining it the way I do on my blog and in my *Faith Without Illusions*. See Dawn's *Unfettered Hope*, 80–81, 149.

CHRIST OUR ASCENDED MEDIATOR

Perhaps the most important media reality for any Christian to under-stand today is this: "There is one God; there is also one mediator between God and humankind, Christ Jesus, himself human, who gave himself a ransom for all" (1 Tim 2:5–6a).

The first mediator between God and humankind was Satan. Jesus has made an heroic entry into the realm of sin and death to make rela-tional repairs, to reverse the mediation of the serpent, to rip all the veils, to lay siege against every relational wall, and to smash them to dust like a fierce king on a rampage to deliver his people (though making his initial appearance as a baby and conquering in the appearance of a slain Lamb).

When Moses was the mediator between God and Israel, Sinai's base was off limits and the people shook with fear. But now,

> You have not come to something that can be touched, a blazing fire, and darkness, and gloom, and a tempest, and the sound of a trumpet, and a voice whose words made the hearers beg that not another word be spoken to them. (For they could not endure the order that was given, "If even an animal touches the mountain, it shall be stoned to death." Indeed, so terrifying was the sight that Moses said, "I tremble with fear.") But you have come to Mount Zion and to the city of the living God, the heavenly Je-rusalem, and to innumerable angels in festal gathering, and to the assembly of the firstborn who are enrolled in heaven, and to God the judge of all, and to the spirits of the righteous made perfect, and to Jesus, the mediator of a new covenant. (Heb 12:18–24b; cf. 8:6; 9:15)

The End of Mediation is near. It comes on that Day when, as stated earlier, Jesus will respond to Satan's "Did God actually say?" with, "Behold, I am making all things new" (Gen 3:1 and Rev 21:5 ESV, respectively). Until we hear those words and see the radiant face from which they come, we live in a time of waiting while Jesus intercedes for us at the right hand of God (Rom 8:34; Heb 7:25; cf. Gal 3:19–20).

"Do not hold on to me," said the risen Christ to Mary in the garden. But now "we have a great high priest who has passed through the heav-ens, Jesus, the Son of God" (Heb 4:14). So let us "approach the throne of grace with boldness, so that we may receive mercy and find grace to help in time of need" (Heb 4:16).

This heavenly mediation and our welcomed access to the throne of God encourage a range of communication forms particular to religious life: spiritual disciplines. And the outpouring of God's Spirit while we await Christ's return also encourages a distinct range of communication forms: spiritual gifts.

FOCAL MEDIA PRACTICES OF THE ASCENSION: SPIRITUAL DISCIPLINES AND SPIRITUAL GIFTS

In our interface of Christology and media we are learning dispositions and patterns that are to shape the church's understanding and practice of media in the twenty-first century. The gospel infuses the joy of eucatastrophe into our communicative enterprises. The Incarnation encourages the church's relational extension into the sphere of the Internet, along with a commitment to physical, face-to-face interaction within the neighborhood and marketplace. Crucifixion offers a haunting cross-visuality that reminds us that Christian media practice is to be selfless, not self-promoting. Sacraments like the Eucharist and baptism are focal media practices reminding us not only of Christ's death, but also of the new life in which we share and by which we can view the world through the resurrection lens of hopeful realism. We now turn briefly to the media practices of spiritual disciplines and spiritual gifts encouraged by Christ's Ascension.

Spiritual disciplines are communicative. The practices of prayer and worship involve our direct address to God and our posture of listening and discerning his call and his response. Fasting communicates to our Lord that we long for his face-to-face interaction (Luke 5:33–35). Our practice of *lectio divina* (basically, "spiritual reading") is a relational interchange as we seek to hear from God through the textual media of scripture, theological writing, and the spiritual classics. These disciplines are vertical in nature, meaning that they are concerned with our interaction with God. Some teachers of spirituality would include horizontal disciplines, those that are concerned with our direct interaction with others (such as giving or service).

As means by which God addresses and edifies his church, the spiritual gifts are also communicative. We have taken a glimpse at Jesus's sending of his Spirit in John's Gospel. In Acts, Luke provides us with the dramatic, multimedia scene of Pentecost. The Sinai theophanies of

Exodus 19–20 (with Moses and Israel) and of 1 Kings 19 (with Elijah) are recalled[17] as God's presence came to inhabit not a distant mountain summit or a physical sanctuary, but the new humanity of the church. In what might be understood as a reversal of the media scourge God assigned to humanity after Babel's Tower, the international passersby in Jerusalem heard preaching in their native tongues. And the continued presence of the Holy Spirit within individual Christians means that he is regularly operating in and through us for the strengthening of his church.

We ourselves are TheoMedia. The church comprises fractured image bearers who are being restored to the image of Jesus, the perfect image of God.[18]

By the indwelling presence of Christ's Spirit, every Christian is now a communicative means by whom God communicates within the church and reveals himself to the world. In Jesus's bodily absence, we draw near the heavenly throne through his mediation, engaging the Triune God through spiritual disciplines. And in the practice of spiritual gifts we render ourselves serviceable to his communicative and self-revelatory work in the life of our faith communities and beyond.

These practices have profound implications for our use of new media in the digital age. If we ourselves are TheoMedia, means by which God communicates and reveals himself through his Spirit, then our blog posts, status updates, tweets, artistic images, and online comments should be products of a life transformed by Christ and indwelled by his Spirit. As restored image bearers, our online presence and activity should image the Triune God. That we are God's own media brings rigorous accountability. It also brings tremendous encouragement: as the wonder and words of God spilled out on the streets of Jerusalem at Pentecost, so can divine reality and wisdom spill out through our social media channels into the Internet and into the ears, minds, and hearts of those on the other end of our communications devices. Even when (perhaps *especially* when!) we are just being silly or playful online, our media practices can be sourced in divine joy.

Another implication for our media-saturated lives deriving from the practice of spiritual gifts and spiritual disciplines has to do with the question of media sources. The bombardment of media we encounter each day comes from an expansive array of producers: corporations and their

17. Johnson, *The Acts of the Apostles*, 42.

18. On the church and the divine image, see Rom 8:29; 1 Cor 15:49; 2 Cor 3:18; Eph 4:2; Col 3:9; and 1 John 3:2–3.

marketing departments; the film industry; private donors campaigning for pet projects; government offices promoting new legislation; political parties hoping to win our vote; television producers hoping to gain our nightly focus; etc. These media sources are hoping to arrest our attention, to influence our thoughts, and to shape our actions.

When it comes to spiritual gifts, the source of communication is God himself. When it comes to spiritual disciplines, we are giving *God* our attention and asking how *he* wants to influence our thoughts and alter our actions. Spiritual gifts are means by which God engages us through our brothers and sisters in Christ. Spiritual disciplines are means by which we directly address God and strain to receive his address to us.

Most of us are quite busy with social media throughout our day. We are active media users. Blipping onto the screens of our smartphones are notifications from Twitter, Facebook, Blogger, or WordPress, letting us know that the online world is thinking about us, interested in us, eager to communicate with us.

Yet no one is eager to communicate more so than God himself. Are we listening? Are we plying the media crafts assigned to the church by which he regularly interacts with us?

There is this simple little policy I try to abide by after I wake up to face a new day. Before opening a screen, my plan is to open my Bible; and before listening to any voice online or on TV, I want to listen out for God's voice through prayer. I hold this policy somewhat loosely—on various occasions I will go online before prayer or study. For the most part, though, my plan is to turn to spiritual disciplines before I turn to social media. With the practice of any spiritual discipline in my life, I find that impure motivations abound. But in this daily media practice of opening scripture and listening for God before opening a screen, I am just trying to make a gesture of sorts, a gesture conveying to God that I wish him to be the primary influence in my life, that I cherish his voice more than any other, that his "updates" are more newsworthy, that his media are those to which I want my senses most attuned.[19]

19. As I mentioned in TheoMedia Note 2, I know God can speak to us through screens. I am not prescribing this discipline to everyone. But I do think we should acknowledge that screens often serve as oracular portals for so many other voices and influences. God may speak to us through social media, but he has quite a bit of competition among other sources when we go online. (I also acknowledge that some of us will open a screen first thing in the morning to use a Bible app, which, though I prefer the codex, is something I sometimes do as well).

TheoMedia Note 9

Word versus Image?

Dismembering the Sensorium . . . and Christ's Body?

The digital age has made us aware of something which perhaps we were not aware before. And this danger is not the disappearance of words. This danger is the idolatry of words.

On the flip side of imagophobia is grammatolatry: the giving over to the medium the power that rests in the message. Worshipping the words rather than the Word-giver, the creation rather than the created; there is also something about that in the Ten Commandments.[1]

—SUSAN WISE BAUER

A thematic thread running throughout our study has been the theological tension between various media forms. Namely, I am referring to the tensions between the eye and the ear, between seeing images and hearing/reading words. These tensions are manifest today in the postmodern word anxieties mentioned in chapter 7, in modernist anxieties over multimedia technologies, and in Protestant suspicions toward visuality and imagery.

But if Jesus is both the Word of God and the Image of God (2 Cor 4:4; Col 1:15; cf. Heb 1:3), should our senses really be at war with one

---

1. Bauer, "Disappearing Words, Part IV."

another? Should there be a rivalry between our various faculties of perception? Is our "sensorium" destined for internal conflict?

Many of the deepest divisions in the church are media related. We have established "sensory regimes," a phrase referring to the particular senses privileged by our particular religious groupings.[2] Denominational lines have been drawn according to emphases on specific sensory practices. Some Christians have championed liturgy or preaching (appealing to the ear) while others have found them too stifling and opted for more visual media forms (appealing to the eye). As focal media practices appealing to the senses of sight and touch, the sacraments have been fiercely contested resulting in violent schisms. A sensory regime selectively honors certain media practices while disparaging others.

It amounts to an attack on the "sensorium" of Christ. Now that Jesus has ascended, his body is the church. And in this body,

> if the ear would say, "Because I am not an eye, I do not belong to the body," that would not make it any less a part of the body. If the whole body were an eye, where would the hearing be? If the whole body were hearing, where would the sense of smell be? But as it is, God arranged the members in the body, each one of them, as he chose. . . . The eye cannot say to the hand, "I have no need of you," nor again the head to the feet, "I have no need of you." (1 Cor 12:16–18, 21)

Our media emphases run the risk of dismembering the body of Christ.

As the church, our sensorium is not ours to order as we please. We are to manifest the sensorium of Christ according to the sensory regime established in scripture. The ear is certainly privileged in 1 Corinthians 12–14, with prophecy identified as the most important spiritual gift. But we should remember that "the members of the body that seem to be weaker are indispensable" (1 Cor 12:22). Prioritizing one sense perception over another in our service as divine media agents cannot be a disparaging of other senses. The sensorium of Christ maintains various emphases, but there is to be no sensory persecution in the church.

I have been asserting the prioritization of verbal TheoMedia in this book. Yet we found in chapter 7 that God himself seems to acknowledge textual limitations. Pages and ink cannot bear the full brunt of divine revelation. In spite of the strong affirmation of textual media in John's

---

2. I first came across this phrase while reading Meyer's article "Religious Sensations."

Gospel ("these are written . . ."), the fourth evangelist also acknowledges the incapacity of written documents to convey in totality the identity of Christ:

> This is the disciple who is testifying to these things and has written them, and we know that his testimony is true. But there are also many other things that Jesus did; if every one of them were written down, I suppose that the world itself could not contain the books that would be written. (John 21:24–25)

The Apostle Paul also offered a critique of textual media, praising over ink and tablet the Spirit as a writing instrument and human hearts as pages. In spite of the strong emphasis on oral media and *fides ex auditu* (faith from hearing) so championed in the Protestant tradition,[3] we find in 2 Corinthians that Paul encourages a visual beholding of Christ as the image of God (2 Cor 3:18). This "metamorphosis of the beholder," as Jane Heath puts it, is a call to visual piety by which we are transformed into Christ's likeness.[4]

So why the prioritization of verbal TheoMedia and the spiritual sense perception of "the ear"?

Along with the limitations of words and texts, we must also acknowledge the limitations of our vision. Though Jesus was seeable as God Incarnate, the Ascension has taken him out of our sight. Paul urges us to behold Jesus, yet he also acknowledges that "now we see in a mirror, dimly, but then we will see face to face" (1 Cor 13:12). Our faculty of sight is spiritually dimmed. We sing with the hymnist "be Thou my vision" because we know we do not see rightly. And we pray for the day that our TheoMedia impairments will be eliminated.

Again, this is not to say that our sense of hearing words by faith is without its limitations. Just before using the metaphor of seeing in a mirror dimly, Paul wrote that "we know only in part, and we prophesy only in part" (1 Cor 13:9). Word-media still retain priority for the reasons presented in Parts 3 and 4 of this book, but verbal TheoMedia must be complemented by other TheoMedia that engage the rest of our senses.

---

3. Murray, "The Image, the Ear, and the Eye in Early Christianity," 17–24. Murray directs attention especially to Luther's lectures on Romans—Martin Luther, *Commentary on the Epistle to the Romans*. See esp. 149–53. See also the chapter, "Luther's Faith and Paul's Sight: Romans 1:17 and 2 Corinthians 3:18" in Heath, *Paul's Visual Piety* (forthcoming).

4. Again, see Heath, *Paul's Visual Piety.*

As we presently come to the scene of New Creation in the book of Revelation, we will find that our entire range of senses will one day be fully engaged with the face-to-face reality of God. The biblical storyline points to a time when visuality, textuality, orality, and materiality will seem to have mutual standing. On that Day, the tension between media forms will be over.

Yet in the meantime, the mélange of TheoMedia are most reliably ordered around divinely sanctioned speech and the church's sacred texts. The Incarnation has certainly provided warrant for a greater mutuality of the senses—early Christians were much more likely to embrace a hodgepodge of visual, material, and verbal media.[5] But the texts of both Testaments guide our understanding and use of all divine media forms, and these texts include warnings against persecuting certain senses in the process of prioritizing others. TheoMedia prioritization—yes (with careful qualifications). TheoMedia persecution? No.

5. Murray, "The Image, the Ear, and the Eye in Early Christianity," 18.

Chapter 13

Christ's Return

Apocalyptic Media and the End of Mediation

He will come again with glory to judge the living and the dead, and his kingdom will have no end.

—FROM THE NICENE CREED

Write in a book what you see.

—REVELATION 1:11

I looked, and behold, a door standing open in heaven!

—REVELATION 4:1 ESV

My oldest daughter respectfully acknowledges that her Christian faith requires some sort of eschatological orientation. At ten years of age, though, she does not really see the need for it. Granted, she wants to see Jesus face-to-face. But she is not quite sure why the world as she knows it must come to a definitive reconfiguration. She lives in a modest "semi-detached" house on the edge of a quaint English city and enjoys excellent health. She has great friends, her relationship with mom and dad is warm and pleasant (except when her dad beats her at board games), and her kid brothers and baby sister are mostly tolerable most of the time.

She has heard of cancer, but she never knew her maternal great-grandmother and paternal great-grandfather who died from it.

She prays for the poor, but she has never known poverty.

She just read an article about Syrian children forced into refugee status by war, but she does not know any of them personally; and Aleppo and Damascus seem far, far removed from her daily circumstances.

She just learned about Anne Frank in school, but the child-friendly curriculum has only offered faint intimations of Nazism's horrors.

We have never told her stories about child abduction, and she does not yet know the definition of "rape."

We have also yet to tell her that twenty children roughly the age of her mostly tolerable brothers were just shot to death in a Connecticut elementary school.

When the news reports of shooting sprees begin to reach her ears, when she learns about Auschwitz, when she sees violent footage from the civil rights movement, and when the daily reality of cancer inevitably brushes against her, it is likely that she will readily embrace the eschatological orientation of her faith and begin praying that ancient prayer that closes our Bibles: *Come, Lord Jesus.*

For Christians, everything points to an eventual ending and then a new beginning. A definitive reconfiguration of the cosmos is on the way and just around the corner. Resolution awaits. Redemption will come in totality—for all of life, for the entire world, for humanity . . . and also for media.

APOCALYPTIC HERMENEUTICS: A NEW WAY OF SEEING

Our final chapter on "Media Christology" before the book's conclusion ends fittingly with the literary document that canonically closes our scriptures and pictures the climactic biblical event of Christ's return. As far as we can tell, the Book of Revelation circulated among ancient Greek-speaking churches under the title "Apocalypse of John." In fact, "apocalypse" is the first word of the entire work.

In today's parlance, "apocalypse" is a cinematically informed concept denoting a world-ending catastrophe from something like an asteroid strike, an alien invasion, or maybe a widescale zombie attack. In the first century CE, an apocalypse was a *revelation*. More specifically, it referred to a revelation about heavenly happenings taking place beyond the scope of the physical senses. It was a glimpse behind the celestial curtain. The purpose of an apocalypse? To bring assurance that redemption and resolution are on the divine program.

Apocalyptic writing was part of a distinct literary genre in early Jewish life (e.g., Daniel, 1 Enoch, 4 Ezra, 2 Baruch). In reading the book of Revelation, we are peering through a peephole gouged into the cosmic veil. We are sneaking a peek into heavenly reality. Remember when Elisha prayed on behalf of his servant, "O LORD, please open his eyes that he may see" (2 Kgs 6:17)? God answered the prayer by allowing the prophet's frightened servant to see the mountains covered in the holy chariots of a divine army. This is the point of the apocalyptic, to cut through the limitations of visible and tangible reality so that heavenly reality might be disclosed.

In terms of literary style, apocalyptic writing incorporates wildly fantastical symbolism to recalibrate how we see what is around us. When realities as understood by our physical senses are desperate and dire, apocalyptic literature extends our faculties of perception via imaginative language to recognize that other forces are gathering strength and will one day vanquish the evil that seems, in our limited sight range, to be so insurmountable. Here is how Richard Bauckham describes the purpose of this type of literature:

> The apocalyptists sought to maintain the faith of God's people in the one, all-powerful and righteous God, in the face of the harsh realities of evil in the world, especially the political evil of the oppression of God's faithful people by the great pagan empires. The answer to this problem was always, essentially, that, despite appearances, it is God who rules his creation and the time is coming soon when he will overthrow the evil empires and establish his kingdom.[1]

Like the gospel proclamation of eucatastrophe, the apocalyptic writing of the sort in Revelation claims that in spite of the sound of screaming, the touch of barbs, the sight of blood, the taste of gall, and the stench of rot and death, a rescue operation is nevertheless underway. Like the Christological hermeneutic of the resurrection, Revelation calls for a perception

---

1. Bauckham, *The Theology of the Book of Revelation*, 8–9.

of the world that extends beyond the registry of our noses, nerve endings, eyes, tongues, and ears.

APOCALYPTIC LITERATURE AND TODAY'S NEWS MEDIA: HOW CHRISTIANS VIEW THE WORLD

Many American Christians perceive the world not through the interpretive lenses of apocalyptic and resurrection hermeneutics, but through the interpretive camera lenses and talking heads of cable news networks (yes, these are indeed "interpretive"[2]). Yet those expensive cameras are ill fitted for capturing fiery chariots on the hillsides; and the talking heads are ill equipped for providing theological and eschatological commentary. I am not bashing the news media here[3]—it would be unfair and unrealistic to expect the news coverage of major media syndicates to present the world through the perspective of hopeful realism. And we would all be suspicious of any footage claiming to depict dragons, sea beasts, and holy chariots on hillsides (specialty topics for the ancient apocalyptists).

My point is simply that the church should be careful in its acceptance of the world's mediation of reality.[4]

Media saturation constructs our worldview. Distortion abounds if we only understand the world through the world's own mechanisms of mediation. *Theo*Media saturation will supplement and often even overturn the concepts of reality offered by news media (even if, perhaps especially if, a media corporation claims to represent conservative values). God himself employs means that are to construct our view of the world. The gospel is a voice piercing a barren deathscape. The resurrection is a sign that doom and gloom are only tomb deep. And the Book of Revelation is a media report that no matter the brutality visible to the senses, something redemptive is brewing offstage.

---

2. The most incisive, unrelenting critique of media's interpretive lenses by a Christian thinker is Malcolm Muggeridge's *Christ and the Media*. For a more contemporary, secular critique along similar lines, see Hedges, *Empire of Illusion* (esp. the chapter, "The Illusion of America," 141–93).

3. See Postman's chapter "Now . . . This" in *Amusing Ourselves to Death* (99–113).

4. And let us also beware of the reportage offered by *Christian* cable news networks. Some of their reporting *does* attempt an interpretation of global events based on the Book of Revelation, but often the hermeneutical lens is one of searching for predictions and fulfillments without recognizing the theological perspective of apocalyptic literature.

There are ways of viewing the world that the world knows not of, and we cannot expect the news media to help us "see" the full picture or to "hear" the full story, no matter their promises of continuous coverage.[5]

The interpretive lenses of a hermeneutic of resurrection and apocalypse, however, are not rose colored.

Elisha did not ignore the fact that the hills were covered not only with an invisible heavenly host but also with legions of soldiers armed to the teeth with his "wanted" poster in hand. The crude entry of evil into our world through sin has rendered idealism untenable and even un-Christian. Any attempt made by the church to minimize the grim realities of darkness and death will explode when confronted with the visual symbol of those gruesome perpendicular bars. When children sitting in a classroom daydreaming about Christmas toys are suddenly murdered, we do not respond with platitudes like, "God needed some wonderful new angels."[6] Trite sentimentality has no place amidst a cross-haunted people. A resurrection hermeneutic is ever marked by the imprint of nails hammered into flesh, and an apocalyptic hermeneutic is ever attuned to the triumphant cacophonies erupting out of hell. The sound of women weeping for slain children is not ignored. The din of war is not silenced. There is no turning away from the sight of blood, no pinching the nose in the presence of death, no plugging the ears to avoid the screams.

It is just that the empty tomb of Jesus has released an otherworldly fragrance into our deathscape, and we can just faintly make it out. It is that the peephole in the celestial curtain gives us just enough of a vantage point to see a rescuing Champion on the horizon. It is that our ears are picking up a new song, a song to the Lamb, amidst the sounds of terror and murderous raging.[7] Realism that is hopeful takes in the full blast of ex-Eden pain while scanning the horizon with a sense that, somehow, Someone will soon appear.

There is a hole in the ground and a hole in the sky. Through the empty tomb and through the punctured heavens, there is just enough

5. For a disturbing example of how continuous coverage can distort reality, see the incisive online essay at *Christianity Today* by Andy Crouch: "The Media and the Massacre."

6. This comment was apparently intended to console grief over the shooting massacre in Newtown, Connecticut (December 14, 2012). Again, see Crouch's article cited above (n. 5).

7. In this paragraph I am relying once more on my previous book *Faith Without Illusions* (see esp. chapters 3 and 12).

eschatological beauty and glory dripping into our world that we cannot view it the same again. The sound of heaven singing is just barely audible. The aroma of incense offered in the divine throne room is just barely perceptible. And while heaven is leaking into our world through Christ's empty tomb and through the blown open sky, the media crews of the world will often miss it.

They will also miss the bad news leaking out of heaven.

Rome certainly did. The "hear ye, hear ye" on those elegant stone streets was "All is well."

Good news for one group is often bad news for another. The gospel is an announcement of a new, in-breaking reign. This is eucatastrophic for those oppressed by tyrannical regimes, but catastrophic for the tyrants and those aligned with them. To proclaim the arrival of the reign of God is to declare an end to all other reigns.

John the Seer wrote Revelation for early Christians struggling beneath the powering weight of political and economic oppression in Asia Minor. Exiled on the Mediterranean isle of Patmos, he experienced a multimedia visionary event, peering through propped open heavenly doors and getting a blessed earful about the divine program for dealing with Rome-sponsored injustice. Apocalyptic writing suited the pastoral task of presenting an alternative way of perceiving the world to his brothers and sisters in Christ. It was good news for the struggling churches, bad news for the power brokers.

These power brokers were also the media brokers. If you listened to the imperial broadcasts you were assured that the *Pax Romana* (peace of Rome) was intact and unassailable. If you passed through any respectable Roman city on the way to market or even glanced at a coin in your hand, the visual media of the day—statues, temples, monuments, the imagery on the currency—would have likely confirmed that Caesar's lordship was beneficial and even divine. The joyful cheers in the colosseums and hippodromes were the sounds of a happily entertained citizenry, safe and sound in their stage seats.

The apocalyptic sounds and images of Revelation were alternative media telling a different story. They amplified for those with ears to hear the muffled cries of martyrs burning and clawing the ground in those noisy arenas. They highlighted the ugly reality of human trafficking and economic exploitation.

Revelation is a literary medium that makes a statement about media. As we come to the redemptive denouement of media in the biblical story, we are confronted with the ancient media form of apocalypse that calls us to distrust the media coverage of the power brokers.[8]

Much of what the New Testament reveals to us about the return of Christ[9] is presented through a literary medium that compels an alternative view of reality. As we look to the End of Mediation in our study, we learn a new media practice, that of *developing spiritual faculties of perception that extend beyond the continuous network footage and interpret the world in terms of a returning Lord.* Our means of apprehending reality are insufficient if they do not take into account the divine perspective . . . something our favorite cable news networks are unlikely to supply.

THE SIGHTS AND SOUNDS OF APOCALYPSE: THE SENSORIUM MOVING INTO EQUILIBRIUM?

The Christian canon ends with the most multimedia of all biblical books. Revelation is so multimedia, in fact, that it comprises at least three different literary genres. Though most obviously an apocalypse, as discussed above, Revelation is also a *prophecy* (1:3; 22:7, 10, 18–19) and most certainly a *letter* as well (1:4; 2:1—3:22). This span of genres attests to the multimedia dimension encoded throughout the book. While John was on Patmos, God opened a cosmic portal and the sights, sounds, events, and words of heaven were almost too much for him to handle. Reading about them can bring us into sensory overload.

In Revelation, the entire "sensorium"—the full range of our varied senses—is engaged beyond capacity, even to the point that a distinction between the senses gets blurred along with the blurring of the genres. For instance, John reports that he "turned to see the voice" (Rev 1:12 ESV; cf. 5:11) and that he was later told to eat a scroll (10:8–10). How does one lay eyes on speech or taste a text? In *seeing a voice*, the verbal and the visual are tied together.[10] In *eating a scroll*, textual media and the sense of taste are tied together. For Revelation, the range, scope, and function of the senses blend and fade into each other.

8. Again, see Hedges's chapter, "The Illusion of America," referenced above (n. 2). Perhaps he is a bit too over-the-top in his criticisms, but as a journalist, he has much to say about the elite's control of what makes the news and what does not.

9. See Matt 24; Mark 13; Luke 21; John 14; 1 Cor 15; 2 Cor 5:10; 1 Thess 4:15—5:11; 2 Thess 1–2; 1 John 3:2; 4:17.

10. See Edith M. Humphrey's study on vision-reports, *And I Turned to See the Voice*, 175–78.

Let's first think about the sounds. Voices are coming from all directions. There are the voices of God and the Lamb that sound like "the roar of many waters." There are the voices of the four living creatures shouting "Come." Angels call out from heaven or from the earth in what is often described as "a loud voice." There is also the rapturous sound of singing, the sonic explosions of all heaven in worship. Martyrs cry out for vengeance and even some mysterious eagles get a few words in while soaring overhead. The stentorian blasts of trumpets intersperse liturgical paeans of praise. Added to the acoustic mix are the "haughty and blasphemous words" (Rev 13:5) of a foul beast, the cursing of God through the gnawed tongues of the impenitent (Rev 16:8–11), and the pleas of the power brokers that the mountains "fall on us" as quickly as possible (6:15–16). There is the pounding of thunder, the rumbling of the earth, and the thudding of monstrous hail. Aside from half an hour's silence in heaven (Rev 8:1), this is a boisterous, noisy book.

Second: the sights. Vivid imagery is a signature of apocalyptic writing. Throughout Revelation we hear over thirty times from John the *Seer* "then I saw" or "and I saw."[11] The sights include angels: sailing through the sky, holding down the four corners of the earth, descending from heaven rainbow crowned and cloud wrapped. And there are monsters, horrific beasts from the ancient world's darkest mythologies. The sight of a great red dragon, hunching with open jowls over a woman in labor and slavering to eat her unborn child—this is the stuff nightmares are made of (12:1–6). Added to the horrifying imagery is a sackcloth sun, a blood moon, a demon army, a trio of frog spirits—the list could go on.

There is also visual beauty so overpowering that John's sight can hardly withstand it: namely, it is the sight of the Lamb and of the Lord God Almighty. The most imaginative language must be employed to portray these sights. To look at the face of the Son of Man is to look straight into the sun in full strength.[12] And the appearance of the enthroned Creator God was such that John must resort to speaking of exotic jewels gleaming in rainbow light.

It is important to recognize that in spite of the visual vantage point from which John writes, he does not describe God's physical characteristics in anthropomorphic terms. The form of YHWH is surely beyond words, but perhaps it is also beyond sight. Visuality is important to John,

11. The Greek is *kai eidon*.

12. For the unfaithful, however, the sight of the coming Lamb will perhaps not be registered as beautiful, but terrifying. See Rev 1:7.

yet he does not offer an ocular description of the visual form of God. The appeal to jewels and rainbow imagery reflects sensitivity to the Second Commandment's prohibition against graven images, but it may also reflect the sensory limitations even of the multimedia genre of apocalypse.

Though the sights and sounds receive more emphases in Revelation than taste and smell, there is the curious command to eat the scroll, and John actually records the taste of the text (10:10; cf. Ps 119:103; Ezek 3:3). We also know that the smoky spice of incense was being wafted all around (Rev 5:8; 8:3; 18:13). There is very little implying the sense of touch throughout the first twenty chapters of Revelation—this is understandable since what is being recorded is understood as a visionary experience. When we get to the scenes of New Creation in Revelation 21–22, however, we will find that tangible materiality is indeed important to John.

The accent on sight and imagery in apocalyptic literature is so strong that it could be suggested that Revelation is so visually oriented that word-media is downplayed.[13] *But textuality is every bit as important as visuality in the book of Revelation.*

We have already "seen" how orality is important: much of what John hears is *speech*: the words of God, Jesus, or their angelic servants. As mentioned, in the curious description of *seeing a voice*, oral word-media and visual imagery bleed together. The same is true for textual word-media and visual imagery. For John, they belong in concert: "Write in a book what you see" (1:11).

To further confirm that textuality is as important as visuality in Revelation, we have to acknowledge that Revelation is itself a book. We know about the visionary experience on Patmos only because God commanded that it be textually preserved—"Now write what you have seen" (1:19). What we know about Jesus and his return in Revelation is textually mediated. With the letters to the seven churches, John is taking down Jesus's dictation. Twelve times in the book he is commanded to "write."[14] The author of this apocalypse/prophecy/letter/book could be known not only as John the Seer but also as John the Scribe.

He is not the only writer in Revelation. Jesus promises the faithful in Pergamum that they will be rewarded with a stone on which a new name

13. Adam acknowledges the possibility of this suggestion in his essay "Interpreting the Bible at the Horizon of Virtual New Worlds," 162.

14. Interestingly, John is told not to write the message associated with the seven thunders (10:4).

has been etched (2:17). To the church in Philadelphia, Jesus claims, "I will write on you the name of my God, and the name of the city of my God, the new Jerusalem that comes down from my God out of heaven, and my own new name" (3:12). The name of God is found later in Revelation on the brows of the 144,000 standing on Mount Zion with the Lamb (14:11).

Textuality also governs the development of much of Revelation's plot. Repeated reference is ominously made to a "book of life," the contents of which serve as a means of identifying the faithful from the unfaithful throughout the narrative flow.[15] Most importantly, Revelation's entire agenda of divine judgment is conducted along the suspenseful opening of a mysterious text. John first eyes this scroll in chapter 5, clutched in the hand of God on his throne. Along its seam are seven wax seals. What are the contents? What is written in this meticulously sealed text? Suspense builds. Who is worthy to open this scroll? An aura of mystique abounds. When the Lamb is presented as the one worthy, John and heaven are overcome with relief. Then the action of divine judgment begins, but it is correlated with the text's opening. As Jesus breaks each seal, portents and ghastly events occur and sometimes lead to series of other portents and ghastly events.

Revelation is a book about the Lamb opening a book.

Textual imagery is used when John describes the sky as rolled back like a scroll (6:14). God and Jesus are both referred to by the letters Alpha and Omega, the "A" and "Z" of the Greek alphabet (1:8; 21:6; 22:13). And the book opens with a blessing on readers: "Blessed is the one who reads aloud the words of the prophecy" (1:3). It closes with a blessing on "the one who keeps the words of the prophecy of this book" (22:7).

The final book of the Bible does not set at odds seeing/hearing, visual/verbal, oral/ textual. What we have, in fact, is a push toward equilibrium among our faculties of perception. The media forms of apocalypse are so intertwined that the conflicting tensions within our sensorium are being redeemed. This multimedia, multisensory book that closes the canon conjoins word and image to describe the most climactic eschatological event of the ages: the second advent of the King of all Kings. His eyes are a visual blaze of fire (1:14; 19:12). His weaponry against evil is a verbal sword that comes from out of his mouth (1:16; 2:12; 19:15).

15. See 3:5; 13:8; 17:8; 20:12; 20:15; 21:27. In 20:12 there are references to multiple other books.

A BRIEF REVIEW: THE MEDIA SAGA OF SCRIPTURE

"In the beginning, God created the heavens and the earth." He also created human beings. Their most elemental vocation was a media vocation: fashioned in God's image, they were to picture and embody divine reality on the stage of creation. Their home was the garden paradise of Eden where the star-forming, sea-creating voice of God mingled with their own.

Then came the voice of another. The most ancient vocation of the serpent was a media vocation. He offered himself as a mediator between the image bearers and their Maker, and took the latter's holy speech, gently tweaked its content, doctored it with the slightest degree of spin, and then rebroadcasted the distorted message into human ears. It is hard to understand what happened next, but we know something was severed, that something was damaged. Communication lines were cut. Our senses were dulled. Dysfunction bled into our relational capacities. Exile.

Soon after, a man named Abel is dying in a field.

Noah, build an ark. But God's renewal of Creation through the flood was short lived. Sin was too systemic, too embedded. More would be required than a renewal of Creation. Perhaps it would need to be remade. The stain of Abel's blood ran too deep.

Before long: *Let us build a tower. A tall one, up to the sky. Technology will save us. Mortar, brick, and crafty engineering will secure our safety, confirm our independence, establish our dominance.* But that just left humanity exiled once more, and this time with a media scourge—our tongues no longer spoke the same words.

Where are you? God kept pursuing humans in their relational dysfunction. *Here am I.* Some responded. Men like Abram and, much later, Moses.

Then one day: *Aaron, make us a god, a bright shiny one that we can see and touch.* Aaron complied, but immediately after the thing came out of the fire, the dust of stone inscribed with words and the dust of metal once coating a calf settled on the ground, ground that still echoed with Abel's crying blood.

Tabernacle, Temple, and tablets of stone—the one whose speech called forth the sun never stopped speaking. Prophets, scrolls, rituals, and signs—God never stopped calling out, "Where are you?" Incarnation, gospel, cross—the Word of God got as close to the ground as possible. And on that ground spilled "the sprinkled blood that speaks a better word than the blood of Abel," the blood of "Jesus, the mediator of a new covenant" (Heb 12:24).

He went to the grave by way of two perpendicular bars, and into the clouds by way of a vacant grave. Disciples stood staring upward.

> "Men of Galilee, why do you stand looking up toward heaven? This Jesus, who has been taken up from you into heaven, will come in the same way as you saw him go into heaven." (Acts 1:11)

Then from Patmos a man named John "saw heaven opened, and there was a white horse! Its rider is called Faithful and True" (21:11a).

UN-MEDIATION AND NEW CREATION MEDIA

That brings us to the final scene of New Creation. We have now followed throughout this book the biblical storyline right up to its climax, searching for a theological framework by which we might understand and use media in our own day. Our trawl through the canon began with the event of creation in Genesis 1–2, a creation that is not renewed at the end of John the Seer's vision, but *remade*: "Then I saw a new heaven and a new earth; for the first heaven and the first earth had passed away" (21:1).[16] Next John sees a city descending from above, a city "whose designer and builder is God" (Heb 11:10 ESV). This New Jerusalem, though, is more than a city. She is also a "Bride."

In Eden, the mediation of Satan led to a damaged relationship between husband and wife. In New Creation, there is (figuratively) the chiming of wedding bells. The Lamb and the Bride of God's people are being forged into an eternal wedlock. The severed ties between God and humanity are relinked in the marriage of the Lamb and the church. In this matrimony the earthly and the heavenly have collided. Cloud and sky veil God no longer. Trees are hiding places for no one. Divine-human distance is obliterated. Mediation between God and humankind is no more:

> And I heard a loud voice from the throne saying,
> "See, the home of God is among mortals.

16. Some commentators believe that a renewal of creation is indeed in view (e.g., Bauckham, *The Theology of the Book of Revelation*, 49–50), yet the language is forceful enough to imply a remaking rather than a renewing. See Aune, *Revelation 17–22*, 1117, 1132–33.

> He will dwell with them as their God;
> they will be his peoples,
> and God himself will be with them. (21:3)

In this resplendent city, the capital of New Creation, there is no Temple (21:22). No mediating structure is necessary.[17] In fact, the four-square design of the city's layout harks back to the design of the holy of holies[18]—the New Jerusalem in which the faithful live in the full presence of God is the expanded inner sanctum of the former Temple!

The divine throne is a central feature of this city. But whereas earth and sky fled from the divine throne in 20:11, the situation is so eschatologically reconfigured in New Creation that mortals can stare directly into the eyes of the One seated on it. This is the definitive moment signaling *un*-mediation, the moment when "they will see his face" (22:4).

When the Lamb of God tenderly wipes with his own hand the tears that sting like hell from our worn eyes, then the epic saga of divine-human mediation has come to its end.

Yet the end of mediation does not necessarily signal the end of media. There is such a thing as "New Creation media." The language John uses to picture the paradise for which we are all waiting is rich with media allusions.

Now, we have to acknowledge that to interpret Revelation literally is to misinterpret. This is a book of imaginative, fantastical language. Is Revelation true? Absolutely . . . though not *literally*.[19] The descriptions of New Creation, therefore, should probably be understood as symbolic. But it is interesting to observe that media feature prominently in the final reconfiguration of all reality.

17. Though the throne of God was encircled by the elders and living creatures in Revelation 4–5, Bauckham points out that there are no reported rings of intermediation in the scene of New Creation (*The Theology of the Book of Revlation*, 142).

18. Compare Revelation 21:16 with 1 Kings 6:20; see Bauckham, *The Theology of the Book of Revelation*, 136.

19. Tolkien would take offense at any attempt to minimize the capacity for fantastical imagery to offer profoundly truthful renderings of reality. I would say that Tolkien's fiction is profoundly true. But I do not read *The Hobbit* or *The Two Towers* as if they were *literally* true. Because "creative fantasy" is trying to "make something new," Tolkien wistfully warns that it just might "open your hoard and let all the locked things fly away like cage-birds" (see once more "On Fairy-Stories," 147). He is trying to point out that imaginative writing employs artful means of expression to help us see the wonder of what is already present in the things we think we know and see. As a media form, an apocalypse opens our faculties of perception to recognize that there is more going on than meets the eye. A tree is not just a tree. It might be the Tree of Life.

We should not be surprised. The verbal media of God's words and the multisensory realm of creation existed before humanity's disastrous Fall. Media is not a concept only among the fallen. Though the relational distance that necessitated mediation between God and humanity is eliminated in New Creation, there are still symbolic media radiating the wonder and glory of the new age to come.

This New Creation media includes textuality. New Jerusalem's city walls and their foundations bear inscriptions of the names of the tribes of Israel and of the apostles. The city's inhabitants have their names "written in the Lamb's book of life" (21:27). As mentioned earlier, God and Jesus are both identified as the Alpha and the Omega (21:6; 22:13). And the name of God is penned on the citizens' foreheads (22:4).

There is also a considerable emphasis on materiality. We observed earlier how the sense of touch is not as heavily emphasized as the senses of sight and hearing. But the eschatological vision on offer in Revelation 21–22 is not one of an ethereal, disembodied existence in the future marked solely by heavenly sounds and visionary sights. New Creation is not depicted as a realm in which spirits float cloud to cloud with mystical harps in hand. There is a rich physicality to this eschatological life. We read of strong, hard walls, of gleaming jewels, and of gold-paved streets. There is a tree—the Tree of Life from Eden—whose leaves can be plucked for the healing of the nations. As a created realm, it is so tangible and physical that it can be measured with hand tools (21:15). Unlike our current created realm, however, this New Creation does not reel, rock, tremble, or groan under the plague of sin.

Sights and sounds continue to abound, of course. Those jeweled structures make for a visually striking cityscape. No sight, however, will be more arresting than the radiance of the Father and the Son, who together replace the sun and moon as sources of light. Alongside the sounds of joyful worship, our ears will also enjoy the rushing flow of the river of life. One particular set of sounds will be missing, though. Never again will be heard the sound of crying and mourning (21:4; cf. Isa 65:19).

Taste and smell are not left out of New Creation media. The taste of that rushing river will be on our lips: "Let the one who is thirsty come; let the one who desires take the water of life without price" (22:17 ESV). And when we allow the prophet Isaiah (on whom John heavily relies) to fill out the eschatological vision, we can also hope for the aroma of a feast like no other: "On this mountain the LORD of hosts will make for all peoples a feast of rich food, a feast of well-aged wines, of rich food filled with marrow, of well-aged wines strained clear" (Isa 25:6). While the mortal myriads sup such luxurious wine and munch on such a lavish spread, God himself will be eating—

> And he will destroy on this mountain
> the shroud that is cast over all peoples,
> the sheet that is spread over all nations;
> *he will swallow up death forever.*
> Then the Lord GOD will wipe away the tears from all faces . . . .
> (Isa 25:7–8a; emphasis added)

While the redeemed and rescued are sitting at a sumptuous table celebrating the salvation of New Creation, God will be having his own meal. Served at the feast of God is Death itself. The massive jowls of the cosmic Lord will be grinding up the squirming, dying enemy of all flesh, that age-old foe so ruefully welcomed into a fresh, teeming world through another meal, a forbidden meal of fruit from a garden tree. Splayed out on a platter and set before the hungry eyes of the Almighty, Death will be the fare of the Great King.

The sensorium will be in equilibrium, the mediation over, and the pleasures of New Creation TheoMedia will be ours forever.

"The Spirit and the bride say, 'Come'" (Rev 22:17).

PART 5

Conclusion

Chapter 14

The Spirit and the Bride

A Rough Theological Framework and "EcclesioMedia"

We believe in the Holy Spirit, the Lord, the giver of life, who proceeds from the Father and the Son. With the Father and the Son he is worshiped and glorified. He has spoken through the Prophets. We believe in one holy catholic and apostolic Church. We acknowledge one baptism for the forgiveness of sins. We look for the resurrection of the dead, and the life of the world to come. Amen.

—FROM THE NICENE CREED

The Bible's claim to truth is not only far more urgent than Homer's, it is tyrannical—it excludes all other claims. The world of the Scripture stories is not satisfied with claiming to be a historically true reality—it insists that it is the only real world, is destined for autocracy. All other scenes, issues, and ordinances have no right to appear independently of it, and it is promised that all of them, the history of all mankind, will be given their due place within its frame, will be subordinated to it. The Scripture stories do not, like Homer's, court our favor, they do not flatter us that they may please us and enchant us—they seek to subject us, and if we refuse to be subjected we are rebels.

—ERICH AUERBACH, *MIMESIS*[1]

1. Auerbach, *Mimesis*, 14–15.

As the page has turned to this concluding chapter, my hope is that we are now dripping wet with biblical ink. In order to understand media in the digital age, we have plunged into the sacred texts of the church with the hope of having our perspectives reoriented around biblical wisdom. Reading scripture trains us for certain "habits of thought—habitual ways of viewing or making sense of the world."[2] This immersing of ourselves in the Bible's theological vision cultivates "cognitive skills and sensibilities, and hence *the ability to see, feel, and taste the world as disclosed in the diverse biblical texts*."[3]

I am hoping that the interpretive lenses by which we apprehend our media culture are being shaped by the reality that God is the ultimate media source and that his means of communication and self-revelation are the media we most desperately need. I am hoping that we are now striving to see our world through the reality that one of Death's locked up tombs has been pried open, that the thickest communicative barrier of all has been breached by One whose tolerance of relational distance has reached its limit. With this hermeneutic of resurrection, I am also hoping that we are being trained to peer through propped open heavenly doors so that our take on our culture might be altered by apocalyptic truth.

Erich Auerbach has observed that scripture coerces a new way of perceiving (see above quote). It compels us to see according to its own vision of reality. So we emerge now from our trawl through the biblical story with our faculties of perception in a state of overhaul and reorientation so that we can make fresh appraisals of our media-saturated lives.

The stated purpose of this book is to provide a rough theological framework for appropriating new media by carefully reading the ancient media of our holy texts. Scripture has been identified as a sufficient source for the church in the digital age, and we have worked through the biblical story of redemption. What the previous three sections have offered is a *reading*, a theological reading of scripture's portrayal of media. In this closing chapter, we are going to try to make some sense of that reading and lay the foundations for a rough theological framework by which the church can use and comprehend media. I am proposing that the foundation of any such theological framework should comprise the Bible's narrative frame of reference for media, the lessons we have taken from our "Media Christology," and the two main points of this book, first

2. Vanhoozer, *The Drama of Doctrine*, 285.
3. Ibid.

mentioned in chapter 1. After briefly revisiting these foundational elements, we will allow the theological framework to gain a bit more definition with the eight "theses" that follow.

The book will close considering the media vocation of the church in our technological culture. Loose ends will remain when we come to the final page. There will be no tidy closure. Questions will persist. The point of this writing project is not to provide the definitive answers to every question the church must ask in a digital culture gone media wild, but to offer an interpretive grid grounded in scripture. There is one question, however, that will *not* go unanswered as we conclude thinking about the church in the digital age: Are we encumbered in the twenty-first century by our first-century media practices?

The answer given will be no.

THE FOUNDATIONS OF A ROUGH THEOLOGICAL FRAMEWORK FOR APPROPRIATING AND UNDERSTANDING DIGITAL MEDIA

My approach in providing an overview of the book is to sketch this rough theological framework I keep referring to, starting with the foundation pieces. This foundation is to be laid with a narrative theology and a propositional theology, and with Christ as the cornerstone binding the two together.

Narrative Theology: The Bible's Narrative Frame of Reference for Media

We are storied people who understand our world and our lives by way of grand sagas or "metanarratives." The epic story of the Bible we have worked through in this book should frame our understanding of media in the electronic age. We have reviewed that story in the previous chapter, but it is worth revisiting here the Bible's narrative theology of media as understood through the long stretch of salvation history we have just worked through.

God is the Creator, and therefore the first and ultimate source of media. The original and most fundamental purpose of media was to communicate and reveal the wonder and beauty of God. Primal media were TheoMedia. Creation and human beings were endowed with the media vocation of placing God on multisensory display. As a concept, "media" belongs foremost to God.

When sin incited a media catastrophe, the biblical story immediately darkened. Media did not become a corrupt concept, but human beings and the rest of creation were debilitated as media forms. Along with the singing of birds came the groaning of the earth. The human vocation of divine image bearing was compromised and our interaction with one another soured. Our senses became dulled to TheoMedia. Ears grew deaf to his voice and eyes became unable (and often unwilling) to detect his splendor. We began hiding from one another, piecing together makeshift screens. As fallen creatures curved in on themselves, humankind's primary engagement with media was with *self-produced* media often marred by sinful values and intentions.

The plot of the Bible is God's dramatic rescue of human beings, fallen media agents, and of creation, a mélange of media tainted in some way by our sinful rebellion. The people of Israel were chosen for salvation and "entrusted with the oracles of God," verbal TheoMedia (Rom 3:2). The sights, sounds, words, and texts of the Creator were manifested to Israel and through Israel in the world. Yet God's people were enchanted with other media sources and forbidden media formats. Turning away from TheoMedia, they almost dissolved as a nation at the hands of Assyrians and Babylonians.

Then Jesus came as God's ultimate Word spoken into a mediascape of emptiness and death. His crucifixion, resurrection, and Ascension are providing a restoration of the senses for those who turn their ears and eyes his way. Divine image bearing has been reassigned to us as the church, God's new media domain in which focal media practices like preaching, sacraments, and spiritual gifts manifest divine reality in our world.

This grand story is one of God employing media to bridge relational distance. The narrative arc is a movement from estrangement to intimacy. Our media use in the digital age should honor and participate in the movement of this arc. Where possible, we are to enact its trajectory, utilizing communications media to bridge and restore fellowship with others. Entertainment, commercial, and news media often distract us; and the devices we use specifically for communicating can still keep other people at arm's length. To honor the Bible's narrative frame of reference for media, we cannot allow our media exposure to occupy our attention to such an extent that we ignore or unwittingly miss TheoMedia. And a use of communications media that is truly redemptive will honor the storied pattern of God's own use of media in extending himself relationally and drawing others near.

Here is a summary (in fewer than 140 characters) of this narrative theology of media: *Our media use should reflect God's media use in the biblical story for reaching outward to others in building and restoring relationships.*

Propositional Theology: The Two Overarching Theses of This Book

Two of what I understand as my most significant assertions appeared in the final paragraph of the introductory chapter and were demonstrated, I trust, throughout all that has followed. First: *if God creates and uses media, then there is a theological logic instructive for how we produce and use media technology today.*

I have spilt quite a bit of ink to show that God's own use and conceptualization of media are instructive for our twenty-first-century lives. The import of this claim is to establish scripture and the church's theological heritage as primary sources for comprehending and engaging media. As we plod on toward the future's unknown horizons, no advance in media technology will remove the concept of media from the Bible's theological purview. Scripture is media savvy and Christian theology is media competent.

I want to make clear that the reading and interpretations I am venturing in this book should be complemented (and perhaps in some cases challenged!) by other interpretive readings. I do hope, however, that this book builds confidence in the Bible's sufficiency for guiding the church in a media culture. We need to be drawing on cultural studies, research data, personal experiences, and practical wisdom for faithful living in the digital age; but not without our sacred "script" as a foundational resource.

Here is the second overarching thesis: *Christians are called to media saturation, but the primary media that are to shape, form, and saturate our lives are the media of God.* Our media exposure today is intense. Many of us are enclosed within a wall of sound bites, images, films, video games, and television shows. We are often too occupied with our communications gadgets to recognize that our senses are overloaded with messages and values sourced solely within our collective selves.

223

So we need an external media source to crack the soundscape and penetrate our field of vision. We need *TheoMedia*, the revelatory and communicative means of the One who is the wisest and best. No other voice is more precious to hear. No sight is more enthralling than a glimpse of his beauty. In the visual field of glowing signage, in our screen-dominated panorama, in the ubiquitous pastiche of glossy ads, our eyes need to catch some glance of the holy. Into the cacophonous din of our age, into the droning buzz of white noise, into the clamor of ringtones and beeps, we need the sonic boom or the gentle whisper of a word from the Lord.

I mentioned in TheoMedia Note 6 that we must learn to "weight" certain media influences. Living in a media-saturated culture means that we must allow the media of God to hold sway over the bombardment of so many other sights, sounds, words, and texts. We do not just need TheoMedia to break into the bubble of our media culture. We need them to saturate us. But many of us cannot spend hours on end reading scripture or listening to praise choruses on our iPods. Our commitments to working faithfully in our contemporary context mean we must engage all sorts of media all throughout the day. If our media intake is such that TheoMedia quantitatively get less press and airtime in our lives, then we at least need to weight them, prioritizing them qualitatively over all other media. If our lives are influenced and shaped by media, then those of us belonging to God are to be influenced and shaped by TheoMedia. Our eyes are devouring images and our ears taking in so many words and sounds each day. But without the sights, sounds, words, and texts of God, we have no life.

"Media Christology": Media Legacies and Corresponding Practices

For the New Testament writers, Jesus was the cornerstone of all reality (see Matt 21:42, Mark 12:10, Luke 20:17, Acts 4:11, Eph 2:20, 1 Pet 2:6–7). The narrative and propositional theologies of media serve as foundational elements of our rough theological framework for understanding media to the extent that they are bound together by the cornerstone of Christ. I will briefly reiterate two of the major points of Part 4's Media Christology and then provide a chart that visually depicts the focal media practices arising from the media legacies established by the life and work of Jesus.

First, we have seen that *Jesus is the consummate TheoMedium*. He is the ultimate revelation of God: "No one has ever seen God. It is God the only Son, who is close to the Father's heart, who has made him known" (John 1:18). The most pristine expression of verbal TheoMedia became not just hearable as the "Word of God," but also touchable, seeable—even killable—since he was the Word who became *flesh*. His Incarnation, crucifixion, resurrection, Ascension, and return reveal who God is and restore us to our vocation of divine image bearing.

I have also emphasized in our study of Media Christology that *it is only through Jesus that we can understand both TheoMedia and our world*. Our faculties of perception are to be baptized in what Richard Hays calls a "hermeneutic of resurrection."[4] TheoMedia make proper sense when appropriated Christologically: our grasp of the scriptures, the Temple, the bronze serpent, creation, and prophetic speech is only complete when we view them through Jesus. And all other media must be Christologically appraised. We cannot allow our interpretation of the world to be governed by the news agencies of our day. The press releases announcing catastrophe are to be weighed against the gospel pronouncement of "eucatastrophe." The reportage of misery by talking heads must be weighed against the apocalyptic reality that behind the celestial curtain God is mightily at work and orchestrating the consummation of all things. Hopeful realism acknowledges the grim realities of ex-Eden life but also acknowledges that a new day dawned when the tomb of our Lord was found vacant.

I made clear in chapter 1 that this book is not a how-to guide. We have mentioned a few practical exercises along the way, but the bulk of our study has been more conceptual than practical. For a list of helpful media practices for Christians, I recommend the closing sections in John Dyer's *From the Garden to the City*, the chapter "Finding and Funding Focal Fundamentals" in Arthur Boers's *Living into Focus*, and Marva Dawn's chapter "Do We and Our Churches Live by Our Focal Concerns" in *Unfettered Hope*.[5] The "focal media practices" suggested in this book have all been directly correlated to the "media legacies" of Jesus. Below is a chart that concisely depicts the conceptual and practical dynamics of the Media Christology from Part 4:

4. See in chapter 12 my discussion of Hays's article, "Reading Scripture in Light of the Resurrection."

5. Dyer, *From the Garden to the City*, 175–79; Boers, *Living Into Focus*, 177–201; Dawn, *Unfettered Hope*, 79–107.

Christological Event	Media Legacy	Focal Media Practices
The Gospel Announcement	The joy of eucatastrophe	Verbal presentation of the gospel (in preaching/discourse/writing)
Incarnation	Relational pursuit to the fullest extent	1) Offline engagement (physical presence and face-to-face interaction in the relational sphere of our home and neighborhood) 2) Online engagement (infiltration within the relational sphere of the Internet)
Crucifixion	Selfless Media Ethic	1) Cross-Visuality 2) Eucharist
Resurrection/ Ascension	The disposition of Hopeful Realism	1) Understanding TheoMedia and all other media through a hermeneutic of resurrection 2) Baptism
	The heavenly mediation of Christ	1) Spiritual Gifts 2) Spiritual Disciplines
Return	The insight and perspective of Apocalyptic Media	1) Christian worldview 2) Easing the tension of the churches' sensory regimes

BUILDING ON THE FOUNDATION: A FRAMEWORK OF EIGHT THESES

We can now begin piecing together a rough theological framework for the church's engagement with media in the digital age. Our foundation is the Bible's big picture of story of media, the New Testament's Media Christology, and two overarching propositions. More propositions can now follow to give shape to our interpretive grid. The list below is a selection of salient points we have come across in our study plus a couple of claims or observations that I am only making now at the end of our journey through scripture. The list of theses could be longer, of course. The eight below, however, have stood out to me as deserving mention before we turn the final page.

1) Our most elemental vocation as human beings is the media vocation of divine image bearing.

Humans were not just made to be media consumers and users. Every fiber of our being, every motion and action, is to be devoted to communicating and revealing divine reality. The reason media are such an intrinsic, unavoidable, dimension to every culture and society is because we human beings have been fashioned as living media forms. But how can we image God if we are being shaped by the images of a fallen world? Recovering our role as divine image bearers has profound bearing on how we use, consume, and produce media.

2) Media are messy: the interplay of our sinfulness and our sharing in God's image means that the media we create are bright and dark.

An unqualified rejection and an uncritical acceptance of media and communications technology are both unwarranted, because we are marked by the divine image (and capable of extraordinary beauty) yet simultaneously marred by sin (and capable of ugly and sinister media products). As fractured image bearers we are both extensions and distortions of God. The contemporary language of "connectedness" can be just as disastrous as it is wondrous. Careful discernment and sensitivity are required if we are going to assess theologically our media culture.

3) God is a multimedia God who sometimes reveals himself through the most unexpected means.

We all have media preferences. God does as well, but we must be careful not to let our predilections for certain media forms cause us to miss the varied and sometimes surprising ways God communicates and reveals himself. We have seen how he staged clamorous events bursting with sounds and abounding in imagery (e.g., the plagues on Egypt, the Sinai theophany). He also utilized the gentleness of a whispering breeze (as with Elijah) and revealed himself through aesthetic craftsmanship (as with the Tabernacle). Though there are formal TheoMedia regularly promoted among the religious and spiritual lives of God's people (like scripture), God can also make just about anything a form of TheoMedia

227

on an ad hoc basis (like that bronze serpent). If he can speak and manifest himself through Balaam's donkey, then we cannot place too many limits on what God will or will not use for his communicative purposes. He might even be audacious enough to use you or me.

4) Verbal TheoMedia are prioritized, but not in a way that persecutes other media forms.

I just stated that God has particular media preferences. Throughout this book it has been argued that word-media is elevated as preeminent among other means of divine communication and revelation. The context of the *Shema* is a call to media saturation with God's words, and the thematic heaviness of that biblical passage in both Testaments compels a rigorous devotion to holy speech and texts. Word anxieties can be valid; and scripture itself attests that textual media are not without weaknesses. Even so, our "script" is textual, and what we know about Jesus is textually mediated to us through the New Testament writings.

The prioritization of word-media, however, is not to lead to sensory persecution. Since God is multimedia in his self-revelation, we must honor and respect other media formats as well. Paul opened his discussion on spiritual gifts in 1 Corinthians by pointing out that the Spirit of God utilizes "varieties of gifts," "varieties of services," and "varieties of activities, but it is the same God who activates all of them in everyone" (1 Cor 12:4–7).

5) The "sensorium" is moving into equilibrium.

Many of the church's internal divisions are motivated by media preferences and the emphases placed on different senses. For example, some Christians champion visuality to the exclusion of textuality, and others vice versa. The sensory organs by which we engage media are not to be at war with one another. Certain tensions need to be held in place as word-media holds preeminence, but we should expect God to engage the full range of our senses in his interaction with us. Also, the New Creation lying at the conclusion of the Bible's narrative arc seems to portray an equilibrium among our senses. The climax of divine-human intermediation ends in a multimedia city full of sights, sounds, tastes, fragrances, words, and texts.

6) God can interrupt our media deluge at any moment with media of his own.

One of the most encouraging finds for me in this writing process is that my own media-saturated life is not out of God's communicative reach. I am responsible for being poised and ready to receive his communication, but at any moment he is capable of breaking through the white noise and ripping through the veils to grasp my attention. Satan is not the only figure who interrupts ongoing media interactions. God also interrupts, as he has done so many times in scripture, appearing on the scene to wrestle a man in the dark, sending an angel to announce an unexpected pregnancy, tearing open the sky to send his presence among us. No mediascape is safe from his divine invasion.

7) TheoMedia are Trinitarian

Though I have not made this observation until now, it should be clear after our journey through the biblical story that the notion of "TheoMedia" accords well with the doctrine of the Trinity. The Holy Spirit was present at the moment of creation (Gen 1:2) and at the moment of re-creation (Mark 1:10, John 20:22, Acts 2, etc.). It was through the agency of the Spirit that Bezalel and his crew of artisans fashioned the material media of the Tabernacle. This Spirit is also "the Spirit of Christ," who inspired the spoken and written words of the Old Testament prophets (1 Pet 1:10–11). Jesus sent that same Spirit into us, the new people of God, who are to place God on display in our world through sacraments, preaching, and spiritual gifts all supplied and guided by this Spirit.

8) The Church is the primary media domain of God

Jesus is the consummate TheoMedium, but the church is the ultimate TheoMedia domain. Just as God was most definitively revealed to the world through Jesus, he is now utilizing the church and its focal media practices to continue his work of redeeming humanity and creation.

The Bible's presentation of the epic saga of salvation ends with the scene of New Creation, but we live just before the denouement of that story, between Christ's Ascension and return. The "happily ever after" of Revelation 20–21 is yet to come. In the meanwhile, God is still employing his TheoMedia to reveal himself and to draw others near. He is still crying out "Where are you?" to silhouetted figures hiding in a dark wood. God can utter that pained question through the groans of creation. He can utilize ad hoc means like donkeys and rainbows, even coarse rap lyrics and back-studio films. But the primary means by which he calls out to the world is now through the ancient media forms of the *church*. We are the primary media domain of God. And this leads to my closing words . . .

"ECCLESIOMEDIA": FIRST-CENTURY MEDIA PRACTICES IN THE TWENTY-FIRST-CENTURY CHURCH

The Western church can be a bit insecure in the digital age. We tend to think of ourselves like a communications device on the verge of becoming outdated or defunct without a significant upgrade. In an effort to stave off our decline into irrelevance, many of us are adopting the newest media technology products as soon as they are on the shelves or ready for download. Local congregations lacking a website are deemed out of touch by more tech-savvy brothers and sisters in the faith. Christians reluctant to embrace media technology are regarded by other Christians as old-fashioned fuddy-duddies. Church leaders without Twitter handles seem like crusty holdovers from a culture now extinct.

I want to close this book calling the church to recognize its unique position in the world as the media domain of God. I want to call us to practice with fresh vigor the TheoMedia specifically assigned to us through the life and work of Jesus: "EcclesioMedia." Making up new words is risky and perhaps a bit presumptuous, but what I mean by "EcclesioMedia" are those media forms repeatedly mentioned that derive from the Media Christology presented in Part 4: the sacraments, gospel-shaped preaching, scripture reading, and spiritual gifts. These are formal means of divine revelation and self-communication commissioned by God for the media domain of his gathered people.

As the church deals with its insecurities in a digital age and tries to reach a media-saturated world, we do not need to lose confidence in the ancient media God has appointed to us as his people. Sure, churches should be considering how to build excellent websites. Many of us should be (carefully and biblically!) using social media. I am supportive of Christian leaders blogging and tweeting, as long as "redirection" and "ecclesial assimilation" (see TheoMedia Note 7) are underway. But there are first-century focal practices intrinsic to who we are as a new temple of the Spirit *that have no expiration date.*

We have seen that no media announcement bears as much power and influence as the gospel: "It is the power of God for salvation" (Rom 1:16). The drum-banging, bell-clanging royal pronouncement of Christ's salvation and triumph can certainly be communicated through blog posts, emails, tweets, status updates, and websites. But the face-to-face proclamation of a preacher before a congregation is an ancient form of EcclesioMedia that needs to be strengthened and accentuated, not dragged to the "Trash" file because it is old. Scripture can be read on massive screens via PowerPoint or on our communication devices via downloadable apps; but the ancient practice of Bible reading is not somehow dignified by the new technological formats.[6] Though the Spirit-anointed interactions of Christians through "a hymn, a lesson, a revelation, a tongue, or an interpretation" can be done via social media to varying degrees of success, there is nothing archaic in Paul's assumption that this would take place in a flesh and blood gathering of local believers (1 Cor 14:26). And the sloshing or dripping of baptismal water, the crunching of unleavened bread, the taste of consecrated wine—these sensory media practices are not ruled irrelevant because they lack the latest technology. The sacraments need not "meet the requirements of contemporary culture."[7]

As we bring new media practices into the life of the church, they must be subordinated to these ancient media practices that hold precedence. The church is the media domain of God, so any media that conflict with or distract from our divinely commissioned focal media are illegitimate. If these latest communication technologies and their underlying

6. It is the other way around—the format is dignified by the practice of Bible reading. What came to my mind in writing this sentence were these words from Jesus in Matthew: "Woe to you, blind guides, who say, 'Whoever swears by the sanctuary is bound by nothing, but whoever swears by the gold of the sanctuary is bound by the oath.' You blind fools! For which is greater, the gold or the sanctuary that has made the gold sacred? And you say, 'Whoever swears by the altar is bound by nothing, but whoever swears by the gift that is on the altar is bound by the oath.' How blind you are! For which is greater, the gift or the altar that makes the gift sacred? So whoever swears by the altar, swears by it and by everything on it; and whoever swears by the sanctuary, swears by it and by the one who dwells in it; and whoever swears by heaven, swears by the throne of God and by the one who is seated upon it" (23:16–22).

7. Borgmann, *Power Failure*, 126.

values cannot be placed in the service of EcclesioMedia, then we must acknowledge that they themselves suffer from that dreaded malady of *irrelevance*. There is an irrelevance worse than the failure to be trendy or cutting edge: it is the failure to be relevant to God and his communicative activity within and through the church.

Tweet, oh people of God. Blog, text, and type status updates. But linger in the TheoMedia domain of the church and cling to the media legacies of Christ's Incarnation, crucifixion, resurrection, Ascension, and return. Hear the gospel. Look to the cross. Feel the embrace of brothers and sisters. Smell the aroma of bread broken and taste the sweet wetness of wine outpoured. Preach and baptize. Exercise spiritual gifts and practice spiritual disciplines that poise our senses before the media of God.

A world drenched in media needs divine image bearers dripping wet with biblical ink and with baptismal waters. The mediascape of emptiness and death needs the media of the One who conquered death and left empty a grave. Those glued to a screen hearing heartrending reports and watching disaster footage need the people of God whose ears can pick up heavenly choruses over worldly dirges and whose eyes are squinting to peer through a ripped open sky. The greatest threat to the church is not our refusal to embrace new media practices but our failure to embrace with joyful vigor our own focal media. And nothing would be more irrelevant to the world than a relevant church that is competent with digital media but inept with the media of God.

Bibliography

Adam, A. K. M. "Interpreting the Bible at the Horizon of Virtual New Worlds." In *The Bible in Ancient and Modern Media: Story and Performance*, edited by Holly E. Hearon and Philip Ruge-Jones, 159–73. Biblical Performance Criticism, 1. Eugene, OR: Cascade, 2009.

Alexander, Bryan. "Schwarzenegger Discusses Violence and Newtown Shootings." *USA Today* (January 14, 2013). No pages. Online: http://www.usatoday.com/story/life/movies/2013/01/14/the-last-stand-movie-violence/1816409/.

Anderson, Gary A. "To See Where God Dwells: The Tabernacle, the Temple, and the Origins of the Christian Mystical Tradition." *Letter & Spirit* 4 (2008) 15–47.

———. "Towards a Theology of the Tabernacle and Its Furniture." In *Text, Thought, and Practice in Qumran and Early Christianity*, edited by Ruth A. Clements and Daniel R. Schwartz, 161–94. Studies on the Texts of the Desert of Judah 84. Leiden: Brill, 2009.

Athanasius. *On the Incarnation*. Translated by John Behr. Popular Patristics Series 44a. Yonkers, NY: St. Vladimir's Seminary Press, 2011.

Auerbach, Erich. *Mimesis: The Representation of Reality in Western Literature*. Translated by Willard R. Trask. Princeton, NJ: Princeton University Press, 1953.

Aune, David E. *Revelation 17–22*. Word Biblical Commentary. Vol. 52C. Nashville: Thomas Nelson, 1998.

Austin, J. L. *How to Do Things With Words*. Oxford: Oxford University Press, 1962.

Bailey, Justin A. "Welcome to the Blogosphere." In *Everyday Theology: How to Read Cultural Texts and Interpret Trends*, edited by Kevin Vanhoozer, et al., 173–89. Grand Rapids: Baker Academic, 2007.

Bailey, Sarah Pulliam. "Twitter Reaches Out to Christian Leaders at Catalyst's 'Be Present' Conference." *Christianity Today*. No Pages. Online: http://www.christianitytoday.com/ct/2011/octoberweb-only/twittercatalyst.html.

Barth, Karl. *Church Dogmatics*. I/1: *The Doctrine of the Word of God*. 1936. Study edition. Translated by G. W. Bromiley, et al. London: T & T Clark, 2009.

————. *Church Dogmatics. I/1: The Doctrine of the Word of God.* 1936. Reprint, translated by G.W. Bromiley et al. Peabody, MA: Hendrickson, 2010.

————. *Evangelical Theology: An Introduction.* Translated by Grover Foley. 1963. Reprint, Grand Rapids: Eerdmans, 1979.

Bauckham, Richard. "God Crucified." In *Jesus and the God of Israel: God Crucified and Other Studies on the New Testament's Christology of Divine Identity.* Grand Rapids: Eerdmans, 2008.

————. *The Theology of the Book of Revelation.* New Testament Theology. Cambridge: Cambridge University Press, 1993.

Bauer, Susan Wise. "Disappearing Words, Part IV: What do We Do About It?" The Well-Trained Mind (May 11, 2011). No Pages. Online: http://www.welltrainedmind.com/disappearing-words-part-iv-what-do-we-do-about-it/.

Beale, G. K. *We Become What We Worship: A Biblical Theology of Idolatry.* Downers Grove, IL: InterVarsity, 2008.

Bennet, Jana Marguerite. *Aquinas on the Web? Doing Theology in an Internet Age.* London: T & T Clark, 2012.

Betz, Hans Dieter. *The Sermon on the Mount Including the Sermon on the Plane (Matthew 5:3–7:27 and Luke 6:20–49).* Hermeneia. Minneapolis: Fortress, 1995.

Boers, Arthur. *Living Into Focus: Choosing What Matters in an Age of Distractions.* Grand Rapids: Brazos, 2012.

Borgmann, Albert. *Power Failure: Christianity in the Culture of Technology.* Grand Rapids: Brazos, 2003.

Bradbury, Ray. *Fahrenheit 451.* 1954. Reprint, London: HarperVoyager, 2008.

Brock, Brian. *Christian Ethics in a Technological Age.* Grand Rapids: Eerdmans, 2010.

Brown, Raymond E. *The Gospel According to John: Introduction, Translation, and Notes.* Anchor Bible. 2 volumes, 29 and 29A. Garden City, NY: Doubleday, 1966.

Brueggeman, Walter. *The Bible and Postmodern Imagination: Texts Under Negotiation.* London: SCM, 1993.

Bultmann, Rudolf. "New Testament and Mythology." In *Kerygma and Myth: A Theological Debate,* edited by Hans-Werner Bartsch, 1–44. Translated by Reginald H. Fuller. London: SPCK, 1972.

————. *Theology of the New Testament.* 2 vols. 1951, 1955. Reprint, translated by Kendrick Grobel. Waco, TX: Baylor University Press, 2007.

Busby, Joel. "Social Media & Theological Discourse [6]: Social Media and 'Incurvatus in Se.'" Hopeful Realism. No pages. Online: http://hopefulrealism.com/2011/04/social-media-theological-discourse-6-social-media-and-incurvatus-in-se/.

Byassee, Jason. "Practicing Virtue with Social Media: An 'Underdetermined' Response." New Media Project (May 10, 2012). Online: http://www.newmediaprojectatunion.org/pages/practicing-virtue-with-social-media/#_ednref14.

Byers, Andrew. *Faith Without Illusions: Following Jesus as a Cynic-Saint.* Downers Grove, IL: InterVarsity, 2011.

————. "From 'Among the Trees' to 'Face to Face': How the Gospel Can Reverse the Disconnect in an Electronic Age." *Youth & Christian Education Leadership* (Summer, 2010) 11–13.

————. "I Believe in God . . . and Monsters" The Ooze (Spring, 2011). No pages. Online: http://theooze.com/culture/god-monsters-part-three/.

————. "Technological Upgrades and Christological Hermeneutics: Is the Bible Sufficient for a Digital Age?" Hopeful Realism (January 16, 2013). No pages. Online:

http://hopefulrealism.com/2013/01/technological-upgrades-and-christological
-hermeneutics-is-the-bible-sufficient-for-a-digital-age/.

Calvin, John. *Institutes of the Christian Religion.* Edited by John T. McNeill. Translated by Ford Lewis Battles. Library of Christian Classics, XX and XXI. Philadelphia: Westminster, 1960.

Campbell, Heidi A. *When Religion Meets New Media.* Media, Religion and Culture Series. London: Routledge, 2010.

Carey, James W. *Communication as Culture: Essays on Media and Society.* 1989. Media and Popular Culture, 1. Reprint, London: Routledge, 1992.

Carr, David M. "Literacy and Reading." In *The Eerdmans Dictionary of Early Judaism,* edited by John J. Collins and Daniel C. Harlow, 888–89. Grand Rapids: Eerdmans, 2010.

———. *Writing on the Tablet of the Heart: Origins of Scripture and Literature.* Oxford: Oxford University Press, 2005.

Carr, Nicolas. *The Shallows: What the Internet Is Doing to Our Brains.* New York: Norton, 2010.

Challies, Tim. *The Next Story: Life and Faith After the Digital Explosion.* Grand Rapids: Zondervan, 2011.

Childs, Brevard S. *Biblical Theology of the Old and New Testaments: Theological Reflections on the Christian Bible.* London: SCM, 1992.

Clapp, Rodney. "New Town and Movie Violence." Running Heads (January 14, 2013). No pages. Online: http://www.runningheads.net/2013/01/14/newtown-and-movie-violence/.

Corley, Kathleen E., and Robert L. Webb. *Jesus and Mel Gibson's* The Passion of the Christ: *The Film, the Gospels and the Claims of History.* London: Continuum, 2004.

Crouch, Andy. *Culture Making: Recovering Our Creative Calling.* Downers Grove, IL: InterVarsity, 2008.

———. "The Media and the Massacre." *Christianity Today.* No pages. Online: http://www.christianitytoday.com/ct/2012/december-web-only/media-and-massacre.html.

De Boer, Martinus C. *Galatians: A Commentary.* The New Testament Library. Louisville: Westminster John Knox, 2011.

Dalrymple, Timothy. "The Indignation Industry, or the Art of Blogging Controversies." Philosophical Fragments (February 14, 2012). No pages. Online: http://www.patheos.com/blogs/philosophicalfragments/2012/02/14/the-indignation-industry-or-the-art-of-blogging-controversies/.

Dawn, Marva J. *Unfettered Hope: A Call to Faithful Living in an Affluent Society.* Louisville: Westminster John Knox, 2003.

DeLillo, Don. *White Noise.* New York: Penguin, 1985.

Dines, Gail. *Pornland: How Pornography Has Hijacked Our Sexuality.* Boston: Beacon, 2010.

Dodd, C. H. *The Apostolic Preaching and Its Developments: Three Lectures with an Appendix on Eschatology and History.* London: Hodder and Stoughton, 1963.

Douglas, Torin. "Social Media's Role in the Riots." *BBC News.* No Pages. Online: http://www.bbc.co.uk/news/entertainment-arts-14457809.

Drescher, Elizabeth. *Tweet If You Heart Jesus: Practicing Church in the Digital Reformation.* New York: Morehouse, 2011.

Dyer, John. *From the Garden to the City: The Redeeming and Corrupting Power of Technology*. Grand Rapids: Kregel, 2011.

Ellul, Jacques. *Propaganda: The Formation of Men's Attitudes*. New York: Vintage, 1964.

———. *The Technological Society*. Translated by John Wilkinson. London: Jonathan Cape, 1964.

———. "Technology and the Gospel." *International Review of Mission* 66, 262 (April 1, 1977) 109–17.

Ferré, John P. "The Media of Popular Piety." In *Mediating Religion: Conversations in Media, Religion and Culture*, edited by Joylon Mitchell and Sophia Marriage, 83–91. London: T & T Clark, 2003.

Forster, E. M. *The Machine Stops*. 1928. Reprint, New York: Penguin, 2011.

Fowler, Robert M. "Why Everything We Know About the Bible Is Wrong: Lessons from the Media History of the Bible." In *The Bible in Ancient and Modern Media: Story and Performance*, edited by Holly E. Hearon and Philip Ruge-Jones, 3–18. Biblical Performance Criticism, 1. Eugene, OR: Cascade, 2009.

Fowl, Stephen E. "Stories of Interpretation." In *Engaging Scripture*, 32–61. Malden, MA: Blackwell, 1998.

Freitheim, Terence. *Creation Untamed: The Bible, God and Natural Disasters*. Theological Explorations for the Church Catholic. Grand Rapids: Baker Academic, 2010.

Gorman, Michael J. *Cruciformity: Paul's Narrative Spirituality of the Cross*. Grand Rapids: Eerdmans, 2001.

Grant, Myrna R. "Christ and the Media: Considerations on the Negotiation of Meaning in Religious Television." In *Mediating Religion: Conversations in Media, Religion and Culture*, edited by Joylon Mitchell and Sophia Marriage, 121–30. London: T & T Clark, 2003.

Grenz, Stanley J., and John R. Franke. *Beyond Foundationalism: Shaping Theology in a Postmodern Context*. Louisville: Westminster John Knox, 2001.

Harris, Elizabeth. *Prologue and Gospel: The Theology of the Fourth Evangelist*. Journal for the Study of the New Testament Supplemental Series, 107. Sheffield: Sheffield University Press, 1994.

Hatch, Derek C., and Brad J. Kallenberg. "Technology." In *Dictionary of Scripture and Ethics*, edited by Joel B. Green, 763–66. Grand Rapids: Baker Academic, 2001.

Hays, Richard B. "Reading Scripture in Light of the Resurrection." In *The Art of Reading Scripture*, edited by Ellen F. Davis and Richard B. Hays, 216–38. Grand Rapids: Eerdmans, 2003.

Hayward, Robert. "Observations on Idols in Septuagint Pentateuch." In *Idolatry: False Worship in the Bible, Early Judaism and Christianity*, edited by Stephen C. Barton, 40–57. London: T & T Clark, 2007.

Heath, J. M. F. *Paul's Visual Piety: The Metamorphosis of the Beholder*. Cambridge: Cambridge University Press, 2013.

Hedges, Chris. *Empire of Illusion: The End of Literacy and the Triumph of Spectacle*. New York: Nation Books, 2009.

Hipps, Shane. *Flickering Pixels: How Technology Shapes Your Faith*. Grand Rapids: Zondervan, 2009.

Hoover, Stewart M. *Religion in the Media Age*. Media, Religion & Culture. New York: Routledge, 2006.

Horsley, Richard A. *Scribes, Visionaries, and the Politics of Second Temple Judaism*. Louisville: Westminster John Knox, 2007.

Hoskyns, Edwin C. *The Fourth Gospel*. Edited by Francis Noel Davey. London: Faber and Faber, 1947.

————. "Genesis I–III and St John's Gospel." *JTS* 21 (1920) 210–18.

Humphrey, Edith M. *And I Turned to See the Voice: The Rhetoric of Vision in the New Testament. Studies in Theological Interpretation*. Grand Rapids: Baker Academic, 2007.

Hunt, R. J. H. "Letter of Aristeas: A New Translation and Introduction." In *The Old Testament Pseudepigrapha: Expansions of the "Old Testament" and Legends, Wisdom and Philosophical Literature, Prayers, Psalms, and Odes, Fragments of Lost Judeo-Hellenistic Works*, edited by James H. Charlesworth, 2:7–11. 2 vols. New York: Doubleday, 1985.

Hutchings, Tim. "Wiring Death: Dying, Grieving and Remembering on the Internet." In *Emotion, Identity and Death: Mortality Across Disciplines*, edited by Douglas Davies and Chang-Won Park, 43–58. Burlington, VT: Ashgate, 2012.

Huxley, Aldous. *Brave New World*. 1932. Reprint, New York: HarperCollins, 2010.

Jacobs, Alan. "Christianity and the Future of the Book." *The New Atlantis* (Fall, 2011) 19–36. Online: http://www.thenewatlantis.com/publications/christianity-and-the-future-of-the-book.

————. "Goodbye, Blog: The Friend of Information, but the Enemy of Thought." *Books and Culture* (May/June, 2006). No pages. Online: http://www.booksandculture.com/articles/2006/mayjun/17.36.html

————. *The Pleasures of Reading in an Age of Distraction*. Oxford: Oxford University Press, 2011.

————. "Why Bother with Marshall McLuhan?" *The New Atlantis* (Spring, 2011) 123–35. Online: http://www.thenewatlantis.com/publications/why-bother-with-marshall-mcluhan.

James, E. L. *Fifty Shades of Grey*. New York: Vintage, 2011.

Jensen, Matt. *The Gravity of Sin: Augustine, Luther and Barth on* Homo Incurvatus in Se. London: T&T Clark, 2006.

Jensen, Robin Margaret. *Understanding Early Christian Art*. London: Routledge, 2000.

St. John of Damascus. *Three Treatises on the Divine Images*. Translated by Andrew Louth. Popular Patristics Series. Crestwood, NY: St Vladimir's Seminary Press, 2003.

Johnson, Luke Timothy. *The Acts of the Apostles*. Sacra Pagina, 5. Collegeville, MN: Liturgical Press, 1992.

Johnson, Steven. *Everything Bad is Good for You: How Today's Popular Culture Is Actually Making us Smarter*. New York: Penguin, 2006.

Jones, Tony *The New Christians: Dispatches from the Emergent Frontier*. San Francisco: Jossey-Bass, 2008.

Josephus, Flavius. *Antiquities of the Jews*. In *The Works of Josephus*, edited and translated by William Whiston. Peabody, MA: Hendrickson, 1987.

Kuyper, Abraham. *Lectures on Calvinism*. New York: Cosimo Classics, 2009.

Laytham, D. Brent. *iPod, Youtube, WiiPlay: Theological Engagements with Entertainment*. Eugene, OR: Cascade, 2012.

Leithart, Peter J. *1 and 2 Kings: SCM Theological Commentary on the Bible*. London: SCM, 2006.

Lewis, C. S. *The Magician's Nephew*. New York: HarperCollins, 1955.

Lincoln, Andrew T. *The Gospel According to Saint John*. Blackwell New Testament Commentary, IV. London: Continuum, 2005.

Luther, Martin. *Commentary on the Epistle to the Romans*. Translated by J. Theodore Mueller. Grand Rapids: Kregel, 1976.

MacDonald, Nathan. "Recasting the Golden Calf: The Imaginative Potential of the Old Testament's Portrayal of Idolatry." In *Idolatry: False Worship in the Bible, Early Judaism and Christianity*, edited by Stephen C. Barton, 22–39. London: T & T Clark, 2007.

Marcus, Joel. *Mark 1–8: A New Translation with Introduction and Commentary*. The Anchor Yale Bible, 27. New Haven: Doubleday, 2000.

Martyn, J. Louis. *Galatians: A New Translation with Introduction and Commentary*. The Anchor Yale Bible, 33A. New Haven: Yale University Press, 1997.

McConville, J. Gordon. *Grace in the End: A Study in Deuteronomic Theology*. Studies in Old Testament Biblical Theology. Carlisle, UK: Paternoster, 1993.

McLaren, Brian D. *A Generous Orthodoxy: Why I am a missional, evangelical, post/ Protestant, liberal/conservative, mystical/poetic, biblical, charismatic/contemplative, Fundamentalist/Calvinist, Anabaptist/Anglican, Methodist, Catholic, Green, incarnational, depressed-yet-hopeful, emergent, unfinished Christian*. Grand Rapids: Zondervan, 2004.

McLuhan, Marshall. "The Medium is the Message." In *Media Studies: A Reader*, edited by Paul Marris and Sue Thornham, 38–43. 2nd edition. Edinburgh: Edinburgh University Press, 1999.

———. *Understanding Media: The Extensions of Man*. New York: Routledge, 1964.

Mettinger, Tryggve N.D. "Israelite Aniconism." In *The Image and the Book: Iconic Cults, Aniconism, and the Rise of Book Religion in Israel and the Ancient Near East*, edited by Karel van der Toorn, 173–204. Contributions to Biblical Exegesis & Theology. Leuven: Peeters, 1997.

Meyer, Birgit. "Religious Sensations: Media, Aesthetics, and the Study of Contemporary Religion." In *Religion, Media and Culture: A Reader*, edited by Gordon Lynch, et al., 159–70. London: Routledge, 2012.

Middleton, J. Richard. *The Liberating Image:* The Imago Dei *in Genesis 1*. Grand Rapids: Brazos, 2005.

Miller, Patrick. *The Ten Commandments*. Interpretation: Resources for the Use of Scripture in the Church. Louisville: Westminster John Knox, 2009.

Moberly, R. W. L. *Old Testament Theology: Reading the Hebrew Bible as Christian Scripture*. Grand Rapids: Baker Academic, forthcoming.

———. "Toward an Interpretation of the Shema." In *Theological Exegesis: Essays in Honor of Brevard S. Childs*, edited by Christopher Seitz and Kathryn Greene-McCreight, 124–44. Grand Rapids: Eerdmans, 1999.

Muggeridge, Malcolm. *Christ and the Media*. Grand Rapids: Eerdmans, 1977.

Murray, Mary Charles. "The Image, the Ear, and the Eye in Early Christianity." *Arts* 9, 1 (January 1, 1997) 17–24.

Ong, Walter J. *Orality and Literacy: The Technologizing of the Word*. 1982. Reprint, London: Routledge, 2002.

———. *The Presence of the Word: Some Prolegomena for Cultural and Religious History*. London: Yale University Press, 1967.

Orwell, George. *1984*. 1949. Reprint, New York: Plume/Harcourt Brace, 1983.

Penner, Milton Bradley, and Hunter Barnes. *A New Kind of Conversation: Blogging Toward a Postmodern Faith.* Milton Keynes, UK: Paternoster, 2006.

Postman, Neil. *Amusing Ourselves to Death: Public Discourse in the Age of Show Business.* New York: Penguin, 1985.

————. *Technopoly: The Surrender of Culture to Technology.* New York: Vintage, 1993.

Potok, Chaim. *My Name Is Asher Lev.* London: Penguin, 1972.

Rice, Jesse. *The Church of Facebook: How the Hyperconnected Are Redefining Community.* Colorado Springs: David C. Cook, 2009.

Rowe, C. Kavin. "New Testament Iconography? Situating Paul in the Absence of Material Evidence." In *Picturing the New Testament: Studies in Ancient Visual Images,* edited by Annette Weissenrieder, 289–312. Göttingen: Mohr Siebeck, 2005.

Schultze, Quentin J. *Habits of the High-Tech Heart: Living Virtuously in the Information Age.* Grand Rapids: Baker, 2002.

Schwartz, Barry. "What Difference Does the Medium Make?" In *The Fourth Gospel in First-Century Media Culture,* edited by Anthony le Donne and Tom Thatcher, 225–38. Library of New Testament Studies, 426. London: T & T Clark, 2011.

Shirky, Clay. *Here Comes Everybody: How Change Happens When People Come Together.* London: Penguin, 2008.

Sweet, Leonard. "In the Beginning Was the Tweet." *Relevant Magazine.* No Pages. Online: http://www.relevantmagazine.com/god/god-our-generation/beginning-was-tweet).

————. *Viral: How Social Networking Is Poised to Ignite Revival.* Colorado Springs: WaterBrook, 2012.

Thompson, Marianne Meye. "The Breath of Life: John 20:22–23 Once More." In *The Holy Spirit and Christian Origins: Essays in Honor of James D. G. Dunn,* edited by Graham N. Stanton, et al., 69–78. Grand Rapids: Eerdmans, 2004.

Thompson, Michael B. "The Holy Internet: Communication Between Churches in the First Christian Generation." In *The Gospels for All Christians: Rethinking the Gospel Audiences,* edited by Richard Bauckham, 49–70. Grand Rapids: Eerdmans, 1998.

Tolkien, J. R. R. "On Fairy-Stories." In *The Monsters and the Critics and Other Essays,* edited by Christopher Tolkien, 109–61. London: HarperCollins, 2006.

Turkle, Sherry. *Alone Together: Why We Expect More from Technology and Less from Each Other.* New York: Basic, 2011.

Uehlinger, Christoph, and Othmar Keel. *Gods, Goddesses, and Images of God in Ancient Israel.* Translated by Thomas H. Trapp. Minneapolis: Fortress, 1998.

Van der Toorn, Karel. "The Iconic Book: Analogies between the Babylonian Cult of Images and the Veneration of the Torah." In *The Image and the Book: Iconic Cults, Aniconism, and the Rise of Book Religion in Israel and the Ancient near East,* edited by Karel van der Toorn, 229–48. Contributions to Biblical Exegesis and Theology. Leuven: Peeters, 1997.

Vanhoozer, Kevin J. *The Drama of Doctrine: A Canonical Linguistic Approach to Christian Theology.* Louisville: Westminster John Knox, 2005.

————, et al. *Everyday Theology: How to Read Cultural Texts and Interpret Trends.* Grand Rapids: Baker Academic, 2007.

————. "The Voice and the Actor: A Dramatic Proposal About the Ministry and Minstrelsy of Theology." In *Evangelical Futures: A Conversation on Theological Method,* edited by John G. Stackhouse, 61–106. Grand Rapids: Baker Academic, 2000.

Von Rad, Gerhard. *Genesis: A Commentary.* Translated by John Marks. Old Testament Library. London: SCM, 1972.

Wallace, David Foster. "Big Red Son." In *Consider The Lobster and Other Essays.* New York: Back Bay, 2006.

Ward, Pete. *Gods Behaving Badly: Media, Religion, and Celebrity Culture.* London: SCM, 2011.

Watson, Francis B. "Are There Still Four Gospels?" In *Reading Scripture with the Church: Toward a Hermeneutic for Theological Interpretation,* edited by A. K. M. Adam, et al., 95–116. Grand Rapids: Baker Academic, 2006.

———. *Text and Truth: Redefining Biblical Theology.* Grand Rapids: Eerdmans, 1997.

———. *Text, Church, and World: Biblical Interpretation in Theological Perspective.* Grand Rapids: Eerdmans, 1994.

Webb, Stephen H. *The Divine Voice: Christian Proclamation and the Theology of Sound.* Grand Rapids: Brazos, 2004.

Weeks, Stuart. "Man-Made Gods? Idolatry in the Old Testament." In *Idolatry: False Worship in the Bible, Early Judaism and Christianity,* edited by Stephen C. Barton, 7–21. London: T & T Clark, 2007.

Wells, Samuel. *Improvisation: The Drama of Christian Ethics.* London: SPCK, 2004.

Wink, Walter. *John the Baptist in the Gospel Tradition.* Society for New Testament Studies Monograph Series, 7. Cambridge: Cambridge University Press, 1968.

Wolf, Naomi. "The Porn Myth." *New York* (October 20, 2013). No pages. Online: http://nymag.com/nymetro/news/trends/n_9437/.

Wolterstorff, Nicholas. *Divine Discourse: Philosophical Reflections on the Claim that God Speaks.* Cambridge: Cambridge University Press, 1995.